Praise for *Luther's Rome, Rome's Luther*

"Springer interweaves Martin Luther's biography and thought with the city of Rome in several cultural manifestations, providing a model for sketching unique perspectives on the person and the metropolis. Springer's masterful craftsmanship in English combines with his mastery of Latin literature and historical data to present the reformer's life and the fascination of the 'eternal city' in a lively, fresh experiment in cultural history."

—Robert Kolb, Concordia Seminary

"*Luther's Rome, Rome's Luther* is a masterpiece of Renaissance/ Reformation scholarship. Springer's rich interpretive work provides the reader with a font of information about Luther and his complex relationship with Rome qua historic cultural hub, charming but corrupt capital, and sinful seat of sacred power. Springer follows the steps of Luther's pilgrimage, producing four carefully coordinated chapters that tease out the nuanced relationship that Luther had with Rome, noting his love for the eternal city, his hatred of the Catholic Church's grip on it, and the struggle he had with the grasp that the city, and all that it represented, had on him. As that influence grew and changed, Luther came increasingly to value his memory of the city. Springer thus thoughtfully shows how Luther's relationship with the city matured over time, a city that, as Luther himself understood, offered so much, both good and bad, to Christendom and to the world. All in all, *Luther's Rome, Rome's Luther* stands and will stand as an important contribution by one of today's leading Luther scholars. Surely it can do no other."

—R. Alden Smith, Baylor University

"The ranking authority on Luther and the classics, Springer revises the half-truth of Luther's hatred of Rome by retelling the story of the reformer's visit to the city and his lifelong engagement with its associated culture, literature, and traditions. This is an essential work for intellectual historians and enjoyable for the lay reader."
—Andrew Weeks, editor of *The Forgotten Reformation*

Luther's Rome,
Rome's Luther

Luther's Rome, Rome's Luther

How the City Shaped the Reformer

Carl P. E. Springer

FORTRESS PRESS

MINNEAPOLIS

LUTHER'S ROME, ROME'S LUTHER
How the City Shaped the Reformer

All Scripture quotations are from the King James Version.

Cover image: Rogers Fund, Transferred from the Library, 1941
Cover design: Landerholm

Print ISBN: 978-1-5064-7202-7
eBook ISBN: 978-1-5064-7203-4

This book is dedicated to my daughter, Anna Magdalena,
and her husband, Daniel, who for the time being live in Rome
but have thought more than once about moving to Oslo.

Contents

Preface

MY SINCERE THANKS TO the Provost's Office, the College of Arts and Sciences, and the Department of Modern and Classical Languages at the University of Tennessee Chattanooga for their generous and consistent support of this project. The SunTrust Chair of Excellence in the Humanities, which I currently hold, made it possible for me in 2018–19 to spend roughly six months trying to retrace Luther's footsteps while on his way to and from Rome and in the city itself.

Some of the central ideas of the book were presented in papers delivered at the fiftieth meeting of the Sixteenth Century Society and Conference in St. Louis in 2019 (panel on "Luther and the Church") and at the annual meeting of the Society of Classical Studies in Washington, DC, in 2020 (panel on "Neo-Latin in the Old and New Worlds"). To Rick Serina and Frederick J. Booth, who organized the panels, as well as those in attendance who offered their observations and critiques, I owe a debt of thanks. Fiammetta Terlizzi, director of the Biblioteca Angelica in Rome, the staff of the American Academy in Rome, and the librarians at Concordia Seminary in St. Louis were very helpful in answering queries and providing access to materials. I commend my faculty colleagues at the University of Tennessee Chattanooga—Justin Colvin, Kody Cooper, Lucien Ellington, Jose-Luis Gastañaga Ponce de Leon, David Pleins, and Norty Wheeler—for their willingness over the past eighteen months to listen patiently to my ideas and offer suggestions.

Profound thanks to my wife, Avery, *dimidium animae meae*, for her faithful companionship and support throughout the process of researching and writing this book. I also want to express my gratitude to my sister, Christel, for her tireless editorial assistance, as well as to Joshua Davies, Ralph Hood, Robert Kolb, Alden Smith, and Andy Weeks for their willingness to read a first draft of the manuscript, and finally to Daniel Andrews, my undergraduate research assistant, for his help in the initial stages of this project.

Prolegomena

*It is a curious subject of observation and inquiry, whether
hatred and love be not the same thing at bottom. Each, in its
utmost development, supposes a high degree of intimacy and
heart-knowledge; each renders one individual dependent for the
food of his affections and spiritual life upon another; each leaves
the passionate lover, or the no less passionate hater, forlorn
and desolate by the withdrawal of his subject. Philosophically
considered, therefore, the two passions seem essentially the
same, except that one happens to be seen in a celestial radiance,
and the other in a dusky and lurid glow.*

—Nathaniel Hawthorne, *The Scarlet Letter*[1]

THIS IS A BOOK about the tempestuous relationship that Martin Luther had with Rome. By "Rome," I mean all of what its most familiar manifestations would have been for Luther: the early sixteenth-century city that he visited as a young man, the ancient republic and empire whose language he used throughout his life and whose literature and history he considered exemplary, the Holy Roman Empire of which Luther was a subject, and above all, the city that served as the sacred seat of the bishop of Rome, the supreme pontiff, the leader of what is regularly referred to today as the Roman Catholic Church.

For anyone already somewhat acquainted with the subject, it might be supposed that a study such as this would be fairly straightforward. The French historian Lucien Febvre, one of the founders of the famous Annales school, describes Luther's trip to Rome as a young man thus:

Toward the end of 1510, on behalf of his order, Friar Martin Luther went to Rome. A huge sense of hope sustained him. He made his way as a pious pilgrim to the city of distinguished pilgrims, the Rome of the martyrs, the vital center of Christianity, the common fatherland of the faithful, the august residence of the vicar of God. What did he find there? The Rome that had belonged to the Borgias and had just lately become the Rome of Pope Julius. When aghast, Luther fled execrable Babylon, with its courtiers, its bullies, its ruffians, its simoniac clergymen, its cardinals devoid of law and morality, and returned to his native Germany, he carried along with him in his heart inexpiable hatred for "The Great Prostitute."[2]

At an early and critical turning point in the pious young friar's spiritual life, according to this account, Luther's hopeful attitude toward Rome was suddenly changed into a hatred that would remain "inexpiable" (*la haine inexpiable*) for the rest of his life.

That the youthful Luther went through such an apparently uncomplicated and immediate emotional transformation as Febvre suggests is an idea that is still commonly held. But while this assessment of Luther's relationship with Rome may be useful enough for most general studies of Luther's life and thought, for anyone who is wary of "premature intellectual closure," it will not prove completely satisfying.[3] In the following pages, I suggest that Luther's attitude toward Rome was much more complicated than has often been supposed by Febvre and others. For one thing, the trip to Rome itself was probably *not* an instant catalyst, dramatically changing Luther's view of the city immediately and forever.

It is certainly true that Luther's antipathy to Rome became more and more pronounced as he grew older. His increasing aversion was often and vituperatively expressed, especially insofar as the city was so firmly identified in his mind with the papacy. It is not at all my intention to downplay Luther's "hatred" of the city of the pope here. What I do want to suggest, however, is that it is best understood as an inverse product of a set of dashed expectations about the city that he once regarded as so very holy. If the idea of Rome and what it represented had not once been so very positive for Luther, it is unlikely that his later animosity toward the city would have been so intensely negative. Indeed, one could say in general that there is a direct proportionality between the level of our initial idealistic expectations and the subsequent degree of bitter disillusionment and disappointment when a darker reality dawns upon us later on.

One of my chief reasons for thinking so is the following: we must acknowledge and account for the fact that Rome continued to loom so very large in Luther's imagination long after his official ties to it were decisively severed. In December 1520, he publicly burned the papal bull issued in June, "Arise, O Lord" (*Exsurge, Domine*), ordering him to recant.[4] Shortly thereafter, in January 1521, Luther was formally excommunicated by Leo X with a second bull. And later in the same year, he was condemned by Charles V, the Holy Roman emperor, after the Diet of Worms (the imperial edict was issued in May 1521). But in the following years, even as his youthful trip to the holy city became a distant memory, it is clear that Rome continued to fascinate the older Luther. There are few cities mentioned more often in the 1530s and 1540s in the *Tischreden*, his famous "Table Talks." Not even Jerusalem, the quintessential holy city of Christianity, is brought up more frequently. Indeed, Luther thought Rome "far more distinguished" (*longe nobilior*) than Jerusalem as a physical city, "if you look at the walls and other buildings."[5] And his interest in ancient and contemporary Rome continued unabated right up to the very end of his life in 1546. In what are very likely his last written words, Luther makes mention of the poetry of Virgil and the letters of Cicero. He suggests that to read the latter aright, one must have been involved like the Roman orator and statesman "for twenty years" in the affairs of "an important republic" (*republica aliqua insigni*).[6] Even on the verge of death, Luther still had Rome on his mind.

So this is not a book that will simply be about his initial "love" and then his later "hatred" of Rome, as though these were mutually exclusive alternatives for Luther. The observations of the nineteenth-century American novelist Nathaniel Hawthorne quoted above regarding the similarities that exist between love and hate despite their apparently disparate natures not only are quite true in general but also apply most aptly to the subject of our study. The opposite of love is not hatred, as the Holocaust survivor Elie Wiesel once wisely observed, but indifference.[7] Hatred has little in common with apathy. Few would disagree that Luther was a man who loved and who hated, but rarely has he been accused of apathetic indifference.

If the relationship between love and hatred is complicated, so was Luther. He once likened himself to a planet following its own erratic path (*planeta errans*), as opposed to a "fixed star," which others, especially his doctors, wanted him to be.[8] His views on Rome expressed over the years are by no means uniform or consistent with each other. They vary considerably depending on attendant circumstances and what aspect of Rome Luther is considering. Not only did Luther's thought evolve considerably over the course of his exciting life, but he also was quite comfortable with paradox. His theology conjoined apparently incompatible binaries (*duo incompatibilia*).[9] As a literary artist, he was inclined to express himself colorfully, intensely, and spontaneously. His writings are replete with hyperbole. It is not always easy, as a result, to state simply where he stood on any given subject. Luther was a complex personage, playing a larger-than-life role in his own times and thereafter as a theologian, a humanistic *littérateur*, an academic, a preacher, a political figure, a family man, and an ecclesiastical leader. There are many "Luthers," one could very well say. The Freudian biographer of Luther, Erik Erikson, distinguished the young Luther from the old so completely that he referred to the former as "Martin" and the latter as "Luther."[10] Not only his age and his health but rapidly changing ecclesiastical and political circumstances must be taken into account when one attempts to determine how Luther may have felt about Rome at any given time in his life.

Furthermore, we must take into consideration how his auditors and editors understood and represented the words Luther wrote at his desk and spoke in the pulpit, at the lectern, and at the table. Luther became one of the most famous celebrities of his age, and eventually he was surrounded by a small army of scribes eager to record his spoken words as well as translators and editors working diligently to put as many as possible of his words, whether spoken or written, into print. Of course, no matter how conscientious any scribe, translator, editor, or even a printer may be, each is as subject to conscious or unconscious bias and outright error as authors themselves can be. Each of them has had his or her own "Luther," just as surely as every biographer has had his or hers. More so than the literary products of modern authors who work relatively independently, then, many of the works we attribute to Luther not only are the product of his own original, independent genius but also reflect the corrections and elaborations of those around him.

Every transcription, edition, or translation is an interpretation to some degree. This said, the inevitability of interpretation does not mean that Luther's words as they have come down to us have only a tenuous connection with his *ipsissima verba* or that the various texts that bear Luther's name, sometimes in multiple versions, were constructed ex nihilo. As Jaroslav Pelikan observes, "The extreme skepticism of certain scholars regarding the general reliability" of some of Luther's works (such as the sermons he preached on the Gospel of St. John) is "unwarranted." Using one of Luther's "favorite" expressions, Pelikan concludes, "The hands may sometimes be the hands of Aurifaber [Luther's *famulus* late in his life]; but the voice is the voice of Luther."[11] There is at the fundament of all the various words assembled in the *Weimarer Ausgabe* and attributed to him a single literary construct that we have little choice but to refer to as "Luther," even as we acknowledge the contributions of those around him in helping constitute it. We do not discount the unique genius of an artist like Peter Paul Rubens simply because he had multiple assistants who did much of the actual work of painting in his busy and successful studio in Antwerp.

If the overriding disciplinary perspective that informs this book as a whole were to be described in a word, it would most likely be as a variety of "textualism," to adopt Luther's own terminology.[12] Throughout the following pages, the reader will be introduced to a variety of texts, both prose and poetry, most of them Luther's and most of them about Rome. Sometimes these will simply be allowed to speak for themselves, with little or no commentary, almost always in my own translation. Luther is eminently quotable. But in the case of other texts, the reader will be invited to examine specific words and expressions in order to tease out their possible meaning(s). At the same time, other disciplinary perspectives will of necessity also be involved. The topic under consideration is inherently interdisciplinary, and in the following chapters, the question of Luther's relationship with Rome will be considered from distinctly different viewpoints in order to help us approach this complex problem as comprehensively as possible. Always, however, the primary emphasis will be on what the relevant texts themselves may have had to say to their first readers—and what they may still have to say to us. Again and again we will return to the words Luther used to construct his Rome and represent it to his various audiences, even as we attempt to situate these words within their most illuminating and relevant contexts: biographical, cultural, geographical, literary, political, rhetorical, psychological, theological, and so on.

The first (and longest) of these chapters will scrutinize Luther's trip to Rome from a more or less traditional biographical or "psychohistorical" (if you will) point of view.[13] What can we really know for certain—or at least reasonably surmise—about the young man's journey to and from Rome and his stay in the city itself? How did Luther describe the trip and its effects on him? As the years passed why did this youthful pilgrimage become so meaningful to him, and just as important, how did he make it so meaningful to others? How do Luther's experiences in Rome compare with those of other travelers to the same city before and since? In what ways may Luther's Rome have shaped our own?

Chapter 2 is an exercise in reception studies, specifically applied to Luther's understanding of and appreciation for ancient Rome. The term "deep classics," proposed by Shane Butler and others to describe this emerging disciplinary area, makes special sense when applied to such a layered city as Rome.[14] Instead of "reception," some scholars prefer to use terms such as "transformation" or "reciprocal creation" in order to avoid giving the impression that any tradition is merely received passively.[15] How did Luther, born over a millennium after the last emperor in the western half of the Roman Empire was deposed, actively reappropriate for himself and his audiences the history and culture, the language and literature of ancient Rome? What did he understand to be the meaning of Rome's virtues and vices, the rise and fall of its empire? How do his perspectives in this regard compare with those of church fathers, medieval visitors to the city, contemporary humanists, and others? The ruins of this great wrecked city certainly had a dramatic effect on later travelers from Germany and elsewhere who followed in Luther's footsteps.

In chapter 3, I adopt a more political point of view as I examine Luther's relationship with the Holy Roman Empire. How did he regard the claims of this political entity as opposed to those of the papacy? What were his attitudes toward magisterial authorities like the electors of Saxony to whom he literally owed his life? How should we characterize his views of Rome in light of the long-standing tension that existed between Germans and Italians and between the empire and the papacy, culminating in the sack of Rome in 1527? How did Luther's doctrine of the "two kingdoms" inform his understanding of what it means to be a "holy" place, whether that be Rome or Wittenberg or elsewhere?

Finally, the last chapter will take up the question of Luther's invective against the Roman pope whom he once called father and the Roman church that he regarded as his mother. Perhaps, following his ecclesiastical uprooting, he suffered from some form of what is referred to today as post-traumatic stress disorder. How much of his coarse, abusive language was due to Freudian neuroses or exacerbated by old age and illness? How much of his scatology was customary, even expected, in his Rabelaisian times?[16] From the perspective of literary criticism, how seriously should we take Luther's anti-Roman virulence? Can some of it be viewed as the expression of a literary persona, the product of a set of expectations imposed upon him by others or even (consciously or unconsciously) self-imposed? Does Luther's persona—that of the angry, hyperbolic, witty polemicist—represent his real or full identity? Furthermore, how might the distinction between law and gospel, so important for Luther's theology, account for what seems to be his "love-hate" relationship with Rome? And finally, what are we to make of the presence of ancient Rome in Luther's famous last written words?

Each chapter in this book is as much about a place as it is about a person. Even as Luther shaped the way in which Rome would be envisioned by his own and coming generations, so also Rome most certainly shaped Luther. The recent "spatial turn" in the study of the humanities has galvanized scholarly interest in such concepts as "space" and "place" (the one more neutral and general, the other more particularized), thereby helping us situate authors and texts more securely within their geographical contexts.[17] What makes one place "holy" or "most holy" for believers, and what does it mean when such a place is lost for them?[18] How does Luther's view of the sacred but doomed city of Rome correspond with the premodern topos of the praise of a city (*laus urbis*), especially as applied to Rome?[19] Why did utopian visions of community inspire Luther less than they did other Protestants? What could have possibly replaced Rome, the seat of Peter, the rock of the church, as a "holy place" in the mind of Luther in the years following his visit there?

In the pages of this book, the historic city itself almost takes on a kind of agency, as it were. Rome is, of course, a place, not a person, but it is a place that has exerted an uncanny attraction upon many besides Luther over the course of the centuries. The name of Rome in Latin (*Roma*) spelled backward is *amor*, the Latin word for love. Luther himself was aware of this playful association.[20] Aeneas, the Trojan who came to Italy looking to found a city for himself and his fellow refugees, was the son of Venus, the Roman goddess of love. The *amor* of *Roma* has always had a kind of promiscuous quality or, more kindly put, an all-embracing, completely absorbing dimension. This is a city that seemed destined from early on to become much more than a modest collection of farmers living in huts on the Palatine Hill, just one among many such thriving but relatively unambitious settlements all over Italy.

Instead, from early on, at least as its story was told by Livy and other ancient historians, Rome seems always to have been lustily extending its presence and projecting its dominance in one way or another.[21] Whether by employing subtle and not-so-subtle forms of political and military coercion up and down the Italian peninsula or extending its hegemonic reach throughout its immediate Mediterranean neighborhood and beyond, Rome expanded dramatically in a way few cities in the history of the world ever have. In the first book of Virgil's *Aeneid* (1.279), Jupiter promises that Rome's mighty empire will be "without limit" (*sine fine*). Luther interprets this expression temporally (not spatially) in 1526: "The Romans also had it in mind to construct an eternal kingdom, as Virgil says: *imperium sine fine*."[22]

By the time of the reign of the emperor Trajan, Rome had become the bustling center of a vast empire that is invariably referred to by its capital city's name, stretching from Britain in the northwest to Mesopotamia in the southeast. Within a few centuries, however, the city's power and prestige had begun to fade. The new capital of the Roman Empire was Constantinople, *Nova Roma*. But even as its former empire slipped from its grasp in late antiquity, the city of Rome itself was not entirely diminished. It was the location of the see of the successor to the apostle Peter, the pope. In the coming centuries, Rome was to serve as the headquarters of a church that was arguably the single most powerful spiritual and political force in western Europe.

The medieval city of Rome was a mere vestige of its former grand self, with a population that by some estimations had shrunk at one point to under twenty thousand inhabitants (at its height, there were as many as one million). After the catastrophic fourteenth century (when the home of the papacy was temporarily moved from Rome to Avignon in France), the city began gradually to grow again, thanks in large part to its appeal to pious pilgrims. Many from northern Europe and elsewhere were eager to visit the holy sites where the apostles Paul and Peter and other early Christian martyrs were supposedly buried and to venerate relics from the Holy Land. By the time of Luther's visit to Rome in the early 1500s, the pope had long since come back from France (1377), and the city had already begun to take the first steps in a long process of redevelopment. Its progress was not always smooth, to be sure, but eventually Rome became the thriving metropolitan area that it is today, the capital city of Italy, with over four million inhabitants. At the time of Luther's visit, however, even despite some recent positive developments, Rome still more closely resembled the medieval city than the modern one.

Rome is the ultimate diachronic city. In *Civilization and Its Discontents*, Sigmund Freud tries imagining Rome not as "a human dwelling-place, but a mental entity with just as long and varied a past history: that is, in which nothing once constructed had perished, and all the earlier stages of development had survived alongside the latest."[23] Its deeply layered history is on display for the casual visitor, not just the professional archeologist. "The very dust is historic," Hawthorne observes in his 1860 romance set in Rome, *The Marble Faun*.[24] One cannot possibly overlook the past here. The historical layers stare one in the face at every turn. The ancient theater of Marcellus, originally planned by Julius Caesar and completed by Caesar Augustus, still has tenants today living in luxury apartments in its upper tiers, as tenants have for centuries. (The Savelli family took it over in the fourteenth century, and it was later inhabited by the Orsini.)[25] The deep and evident historicity of the city has always been one of its most distinctive aspects, as noticed by Luther and many others who have visited it over the years.

By the same token, however, there is also a mature (possibly overmature) ripeness about Rome that may not necessarily sit well with those who appreciate modernity. The rich accumulation of sensual stimuli—some old, others new—and all of the varied sights and sounds and smells of this ancient city can leave the visitor today missing the clean simplicity of a northern European city with hotel rooms fitted out in modern Scandinavian decor. Fusty baroque charm only goes so far when one is interested primarily in a good night's sleep. Of the area around the Palazzo dei Cenci (to the northeast of the great synagogue, Tempio Maggiore, near the Tiber River), Hawthorne observes, "Dirt was everywhere, strewing the narrow streets, and incrusting the tall shabbiness of the edifices, from the foundations to the roofs; it lay upon the thresholds, and looked out of the windows and assumed the guise of human life in the children that seemed to be engendered out of it. Their father was the sun, and their mother—a heap of Roman mud."[26]

Not only tourists but residents themselves have expressed their distaste for Rome over the years, beginning already with Juvenal's Umbricius (*Satire* 3), a disgruntled Roman whom the satirical poet imagines leaving the squalid, noisy, expensive, and dangerous city, swelled with immigrants, for the more peaceful setting of rural Cumae.[27] At the time of this writing, the problems with trash accumulating in the streets of Rome verge on the acute. The current garbage crisis is so extreme that a group called "Rome sucks" (*Roma fa schifo*), which has been documenting the issue, has a Facebook page with hundreds of thousands of followers.[28]

Luther was not the only German of his time, of course, who had a complicated emotional relationship with Italy. His views were not so very different from those of many of his fellow countrymen north of the Alps who were just as intrigued as he by the city about which they had heard and read so much. Nor, most certainly, was he the only visitor to Rome from colder climes who has returned home from the city disappointed and even appalled. And the animosity went both ways. We will not leave unexamined the historic prejudices of Italy against its "barbaric" northern neighbors. At the same time, there is an element not only of repulsion but also of fascination with the Germanic "other," which for Romans goes back at least as far as Tacitus's *Germania*.[29]

The tension between northern and southern Europe in Luther's time continued in the following centuries and has not disappeared even today, although with the formation of the European Union, some of the most dramatic cultural differences have begun to be papered over in recent decades. The juxtaposed antipodes that are apparent in the two words of the title of Thomas Mann's 1901 novella, *Tonio Kröger*—whose young hero with the Italian first name has a vivacious "southern" mother and a serious, businesslike German father (his last name means "innkeeper" literally) and whose shifting sense of identity is held in the balance—will be in evidence everywhere in the pages that follow.

How might Luther's views on Rome have influenced not only his immediate audiences but others thereafter who have followed in his footsteps, making their own pilgrimages or taking sightseeing tours to the great ruined city? How long a shadow does Luther cast on those after him who have shared his respect for Rome's ancient paragons of virtue and literary genius or who have felt just as vehemently opposed as he eventually became to the claims of the bishop of Rome to be the ultimate ecclesial authority on earth? This question of influence, whether direct or indirect, is not the least interesting of the questions—even though it is more sweeping and speculative than others—that may interest readers as we explore the particulars of the specific issue at hand: Luther's relationship with Rome.

If we are "autobiographical animals," with our own selves inevitably intruding, however unconsciously or unintentionally, into whatever genre of writing in which we might be engaged, no matter how objective, scientific, or scholarly we may aim for our words to be, it would be remiss of me not to say something here about my own relationship with Rome.[30] Rome "is one of those rare cities, like Jerusalem or Paris, which exist just as much in the mind as in the world," as Adam Kirsch observes. "Every portrait of the city, one might say, is partly a self-portrait."[31]

It was the first European city I ever visited, and like Luther when he traveled to Rome, I was in my late twenties. The year was 1983, by chance the five hundredth anniversary of Luther's birth. While I myself had originally planned to follow my father's career path and prepare for the Lutheran ministry, I was in a doctoral program in the classics at the University of Wisconsin–Madison. The purpose of my visit to Rome was to study the art of the catacombs. It was January, and whenever I stepped out of the convent where I was staying, just off Saint Peter's Square, the crisp air, redolent of fresh *bomboloni* and cigarette fumes, would beckon me to explore Rome on foot (as one really should in order to enjoy fully the charms of the large but surprisingly compact area enclosed by the Aurelian Walls). And so I did for over a month, experiencing with all the enthusiasm of a novice the famous attractions of the city: snow descending through the *oculus* of the Pantheon, the musty warmth of the catacombs, the towering ruins and umbrella pines of the Baths of Caracalla. The sensual delights of gelato, cappuccino, and pizza rustica, all pleasures as yet unsampled by this callow youth fresh from the upper Midwest of the United States of America, made a positive and lasting impression.

Several years later I returned to Rome and had a completely different experience. It was late August, and the city was hot, noisy, and smelly, reeking of trash and sometimes even of human waste.[32] The hotel that I thought I had booked in advance had never heard of me and was full. Many of the churches that I had hoped to visit seemed always to be closed whenever I passed their doors. The basilica of Saint Peter's was still impressive, but I began to wonder whether the expense to build and maintain the enormous edifice and the associated complex was at all in keeping with the lifestyle of its namesake, the fisherman of the Gospels, or the Galilean rabbi whose disciple he was. The *pensione* where I ended up staying was infested with fleas, and I found myself unable to sleep at night. Instead, I napped intermittently during the sessions of the conference (held to commemorate the conversion of Saint Augustine at the Institutum Augustinianum, not far from Saint Peter's) that I was attending. By the end of the week, I was completely miserable, quite eager to leave Rome and content never to see it again.

Since then, I have revisited the city many times—it continues to fascinate me still, much more so than any other city—but ever since these two dramatically different encounters with Rome, I have never taken it for granted that any time spent there will be a wholly unmitigated pleasure. As the nineteenth-century novelist Richard Bagot once observed cynically, "One of the principal charms of Rome consists in the getting out of it."[33]

Perhaps no writer has ever expressed more fully the scrambled quality of the love-hate relationship that so many visitors have had with this perplexing city than Hawthorne when he describes what one feels upon leaving Rome:

When we have once known Rome, and left her where she lies, like a long-decaying corpse, retaining a trace of the noble shape it was, but with accumulated dust and a fungous growth overspreading all its more admirable features,—left her in utter weariness, no doubt of her narrow, crooked, intricate streets, so uncomfortably paved with little squares of lava that to tread over them is a penitential pilgrimage, so indescribably ugly, moreover, so cold, so alley-like, into which the sun never falls, and where a chill wind forces its deadly breath into our lungs,—left her, tired of the sight of those immense seven-storied, yellow-washed hovels, or call them palaces, where all that is dreary in domestic life seems magnified and multiplied, and weary of climbing those staircases, which ascend from a ground-floor of cook-shops, cobblers' stalls, stables, and regiments of cavalry, to a middle region of princes, cardinals, and ambassadors, and an upper tier of artists, just beneath the unattainable sky,—left her, worn out with shivering at the cheerless and smoky fireside by day, and feasting with our own substance the ravenous little populace of a Roman bed at night,—left her, sick at heart of Italian trickery, which has uprooted whatever faith in man's integrity had endured till now, and sick at stomach of sour bread, sour wine, rancid butter, and bad cookery, needlessly bestowed on evil meats,— left her, disgusted with the pretence of holiness and the reality of nastiness, each equally omnipresent,—left her, half lifeless from the languid atmosphere, the vital prin- ciple of which has been used up long ago, or corrupted by myriads of slaughters,—left her, crushed down in spirit with the desolation of her ruin, and the hopelessness of her future,—left her, in short, hating her with all our might, and adding our individual curse to the infinite anathema which her old crimes have unmistakably brought down,— when we have left Rome in such mood as this, we are astonished by the discovery, by and by, that our heartstrings have mysteriously attached themselves to the Eternal City, and are drawing us thitherward again, as if it were more familiar, more intimately our home, than even the spot where we were born.[34]

A century or so after Hawthorne wrote these words, the Italian cinematographer Pier Paolo Pasolini expressed something of the same ambivalence but more succinctly: "Rome is surely the most beautiful city in Italy, if not the world. But it is also the most ugly, the most welcoming, the most dramatic, the richest, the most wretched."[35] Pasolini's murdered body was found on a beach in Ostia outside of the city of Rome in 1975.

1

"Hail, Holy Rome!"

THE PILGRIM

WHEN HE WAS IN his late twenties, Martin Luther traveled to Rome from Germany and after spending four weeks in the city returned home.[1] Specific details such as the date of the trip, the precise route he followed there and back, the identity of his traveling companion, why exactly he went, and what he did and saw in the city itself have been and continue to be questions subject to vigorous dispute and frequent conjecture.

Of all the trips ever taken over the centuries, Luther's has often been regarded as one of the most significant. It might almost be described as one of those pivotal journeys that changed not only the traveler but the world thereafter, akin to Christopher Columbus's trip westward or Charles Darwin's voyage on the HMS *Beagle*. It would be a pity, therefore, to lose sight of the larger significance of this momentous trip because the reader's attention has become distracted by smaller and controverted issues, important as these may be. I shall try to review the relevant scholarly considerations and arguments in the first part of this chapter, but more or less briefly, referring the reader who is interested in greater detail to the primary and secondary sources indicated in the notes so that the overarching plot of the story of Luther's trip to Rome remains relatively uncluttered.[2]

On the other hand, I shall resist telling this story in the categorical fashion in which it has sometimes been told not only in popular literature but also in serious historical studies.[3] Vexed issues have all too often been confidently discussed as though they are quite settled, assumptions and unknown factors are not taken into full

>>> I <<<

consideration, and the extensive scholarship devoted to the question (not always readily accessible, especially to the Germanless reader) remains largely unconsulted.[4] In detailing Luther's travel experiences, sympathetic biographers have been as susceptible to the siren call of the historical imagination as unsympathetic ones. Luther is a larger-than-life figure who lends himself readily to legendary treatment, both positive and negative, and too many historians in the past have simply made up "entire scenes," as Heinrich Böhmer complains, imagining where he must have gone in Rome and what he must have seen or even how he must have felt. Projecting themselves completely onto the young Luther, these scholars have found it difficult not to represent him anachronistically, "as though he must have duly walked around the eternal city with the eyes and interests of a German professor," consulting his trusty *Baedeker* as he diligently made his way "through all the galleries, churches, and ruins."[5]

The fact is that we know relatively little for certain about this trip, and it behooves the careful writer to use the subjunctive mood more often than the indicative when setting forth details about Luther's journey that are reasonable hypotheses but not established facts.[6] In what follows, we shall focus less on what Luther might have seen or done on his way to and from Rome and in the city itself and more on what he said that he saw or did and, just as important, what the trip came to mean to him and to others thereafter.

"To Rome and Back Again"

Luther would have set out for Rome either from his monastery in Erfurt or from the newly founded university in Wittenberg.[7] His location at the time of his departure depends on whether the trip began in the late fall of 1510, as Heinrich Böhmer argued in 1914 in his influential *Luthers Romfahrt*, or a year later. For many decades after his study appeared, Böhmer's conclusions about the timing of the trip were widely accepted, and only in recent years have they begun to be seriously challenged. In 2011, Hans Schneider made a compelling case for a later date. According to Schneider's *Martin Luthers Reise nach Rom—neu datiert und neu gedeutet*, Luther arrived in Rome in the late fall of 1511.[8]

There are difficulties with both sets of dates. Luther himself is not always clear (or perhaps even sure) exactly what year it was that he went to Rome, contributing to the long-standing confusion on the subject.[9] Near the end of his life, Luther seems to question his own memory of the date: "It was in the year 1510 *anno domini*, if I remember correctly (*ist mir recht*), that I was in Rome."[10] Philipp Melanchthon, Luther's colleague at the University of Wittenberg, puts the trip a year later.[11] One solution has been to posit more than one trip to Rome, although this seems most unlikely given the failure of Luther or any of his early biographers to mention such an important fact.[12]

What was Luther going to do in Rome? The usual explanation is that he was sent there in connection with a serious problem that had arisen within the Augustinian order in Germany at the time.[13] The Augustinian monastery in Erfurt that Luther had joined in 1505 was one of many such houses in Germany, of which twenty-nine were reformed (sometimes called "observant" or "renitent"), with the remainder ("conventuals") following less rigorous practices. The vicar-general of the observant German Augustinians, Johann von Staupitz, was trying to forge a union between the two factions and had already personally traveled to Italy in search of a solution. His efforts, however, had been vigorously opposed by Luther's own house in Erfurt and six others, including those in Nuremberg and Kulmbach, whose members feared that such a union might lead to a relaxation of their own strict religiosity.

If Luther's trip to Rome took place in 1510/11, as Böhmer argued, the young friar in the monastery in Erfurt was most likely chosen by the resistant members of the *congregatio reformata* to represent their cause in Rome because it was thought that he supported their rigorist views and opposed Staupitz's ideas about union.[14] Given the rigid hierarchical structures of the Roman church and the strict expectations for obedience within the Augustinian order, if this was indeed an embassy undertaken to represent the case of the recalcitrant monasteries to the ecclesiastical authorities in Rome "without the express permission of their vicar" (*sine vicarii licentia speciali*), the chances for its success were slim.[15] In the register of the general of the Augustinian order, we find a statement dated to January 1511: "According to the laws, the Germans are forbidden to appeal."[16]

If the journey was made a year later in 1511/12, it is more likely that Luther—now in Wittenberg, where he was being groomed to become a professor—would have been personally handpicked by Staupitz himself. Presumably, he considered his protégé to be amenable to his efforts to unify the order. Perhaps he even hoped that Luther would be able to interact productively with the Augustinian authorities in Rome, consulting with them about the current situation in Germany and seeking their advice.

The date matters. If we opt for 1511/12, the need to explain how Luther could have so quickly switched sides upon returning from Rome in order to support Staupitz, as he did, is eliminated.[17] Indeed, once he was back in Germany, Luther traveled with Staupitz to Cologne—quite amicably, it would seem—to attend a gathering of Augustinians there in May 1512. Luther's faculty position at the University of Wittenberg, *Lectura in Biblia*, Staupitz's former chair, was approved on this occasion. Luther was awarded his doctoral degree on October 19 of the same year and three days later was "accepted into the university senate."[18]

Heiko Oberman argues that even if Luther did go to Rome in 1510 to represent Erfurt's case against his superior, he was not being rebellious in so doing. Rather, he "had dared to stand and be counted against the vicar general's policies, although this was the man who had offered him an academic future." Oberman admits that Luther's sudden reversal of positions once he returned home might make him appear "servile and career-minded," but he defends Luther's character as follows: "Throughout his life he was incorruptible and prepared to place principles before friendships. At such moments he counted neither his interests nor his inclinations."[19] But if Luther went to Rome at the behest of Staupitz and not in opposition to him, a year later than Böhmer and Oberman suppose, such a convoluted explanation becomes unnecessary.

In fact, it is not at all clear that Luther himself was ever especially concerned with restoring or strengthening his order's commitment to poverty, however seriously he may have taken specific ascetic directives for himself while in the monastery.[20] Indeed, later on he could be very critical of his former fellow monks in Erfurt and their strict piety. He called them "little saints" and criticized their "selfish striving for saintliness without regard for the obedience they had pledged in their vows."[21] Nor, at this early stage in his life, was Luther necessarily as inclined to challenge ecclesiastical authority as later. Staupitz was beginning to assume an increasingly important position in Luther's life as a spiritual mentor and his "father in Christ," who not only helped advance his academic career but also led him to a fuller appreciation of the depth of God's mercy (as opposed to the severity of his justice).[22] Perhaps it was not only finding a solution to the Augustinian order's problems that was on Staupitz's mind when he decided to send Luther to Rome, if it was he who did so, but a fond hope that such a journey to such a holy place might be just the thing to help satisfy the troubled young man's spiritual needs—or simply serve to distract him from his pressing theological worries.[23]

We can be quite sure that Luther did not travel alone. According to the *Regula Augustini* and the order's tradition, the friars were not supposed to go out of the monastery alone; they traveled in pairs on long journeys such as this, one walking behind the other, chanting and praying as they proceeded. Given his relative youth, Luther may well have been joined by a more senior *litis procurator*, responsible for arguing the case, for whom he would then have served as a junior "travel companion" (*socius itinerarius*).[24] We do not know this latter detail for certain, because we are not sure of the identity of Luther's companion. Luther describes him simply as a "brother" but never mentions his name. It could have been Anton Kress, a doctor of civil and canon law who served as provost of the church of Saint Lorenz in Nuremberg, where one of the Augustinian houses critical of Staupitz was located.[25] Or if the journey took place in 1510/11, his companion might have been Johann Nathin, a former professor of Luther's at the University of Erfurt.[26] Another possibility, which makes more sense if the visit is dated to 1511/12, is Jan van Mechelen, who had recently received his doctorate at the University of Wittenberg and who we know made a trip to Rome before February 1512.[27]

What itinerary might Luther and his unnamed companion have followed as they made their long trek to Rome?[28] Whether they left from Erfurt or Wittenberg, they probably passed through Nuremberg, a "most wealthy city and very well situated" although "not well fortified," whose impressive mechanical clock, the *Männleinlaufen* (installed between 1506 and 1509 on the Frauenkirche), Luther later mentions.[29] From there they may well have followed one of the routes that merchants regularly took as they made their way from Nuremberg to Milan. If so, the city of Ulm would not have been far out of their way. According to one of the *Tischreden* from 1538, Luther comments on the size of the cathedral there. He describes it as impressively large, like Saint Peter's in Rome and the cathedral in Cologne, but not well suited acoustically for preaching.[30] From Ulm they would likely have proceeded south via Memmingen to the Bodensee.[31] They would have then gone on to the Swiss town of Chur as they made their way south across the Alps, most likely by way of either the Septimer or the Splügen Pass.[32] Without offering specifics, Luther speaks of the "safest path" (*tutissima via*) through the Swiss Alps in one of the *Tischreden* from 1539.[33] He praises the Swiss people for their courage and candor (*animosi, candidi*), but it is not clear from the context of these remarks whether his judgments of them were based on firsthand experience or the reports of others.[34] He also observes that when the Swiss men were not fighting, they did the milking and made cheese, activities usually considered to be women's work.[35]

From Switzerland, Luther and his companion would have made their way into Italy, very likely through the strategically located town of Chiavenna and then down along the west side of Lake Como via Gravedona to Como itself.[36] In each of these last two towns, there was an observant Augustinian monastery where Luther and his companion could have stayed.[37] From Como they would have then proceeded to nearby Milan. In this city, Luther remembers that he was not allowed to say Mass, since he and his companion were unfamiliar with the Ambrosian rite, in which "the canon of the Mass, the elevation of the host, and the exchange of the *Dominus vobiscum* with the people" were omitted: "When I, Martin Luther, along with my brother, wanted to celebrate Mass there, I was prevented from doing so by the officiating priest, who said: 'What are you trying to do? You can't say Mass here because we are Ambrosians.'"[38]

From northern Italy, the two monks likely proceeded to Bologna. There is a fresco in the Augustinian monastery of S. Maria della Misericordia in Bologna that some suppose includes a likeness of the young Luther.[39] In one of the *Tischreden* from 1540, Luther mentions an incident that occurred in Bologna. It seems that some students there had requested papal permission to be excused from saying their prayers, but the pope's only response was to recommend that they get up earlier in the morning and pray faster.[40] It is not clear from this account, however, that Luther meant to suggest that he heard the story while himself in Bologna. From this city, he and his companion would have crossed the Apennines, passing through Florence and Siena, where they would have joined one of the branches of the famous pilgrim route leading from Canterbury to Rome, the Via Francigena, as they headed south to the eternal city.[41]

It was most likely off the ancient Via Cassia just outside of Rome that Luther first caught sight of the venerable city, probably from the elevation of Monte Mario, to the northwest of the city's historic center. On first glimpsing this view of Rome, he told those gathered around his table in Wittenberg years later that he "threw himself to the ground" (*in terram prostratus*). From this position Luther says that he issued a greeting to the city: "Hail, holy Rome!" (*Salve, sancta Roma!*). He then went on to explain why he considered Rome to be holy: "Yes, truly holy because of the holy martyrs with whose blood it is soaked" (*Ja, vere sancta a sanctis martyribus, quorum sanguine madet*) "but which now has been ravaged" (*sed iam lacerata est*).[42]

How accurately Luther remembered what he said at this moment is a fair question. Some of what he recalled may well have been reconstructed for the benefit of those gathered around the table. The records made of his remarks by his table companions on this particular occasion may also not have been completely accurate. Furthermore, if these were indeed the first two sentences that Luther initially exclaimed upon seeing Rome, they may well have been rehearsed in advance. The apostrophe of the city sounds somewhat formulaic, not so very different from one attributed to the Carolingian poet Paulinus of Aquileia, whose address to "happy Rome" (*O Roma felix*) was adapted for the Roman Breviary (the office of Saints Peter and Paul on June 29): "O happy Rome, you who have been stained purple by the precious blood of your princes [i.e., Peter and Paul], you excel all the beauty of the world, not because of the praise you have been rendered, but because of the merits of the saints whom you butchered with bloody swords."[43]

Luther does not simply praise Rome in extravagant terms, like Latin poets of late antiquity such as Claudian, who lauded the towering temples and glorious palaces of the city in his panegyric written in honor of the sixth consulate of Emperor Honorius, or Rutilius Namantianus, who described Rome as "the most beautiful queen of the world" in his *De reditu suo* (416 CE).[44] Like Paulinus before him, Luther qualifies his salutation of the city. Rome is worthy of special reverence not because of its magnificent buildings and former imperial splendor but rather because the blood of so many early Christian martyrs had been shed there.

Immediately following Luther's pious *trisagion* of Rome in Latin (except for one word, *Ja*),[45] we find the following scatological sentiment in German: *und der Teuffel hat dem bapst seinen danck darauf geschissen* ("and the devil shat out his thanks on it for the pope"). The only reward that the venerable city of the martyrs has earned lately, Luther suggests, is the devil's shit, which he has bestowed in gratitude for the pope who has now claimed the city for himself and Satan.

We have a slightly different version (entirely in German) of this event and what Luther said from the pen of Joannes Aurifaber,

Luther's *famulus* during the last two years of his life, who issued his own collection of *Tischreden* (first published in 1566). According to Aurifaber, Luther says that he not only fell to the ground but also lifted his hands up in the air (*hub meine Hände auf*) as he greeted the city. The scatological coda is also somewhat different: *und der Teufel hat den Papst, seinen Dreck, darauf geschissen* ("and the devil has shat on it the pope, his crap").[46] This would seem to make more sense than the other version. "Crap" or even "the pope" is a somewhat more predictable object of the verb "to shit" than "thanks" is. Vulgar woodcuts showing the devil or his minions shitting out the pope (or the Roman curia or monks) were not uncommon during this period.[47] But Aurifaber's *Tischreden* are based on secondhand accounts for the most part and rendered entirely in German rather than the macaronic mix of Latin and German that Luther seems to have preferred to use at table.[48] The wise principle of *lectio difficilior*, often applied to decisions about which of two possible readings is more likely to be correct, suggests that just because a reading is harder to understand does not automatically disqualify it in favor of a more predictable one. In fact, quite the opposite is true. Aurifaber's more heavily edited version is likely the one that has been altered.

Regardless of which version is more accurate, both of these German addenda were almost certainly added long after the fact to what would have been Luther's original exclamation in Latin. Neither one of the scatological additions probably reflects actual words that the pious friar uttered at the time of his visit to Rome. Nonetheless, both of them do make it clear on whose account at a much later date Luther believed the city had been so "ravaged" (*lacerata*). Even though Rome had once been "holy" in his eyes, now after several decades had passed, Luther considered the city to be as thoroughly soaked with the pope's diabolical shit as it once had been with the blood of the ancient martyrs.

To the northeast of Monte Mario, the Via Cassia converges with the Via Flaminia. It is this latter ancient road that Luther most likely took to reach the Milvian Bridge (Ponte Molle), which he would have used to cross the Tiber River and enter the city proper. Luther was familiar with the famous battle that took place there in 312, when Emperor Maxentius tried to defeat his rival, Constantine, but failed, thereby ensuring the subsequent success of Christianity in the Roman Empire. In the course of the conflict, Maxentius had drowned in the Tiber.[49] Like so many other pilgrims coming to Rome from the north, Luther would then have passed through the ancient Aurelian Walls, using the newly reconstructed Porta del Popolo about two miles south of the bridge, built by the order of Pope Sixtus IV (for the Jubilee Year of 1475) on the site of an earlier gate. The gate draws its name either from the financial support that the construction of the nearby church received from the Roman people or from the fact that so many poplar trees grew in the vicinity. After Luther's visit, the gate itself was remodeled (1562–65); the present outer facade takes its cue from the Arch of Titus, and four of its columns come from the old basilica of Saint Peter.[50]

Directly inside the gate, at the northeast corner of the Piazza del Popolo, stands the minor basilica of S. Maria del Popolo. A chapel had already been established on the spot by Pope Paschal II in 1099. The church rebuilt there by Pope Sixtus IV at the end of the fifteenth century is considered by historians of architecture to be "one of the first buildings of the Renaissance" in Rome.[51] Adjoining the church at the foot of the Pincian Hill stood the building (replaced in the nineteenth century) that served as the Augustinian monastery where it has often been supposed, especially since Böhmer's study, that Luther stayed while in Rome. In the thirteenth century, it was at S. Maria del Popolo that some of the first steps were taken toward formally establishing a monastic order dedicated to following the Rule of Saint Augustine.[52] The Franciscans who were there already were moved to the monastery of Ara Coeli on the Capitoline Hill to make room for the Augustinians.

If Luther's visit to Rome was on behalf of his brethren in Erfurt, it would make sense that S. Maria del Popolo would have served as his residence while in the city. In the fifteenth century, it had become "observant" and was assigned to the Lombard Congregation, one of the most important of the Augustinian congregations in Europe.

But Luther never directly mentions S. Maria del Popolo. In one of his sermons on the life of Luther, Johannes Mathesius says that when Luther was celebrating Mass in Rome, he was urged by "the Roman servants of the Mass" to hurry up so that the son could get "back home to our Lady quickly." Herbert Vossberg takes "our Lady" to be an allusion to S. Maria del Popolo and evidence that Luther was staying there. But this was probably no more than a facetious reference to Christ's permanent heavenly home in the company of his now assumed Virgin mother and not to the Augustinian church in Rome named after her.[53] If Luther would just hurry up and finish his Mass, Jesus could more quickly return from the altar on earth to be with Mary in heaven.

If Luther came to Rome a year later at the behest of Staupitz, it is more likely that he would have stayed instead in the Augustinian convent next to the Basilica di Sant'Agostino, where the Biblioteca Angelica now stands.[54] The basilica complex was the headquarters of the entire Augustinian order. The impressive church itself had been rebuilt in the year Luther was born (1483), using travertine marble from the Colosseum. At the time of Luther's visit, S. Agostino was abuzz with humanist activity. Egidio Antonini of Viterbo (also known as Giles), the prior general of the Augustinian order, was himself a warm devotee of Plato.[55] Even if Luther never actually met Giles in person, we know that he considered him "a very learned man" (*virum valde doctum*). Giles was a student of Greek and Hebrew, a historian, and a vocal critic of the rampant corruption in Rome.[56] His tomb is in S. Agostino, as is that of Augustine's mother, Monica, who died in Ostia. This location would certainly have put the two German travelers closer to Giles, but he had left the city in November 1511 and returned only in April 1512.[57]

Luther himself gives no indication of where he stayed while in Rome. Another possible residence, although less often mentioned by scholars, is S. Susanna on the Quirinal Hill, about two kilometers from S. Agostino and administered by Augustinians between 1448 and 1587.[58] There is also the now defunct church S. Matteo on the Via Merulana, along with its priory, which had been entrusted to the care of Augustinian friars starting in 1477. After Luther's visit to Rome, it was revived by Leo X in 1517, and one of its first cardinals was none other than Giles himself. Given the lack of any evidence that they necessarily stayed in Augustinian lodgings while in Rome, it is possible that Luther and his companion may have arranged for private accommodations, although that would surely have been a more expensive option.

Luther himself seems to have regarded his trip to Rome primarily as a religious pilgrimage. He was a pilgrim to Rome (*Romipeta*). This is what he calls in 1537 the "principal" purpose for his trip. To judge from his own words, Luther mostly wanted to go to Rome in order to make a full confession (*eyne gantze beychte*) of all of his sins committed from little on (*von jugent auf*).[59] In his exposition of Psalm 117 (1530), he wrote of how eager he had been to visit the sacred sites of the city and what he hoped to gain by "running" about from holy site to holy site: "Just as it happened to me in Rome, when I also was such a crazy holy man (*ein toller heiliger*), I ran through all the churches and crypts and believed everything, the whole stinking pack of lies there. I also probably said a Mass or ten while in Rome and at the time was almost sorry that my father and mother were still alive. For I would have liked to have released them from purgatory with my Masses and other even more impressive works and prayers."[60]

Luther speaks hardly ever, if at all, about the ostensible reason that he had been sent to Rome: Augustinian order business. If he was there as a representative of the Erfurt monastery and the observants, it seems that his visit was fruitless. He and his companion were probably unsuccessful in their efforts to meet with the appropriate ecclesiastical representatives. If Luther was in Rome on behalf of Staupitz, he is remarkably reticent about what exactly he was supposed to be doing there to serve the interests of his monastic superior. Even the one apparently clear passage where Luther himself says that the issue that brought him to Rome was "the Staupitz dispute" (*contentio Staupitii*) is controverted.[61] The original reading seems to have been *contentio Sat.*, the latter perhaps an abbreviation not for

"Staupitz" but for "Satan." Was the long trek to Rome really about searching for a resolution to a spiritual struggle with Satan for the salvation of Luther's soul and not about serving as an ambassador for Staupitz (or advocating against him) at all?

While we know nothing about any administrative duties that Luther may have undertaken while in Rome, we are better informed about the work he did on behalf of the Augustinian order when he returned to Saxony, serving as subprior and director of the *studium generale* at the Wittenberg monastery (starting in 1512) and later (1515–18) "as district vicar in charge of ten monasteries."[62] There can be no question that later in life Luther was someone who took his administrative responsibilities seriously. To judge from his relative silence about what he was supposed to be doing in Rome as a representative of his monastery or Staupitz, we must assume either that there were very few duties for him to perform, if any (perhaps his senior companion did most or all of whatever actual work had to be done), or that the issues at stake were simply not as interesting or important to Luther in retrospect as the pressing spiritual and theological questions that he was trying to resolve for himself at the time.[63] Certainly, the audiences to whom he was recounting stories about his trip to Rome in later life would have been far more interested in Luther's stirring anecdotes about clerical corruption and moral depravity in the great, wicked city than in the details of a now irrelevant monastic dispute.

Rome had long been one of the most popular pilgrimage destinations for Christians in western Europe.[64] It was, after all, the supposed burial site of both Peter and Paul, and it ranked second only to Jerusalem in the history of Christianity in terms of its importance and prestige as a holy place. There were, to be sure, other popular pilgrimage destinations, such as Canterbury in England and Compostela in Spain, but none of them could rival Rome for the number of early and important martyrs buried there. The city where Jesus was crucified and rose again and where the Holy Spirit descended upon the apostles at Pentecost was arguably "the mother of all churches,"[65] but Jerusalem had fallen under Muslim control (beginning already in the seventh century). This, combined with the fact that it was relatively far removed from northern Europe, made it a less practicable destination for many pilgrims than Rome. The Crusades, which started in the late eleventh century, were intended to help secure access for Christian pilgrims to Jerusalem and other sites in the Holy Land, but they were only intermittently successful in so doing. The holy city was retaken during the First Crusade by Christian princes, but it was subsequently recaptured. In Luther's lifetime, Jerusalem came under the control of the Ottomans, in whose hands it remained until the early twentieth century.[66]

By the time of Luther's visit, there were added incentives for pilgrims to go to Rome. In 1300, Pope Boniface VIII had come up with an idea that proved to be critical for the future fortunes of the city.[67] He declared the centennial year to be a year of Jubilee (cf. Lev 25:8–55). This meant a plenary pardon for anyone who made the trek to the city. It was an immediate success. Vast multitudes of pilgrims flocked to Rome. As many as two hundred thousand might be in the city on any given day.[68] At first the grand event was scheduled to be held every hundred years, but thanks to the idea's popularity (and no doubt the revenue it generated), the Jubilee Year began to be celebrated even more frequently.[69] Luther was aware of the practice and criticized it as a money-making scheme for the pope, but he was not himself there during such a year.[70] Whether pilgrims visited Rome during a Jubilee Year or not, it was their willingness to spend substantial amounts of money while visiting there that helped ensure Rome's rising fortunes as an early modern city, which already at the time of Luther's visit was undergoing a veritable building boom despite occasional setbacks.

The churches of Rome, many of them large and impressive (if not yet decked out in their later Baroque splendor) and associated with the names, remains, and associated relics of famous personages in the history of Christianity, must certainly have been among the chief attractions of the city for Luther, as they have been for so many other pilgrims before and since.[71] By the time of Filippo Neri, who drew up a standardized itinerary for pilgrims to Rome in the 1550s, it had become quite customary to visit all seven "station" churches in one exhausting day (pilgrims would need to walk a total of some twelve miles while fasting). These great pilgrimage churches—the seven *templa*, as Luther calls them in a sermon of 1531—included the basilicas of S. Paolo fuori le Mura, S. Sebastiano, S. Giovanni in Laterano, S. Croce in Gerusalemme, S. Lorenzo fuori le Mura, S. Maria Maggiore, and S. Pietro.[72]

It was not in one of these popular pilgrimage churches in Rome, however, where Luther seems to have felt most at home but rather in S. Maria dell'Anima. This was "the German church" in Rome, as Luther describes it in a sermon of 1538, just off the west side of the Piazza Navona and only three hundred some meters from S. Agostino. Luther declares it to be "the best" church and is especially appreciative of the fact that it had "a German pastor."[73] Originally designed, beginning in 1350, to serve as a hostel for pilgrims, by the time of Luther's visit, S. Maria dell'Anima had become popular with travelers from the northern Holy Roman Empire, especially speakers of German and Dutch. It was established as a church in 1431 and then rebuilt beginning in 1499 in anticipation of the Jubilee Year of 1500. A prominent German banking family, the Fuggers from Augsburg, was associated with the church. A decade after Luther's visit, Giulio Romano painted an altarpiece there for the Fugger family, and the church was frequented by a number of the "clients of the House of Fugger."[74] The only Dutch pope, Adrian VI (Adriaan Floriszoon Boeyens), born in Utrecht and the former tutor of Emperor Charles V, is buried in S. Maria dell'Anima.

Other ecclesiastical institutions to which Luther specifically refers include the Franciscan monastery of S. Maria in Ara Coeli,[75] as well as S. Pancrazio and S. Agnese fuori le Mura.[76] It would have been difficult for any pilgrim to Rome not to have seen S. Maria in Ara Coeli, at least from the outside, because of its central location and prominent situation atop the Capitoline Hill. The impressive steps leading up to the church, constructed in 1348 to celebrate the end of a plague in the city, were already well worn by Luther's time.[77] Both S. Pancrazio and S. Agnese, by contrast, were farther removed from the center of the city, outside of the Aurelian Walls, although certainly not so far as to discourage a pilgrim like Luther, who had walked so many miles already to get to Rome in the first place. The basilica of S. Pancrazio on the Janiculan Hill and the catacomb directly underneath it were known and visited by pilgrims throughout the Middle Ages, especially those wishing to venerate the remains of the popular child martyr Saint Pancras.[78] The catacombs of S. Agnese on the ancient Via Nomentana, however, were rediscovered only after the time of Luther's visit by the indefatigable Augustinian scholar of antiquities Onofrio Panvinio.[79]

It has been suggested that Luther may have consulted a written tour guide while in Rome. Perhaps he used a version of the venerable medieval handbook for pilgrims, the *Mirabilia urbis Romae*, to help orient himself for the visits to the holy sites that he undertook. This is possible, but such a guidebook would hardly have been necessary for an Augustinian visiting Rome, since there were plenty of resident experts handy, fellow friars in his order, who could readily have advised Luther and perhaps even personally accompanied him to popular pilgrimage sites.[80]

One of Luther's best-known pilgrim experiences in Rome took place on the Scala sancta. The Holy Steps at the present time are across a busy street from the major papal basilica of Saint John Lateran, in a building that bears the official title of Pontificio Santuario della Scala Santa. The central set of stairs proper is now flanked by staircases on either side and is often closed to the public.[81] Like so many other pilgrims before and since, Luther climbed on his knees all the way up the twenty-eight steps, which were supposed to be the very ones that Jesus had taken to reach Pontius Pilate's *praetorium* in Jerusalem. Luther makes mention of this experience in a sermon he preached near the end of his life (November 15, 1545):[82] "So when I was in Rome, I wanted to release my grandfather from purgatory, and going up the steps of Pilate I was praying a *pater noster* at each step. For I was convinced that anyone who prayed in this way could redeem a soul. But as I got to the top, I kept thinking: 'Who knows whether it's true?'"[83]

Himself a priest (ordained in Erfurt in 1507), Luther later remembered presiding over a number of Masses for departed souls (*Seelenmessen*) at various altars throughout Rome. There were so many of these, in fact, that he seems to have lost count over the years. Even as early as 1518, Luther is vague about the number of Masses he said in Rome ("more than one").[84] Twelve years later, he says that he probably celebrated "a Mass or ten" while in Rome.[85] But even though he wanted to, he was unable to say Mass at Saint John Lateran because there were too many other visiting priests who wanted to do the same thing. At the time, Saint John's was by far the most important of all of the basilicas in Rome, the "mother and head" (*mater et caput*) of all the churches "of the city and the world" (*urbis et orbis*).[86] In his exposition of the 117th Psalm in 1530 for his friend Hans von Sternberg, who had himself made a pilgrimage to Jerusalem, Luther cited a popular saying to the effect that any mother "whose son could read Mass on Saturday evening at Saint John's is blessed." Luther goes on to say, "How very much I would have liked to have made my mother blessed! But it was too crowded, and I couldn't get through, so I ate a smoked herring instead." He then observes, "Well, that's what we did; we didn't know any better."[87]

Besides the Holy Steps, other relics in Rome that Luther later mentions include the veil of Veronica, which was supposedly used to wipe the face of Jesus on his way to the cross, one of the most celebrated of all such sacred mementos. In a sermon preached in 1531, Luther asked his congregation why they would go to Rome to see the veil when they had baptism right where they were: "See what you have in your own church. The veil of Veronica does not have the word of God. In baptism there is spirit and life, the word. That is what I would say to you. They themselves [the Romans] think that baptism is just a worthless thing: 'Don't I have something greater than every other Christian has? Falling down three thousand times in a row in front of the Veronica veil, that's the greatest thing.'"[88] The veil was one of the main attractions for pilgrims coming to Rome. Dante mentions it in the *Divine Comedy* (*Paradiso* 31.103–8). The Italian poet imagines a pious pilgrim from Croatia coming to Rome and looking at "our Veronica" with rapt attention and wondering whether this was indeed the very likeness of Christ Jesus, God himself.[89] The relic itself may have been destroyed during the sacking of Rome in 1527,[90] but a copy, if not the original, is preserved among other relics at Saint Peter's and is still brought out for display in Rome on the fifth Sunday of Lent.[91]

Luther also refers to the "wooden" heads of Saints Peter and Paul in Saint John Lateran. They are now encased in silver busts in a reliquary above the high altar. Even though the two apostles themselves may both well have been in Rome, it is a "barefaced lie" (*unverschempte Lugen*), according to Luther, that these heads once belonged to Peter and Paul, since their bodies would have been disposed of unceremoniously after their execution.[92] In fact, the heads were not wooden but actual skulls, although whether these were really the heads of Peter and Paul is quite another question. In a sermon preached for "the day of Peter and Paul" in 1539, Luther suggests that God disposed of the bodies of Peter and Paul as he did that of Moses (Deut 34:6) so that no one would know where they were buried lest they be worshipped after their deaths.[93] The two heads were displayed publicly on the feast day of Saints Peter and Paul (June 29), so Luther would not himself have seen them if his visit to Rome took place during the late autumn or early winter months.[94]

Luther dismisses entirely the legends surrounding the head of John the Baptist, which is still on display in S. Silvestro in Capite.[95] The Saracens (who sacked the city in 846), he says, "opened the grave of John and burned everything to powder." Luther was also sure that other relics in Rome, such as "the key" of Peter and "the wood of the cross," were nothing more than "great big lies" (*maxima mendacia*).[96] While in the city, he could hardly have missed seeing some of the many artistic representations, sculpted or painted, of Peter holding the keys to the kingdom given to him, metaphorically, by Christ himself (Matt 16:19). One of the more recent of such paintings at his time, by Pietro Perugino on the northern wall of the Sistine Chapel, was completed in 1481–82. But there were other earlier examples of Peter with his keys to be found everywhere in Rome in the early sixteenth century.[97] As for pieces of the true cross, Luther would most likely have seen them at the church of Santa Croce, one of the seven pilgrim churches, famous to this day for the supposed fragments of the cross in its possession, brought back to Rome from the Holy Land by Helena, the mother of Constantine.[98] Relics that visitors to the church could see included not only part of the true cross itself but one of the nails used to attach Jesus to the cross, thorns from the crown that he wore, part of the cross on which one of the thieves was crucified along with Jesus, and the finger with which Thomas touched Jesus's wounds after his resurrection.[99]

Luther also dismissed as a deliberate "Satanic" lie, not simply a pious mistake, the legend that three fountains sprang up on each of the spots where Saint Paul's head bounced and hit the ground when he was decapitated south of Rome at San Paolo alle Tre Fontane.[100] There is still an abbey (Trappist) on the site, which was first given to the Cluniacs and later to Bernard of Clairvaux and the Cistercians.

To urge his followers not to become so complacent ("sitting in their rose gardens") as to forget "in what dark shadows our elders were immersed" before the Reformation, in one of his *Tischreden*, Luther used the example of the rope in Rome with which Judas was supposed to have hanged himself.[101] The rope (twelve feet in length) had hung from a column in Saint Peter's until the sack of Rome in 1527, when it was carried off to Germany, where it was hung up again in the town of Schorndorf.[102]

Luther's suspicions about the relics on display in Rome and the veracity of the legends surrounding them were by no means unique to him. The celebrated humanist Erasmus of Rotterdam expressed his doubts about the ability of one cross to have so many fragments: "So they say of the cross of Our Lord, which is shown publicly and privately in so many places, that, if all the fragments were collected together, they would appear to form a fair cargo for a merchant ship."[103] The French reformer John Calvin also entertained sensible doubts on this score.

In addition to "running" around to visit the churches themselves, Luther also says that he visited underground burial sites (*klufften*) while in Rome.[104] This experience seems to have made a more positive impression on him than viewing relics housed above the ground. He may very well have visited the catacombs on the Appian Way connected with the basilica of Saint Sebastian. This was one of the seven pilgrimage basilicas, and its associated catacombs have always been accessible to visitors on a continuous basis throughout the centuries.[105] Exploration of most of the other catacombs did not begin until later in the sixteenth century. It was more than a hundred years after Luther's visit that Antonio Bosio's *Roma Sotterranea* was published. Obviously, Luther would not have been able to visit the many catacombs in Rome that have been rediscovered over the years since the time of his visit, such as the catacomb on the Via Latina (only found in 1955).

Luther was particularly struck by the catacombs of Callixtus, the enormous underground burial location for "many thousands of martyrs."[106] While the actual numbers Luther adduces are not always consistent with each other, it is clear that he was deeply impressed by the sheer size and antiquity of this sacred place.[107] Luther says that the *Coemeterium Calixti* "now lies a half mile outside of Rome but was previously situated within the middle of the city." In fact, these catacombs, like others, always lay outside the Aurelian walls, in keeping with ancient Roman scruples against the presence of burial sites within the city proper.[108] Perhaps Luther is referring to the shrinking of the inhabited part of the city in his own time compared to its earlier extent. The holiest relics of the catacombs of Callixtus were transported elsewhere over time, and the great underground complex was virtually abandoned in the later Middle Ages.[109] It was indeed the largest of all of the Roman catacombs, and it is estimated now that Callixtus once contained as many as five hundred thousand bodies, including a number of papal sarcophagi. How many of the burials in Roman catacombs involved actual martyrs—that is to say, those who died as a result of persecution for their faith—is questionable. There are only fifty-two martyrs listed in the fourth-century *Depositio martyrum*.[110] Luther calculated the number of Roman martyrs to be in the thousands, and for him such burial sites were particularly meaningful.

Luther also mentions specifically the crypts of three saints—Sebastian, Lawrence, and Pudentiana—but he does not make it clear whether he actually visited them while in Rome.[111] Sebastian was a soldier who was martyred during the persecutions of Diocletian (his body pierced with arrows was a popular subject for artists in the Renaissance). Originally buried in the catacombs of S. Sebastiano on the Appian Way, his tomb was later moved up to the basilica proper. Lawrence, a deacon in Rome, was supposed to have been roasted alive on a gridiron (see Prudentius, *Peristephanon* 2) during the persecution of the emperor Valerian in the third century. His body was supposedly interred in the *confessio* under the high altar at S. Lorenzo fuori le Mura. Pudentiana was the daughter of Pudens, a Roman senator converted to Christianity by Paul, according to legend. Splendidly decorated churches dedicated to the memory of Pudentiana and her sister, both martyred, are still standing (S. Pudenziana and S. Prassede) not far from the basilica of S. Maria Maggiore. Pudentiana is listed in medieval pilgrim itineraries as buried in the catacombs of Priscilla on the Via Salaria. Even if he had few doubts about these sacred locations and the legends surrounding them while he was in Rome, already by 1518 Luther was confessing that he had begun to grow dubious on this score.[112] At this relatively early date, less than a decade after returning from Rome, he still sounds a little defensive when expressing doubts such as these, explaining that they cannot be considered heretical if the actual facts have not yet been determined by a church council. In later years, Luther was much quicker to dismiss legends about the saints and their remains in Rome as outright lies.

While he was in Rome, did Luther see the pope? At the time Luther visited the city, in the early years of the second decade of the sixteenth century, it would have been the bellicose Julius II who was reigning. If we assume the earlier date for Luther's pilgrimage, he would not have seen Julius in Rome even from afar, because he was off fighting a war in an attempt to recover the city of Ferrara in 1510/11. But the warrior pope was back in Rome in the winter of 1511/12, so it is possible that Luther may have caught sight of him in the city then, if we accept the later date for Luther's journey there. Today, Julius II lies buried in a monumental tomb in the church of Saint Peter in Chains, which he had commissioned Michelangelo to build for him already in 1505. It was only completed in 1545, long after Julius's death and shortly before Luther's.

In one of his *Tischreden*, Luther contrasts an earlier period in his life when he looked at the pope and saw only "his face" with the way in which he now viewed the pope. Divested of his former sanctity, the pope is seen by the mature Luther from quite the opposite perspective, "in the ass" (*in culum*). This crude expression probably finds its origins in a medieval dialogue between the cunning peasant Marcolf and King Solomon. When the king grew tired of him and said that he did not want to see Marcolf's face again, the jokester obeyed the king's orders quite literally and "mooned" him instead.[113] It is not clear, however, in this context whether Luther is talking about actually seeing the pope with his own eyes or simply referring to how differently he regarded the office of the papacy later in his life. Luther does mention pontifical specifics, such as the impressive tiara that the pope wore and the fact that his feet were kissed as a sign of respect, but these are details that he might easily have learned from sources other than the evidence of his own eyes.

Luther says that he saw a "stone monument in a public square" in Rome dedicated to the legendary female pope, Joan (or "Agnes," as Luther calls her).[114] She was supposed to have given birth to a child during a procession from Saint Peter's to Saint John Lateran, along the route regularly taken by popes as they made their way from one papal basilica to the other, not far from the minor basilica of S. Clemente. The spot was marked with a statue (referred to in the early fifteenth century by Adam of Usk, a Welsh chronicler), which is the same one presumably that Luther saw.[115] The statue must have been demolished (or perhaps thrown into the Tiber River) sometime in the decades following Luther's visit. A visitor to Rome later in the same century (around 1595), Elias Hasenmüller, says that he had seen "the place and pedestal" where the statue used to be, but not the statue itself.[116]

Did Luther spend much time in the great basilica of Saint Peter? Established in the first part of the fourth century by order of Constantine on the site where it was thought that Peter's body was buried, it is at the present day arguably the most notable Christian landmark of the city and one of its most popular tourist destinations. The enormous cost of its long and ambitious rebuilding, begun already under Nicholas V in the fifteenth century and continued by Julius II and subsequent popes, was one of the precipitating causes of the Reformation. Luther's objections to the selling of indulgences in Saxony to help fund this expensive project set off a chain reaction that led to some of the most momentous developments in modern European history. The connection between the selling of indulgences and the construction of Saint Peter's is made clear in one of Luther's famous Ninety-Five Theses: "Christians should be taught that if the pope knew of the demands made by the preachers of indulgences, he would prefer that the basilica of Saint Peter be burned to ashes rather than be built using the hide, the flesh, and the bones of his sheep."[117]

Luther refers to the size of the basilica and its prestige frequently in later years. In his Genesis lectures, he remarks, "For we have made much of Peter's basilica in Rome, more than all the other places which have the word and sacraments and the proper use of the keys, even though it should go without saying that where these latter are, there God is present and favorably disposed."[118] He refers to "the construction of Saint Peter's" in a letter of 1517 to Albrecht, archbishop of Mainz, but he has little specific to say about details of the extensive rebuilding project begun in 1506, based on a design by Bramante.[119] At the time of Luther's visit, only part of the impressive dome, eventually to be redesigned and finished by Michelangelo in 1547, had been completed. Indeed, it was only in 1626 that the rebuilt basilica was finally consecrated, with the colonnades of Bernini representing the embracing arms of Mother Church added even later (1656–67).

If Saint Peter's Basilica could claim to be the place where Peter's bones lay buried, there were other sites in Rome dedicated to events that supposedly took place at the end of Peter's life. These include the Mamertine Prison at the northeast foot of the Capitoline Hill, where Peter was supposed to have been imprisoned, and a sanctuary on the Via Appia, where a small church known as Chiesa del Domine Quo Vadis now stands. According to the apocryphal *Acts of Peter*, this is where the apostle, who was trying to flee the persecution in Rome, met Jesus going in the other direction. When Peter asked Jesus, "Lord, where are you going?" (*Domine, quo vadis?*), Jesus told him that he was going into Rome to be recrucified.[120] Ashamed, Peter returned to the city and insisted on being crucified upside down. At the time of Luther's visit to Rome, it was believed by some that Peter had been executed on the Janiculan Hill and not in Nero's circus near Saint Peter's. The exquisite Tempietto, commissioned by Ferdinand and Isabella of Spain and designed by Bramante, was finished as early as 1502 on the site of S. Pietro in Montorio on the Janiculan Hill to commemorate Peter's supposed execution there. Luther, however, does not specifically mention seeing any of these sites.

Luther has little specific to say about any of the artistic and architectural achievements of Italian humanism on display in early sixteenth-century Rome.[121] He does make mention of the Cortile del Belvedere begun by Innocent VIII in 1484 and still unfinished when Bramante died (1514). Julius II made use of it to house his collection of ancient artifacts, including such renowned sculptures as the Laocoön group, the Belvedere Apollo, and the Belvedere Torso, but it was not open to the public at the time of Luther's visit.[122] In this context, Luther does not mention any of the works of art per se, but his silence as to the impropriety of using indulgence money for purely aesthetic purposes is eloquent: "I am also going to keep silent just for the moment about where the indulgence money has gone; at another time, I will inquire further. The Campo de' Fiori and the Belvedere and quite a few other places probably know something about that."[123] The Campo de' Fiori had been paved and the surrounding buildings developed in the fifteenth century. In 1521, Luther comments negatively in general on the "huge expenditure of money wasted on constructing, erecting, adorning, enriching churches, monasteries, shrines, altars, and works of this sort."[124]

While in Rome, it is possible that Luther would have heard about the progress Michelangelo was making on his famous ceiling for the Sistine Chapel (begun in 1508), even if he did not actually see it. He may also have viewed some of Raphael's paintings in the Stanze di Raffaello. In the basilica of S. Agostino, Luther might have had the chance to see Raphael at work on a fresco of Isaiah for the church, commissioned by Johann Goritz and finished in 1512.[125] But he mentions by name none of the famous Renaissance painters and sculptors active at his time in Rome or elsewhere in Italy whose work had a profound influence on other visitors from the north, such as the contemporary German artist Albrecht Dürer, who made two trips to Italy.[126]

His silence in this regard, however, should not necessarily be taken to indicate complete indifference on his part to the Renaissance artists of Italy. In fact, Luther praised the genius of Italian painters in general: "For in such a masterful way and so exactly can they follow and imitate nature in their paintings, that not only do they give the proper natural color and shape to all of their figures, but they also make the forms almost come to life and have the ability to move."[127] Luther goes on to suggest that the Italian painters had served as an inspiration for Flemish artists.

The paintings Luther does specifically mention seeing in Rome were much earlier ones, supposedly from the hand of the evangelist Luke, who according to tradition was an artist as well as a doctor. In a sermon preached in 1539, Luther told his congregation, "I myself saw certain paintings which [were attributed] to Luke."[128] In the Middle Ages, Lukan icons existed in multiple versions and in many locations, including Rome, where a guild of painters known as the Compagnia di San Luca was established in the fourteenth century. In one of the most famous variations of these Lukan icons, often referred to as the Hodogetria ("the way-shower"), Mary is depicted from the waist up holding her divine son in one hand and extending her other hand to point toward him.[129]

One such Lukan icon has been in S. Maria del Popolo since the thirteenth century. Another one, the so-called Salus populi Romani ("Salvation of the people of Rome"), supposedly responsible for lifting a plague on the city in the sixth century, can still be seen in S. Maria Maggiore.[130] There is also an icon of Christ *pantocrator*, which was supposed to have been begun by Luke (but finished by an angel) on the back wall of the private chapel of the popes, the Sancta Sanctorum, in the building that houses the Holy Steps. It is known as the Acheiropoieton (often shortened to Acheropita)—that is, "not made by human hands." Given its fairly secluded location, this last icon is less likely to have been seen by Luther than some of the others. In an annual procession on the eve of the festival of the Assumption (August 14), this icon was carried with due ceremony from Saint John Lateran to S. Maria Maggiore so that the son could be reunited with his mother.[131]

If there are questions about Luther's itinerary to Rome, we are even less sure (if that is possible) about how he got back home from Rome. An eastern route has often been assumed by those who prefer the earlier date (1510/11), which would most likely have taken Luther over the Alps via the Brenner Pass, passing through cities like Mantua, Verona, Trent, and Innsbruck before reaching Germany.[132]

Of all the monastic lodgings where Luther may have stayed on his way to and from Rome, he mentions only one. Interestingly enough, it was not an Augustinian monastery but a Benedictine one, most likely S. Benedetto Po, a splendid cloister on the Po River twenty-two kilometers southeast of Mantua. Even more interesting is the fact that there were two observant Augustinian monasteries in Mantua at which Luther might have stayed instead.[133] It seems that Luther was not himself so dedicated to observant Augustinianism that he felt it necessary to pass up the hospitality of an opulent Benedictine monastery: "In Lombardy near Padua, there is a monastery of Saint Benedict that is very wealthy, which has an annual income of 36,000 ducats. They are so well off there that every year they spend 12,000 ducats on hospitality, 12,000 ducats on infrastructure, and the third part on the convent. I, Martin Luther, was treated as an honored guest there. Ah, the worship of God does not consist in wealth, as the familiar proverb says: 'Religion is a mother that has given birth to riches, but afterward the daughter has devoured her mother, that is to say, religion.'"[134]

Much as he appreciated the generosity of the wealthy Benedictine monastery, at the end of his remarks, Luther cannot help but reflect on the incompatibility of the worship of God and wealth (cf. Luke 16:13), especially in a setting such as a monastery, where poverty was supposed to be considered such a great virtue. The kind of dignified reception that Luther enjoyed at this monastery evidently did not characterize his experiences in all the monasteries at which he stayed, some of which he found "most unholy."[135]

In one of the *Tischreden*, Luther refers to Innsbruck, an Austrian city at the northern end of the Brenner Pass: "Innsbruck is small, but made up of similarly sized buildings, as if it were one continuous house."[136] Even today there is still a row of interconnected houses on the northwest side of the Inn River (in the part of the city known as Mariahilf). From Innsbruck, Luther may well have taken the Scharnitz Pass and traveled north via Partenkirchen and Schongau to Augsburg.[137]

It was in Augsburg that Luther would have met with Anna Laminit, whom he calls "Ursula" in one of his *Tischreden* of 1540. Luther did visit Augsburg one other time in his life, in October 1518, when he was in the city for a conference with Cardinal Cajetan, but since Anna Laminit was already dead by then (she had died earlier in May of that year), any meeting between Luther and her must have happened on a previous trip, and therefore most likely on Luther's way back from Rome. The Augsburg woman had gained a reputation for special saintliness by not eating anything for years.[138] Luther questioned her as to whether she wanted to die (and go to heaven): "The Laminit woman, the virgin Ursula, was not herself deceived, but instead deceived others. I met her in Augsburg and asked whether she wanted to die. She responded, 'Absolutely not! How things work there [the afterlife], I don't know, but how they work here, I do.'"[139]

If Luther's return trip took place in early 1512, a year later than Böhmer and others have argued, the route home from Rome via Bologna would have been even more problematic, since by then the conflict in northern Italy between the Holy League and France had begun to intensify.[140] In January 1512, the city of Bologna, the end point of the road known as the Flaminia militare, one of the best ways to pass through the Apennines when traveling north from Rome (via Arezzo and Florence), was under siege. The dangerous situation did not end until later that year, after a major battle at Ravenna between papal and French troops. It is just possible, therefore, that Luther would have returned home not through the Brenner Pass but by a western route, following one of the variations of the Via Francigena, going northward along the Rhône Valley in southeastern France.[141] We know that Jan van Mechelen, who may have been Luther's companion, traveled from the Austrian city of Salzburg in February 1512 to Cologne.[142] How would Mechelen have gotten to Salzburg from Rome? Possibly he would have gone by ship from Rimini to Venice and from there to Salzburg. Did Luther go with him? He never makes any mention of taking a sea voyage. Schneider suggests that "in these dangerous times, Mechelen and Luther may have traveled home by separate routes to make sure that one of them returned safely."[143]

"Anyone Who Takes a Trip Can Tell a Story"

Later in his life, Luther began more and more frequently to allude to his trip to Rome.[144] He often seems quite eager to tell (and retell) various parts of the experience, whether to friends gathered around his table, students in the lecture hall, or congregants listening to him preach in the city church in Wittenberg. More than once he begins an account with a prefatory statement that makes it clear that it is based on his own personal experiences and observations, such as "When I was in Rome . . ."; or "In Rome, I saw . . ."; or "I also was in Rome."[145] How did the pilgrimage to Rome become so meaningful to Luther and to others as the years passed?

In light of so many scholarly and not-so-scholarly attempts to provide a consistent and complete narrative retelling of Luther's trip to and from Rome or his experiences in the city, it should be emphasized that we do not possess anything like such an account from Luther's own pen or mouth. It is not that fairly detailed descriptions of a trip such as his were unknown in his time. We have the written account of his contemporary, Nikolaus Besler, who went to Rome in 1505 and returned in 1509, as well as that of the Franciscan Konrad Pellikan, who visited Rome in 1517.[146] But from Luther we do not have a journal or even notes containing observations he made at the time of the trip. Nor did he sit down later, as so many other travelers have, in order to recount the trip from beginning to end in sequential detail. What we have instead is a random mass of incidental anecdotes and references told and retold by Luther (sometimes with multiple variations) years and even decades later. Many of these reminiscences were originally offered in oral form, as recorded in the *Tischreden*.

We must certainly take care to treat the accuracy of these *Tischreden*, the "records" of what Luther said in conversations at the table (dating to the 1530s and 1540s), with a healthy degree of skepticism, especially given the free-flowing nature of conversations held in these settings (and considering also the amount of beer and wine that may have been drunk).[147] Careless or selective listening and later editing no doubt took place, as noted above. Joannes Aurifaber was not himself present at many of the conversations he recounts. At the same time, however, it is also important to acknowledge that not everything that is recorded about Luther's trip to Rome in the *Tischreden* should be regarded with suspicion, especially when corroborated elsewhere in his writings or when the same or similar remarks are recorded by more than one scribe or on more than one occasion.[148] It is striking, in fact, that more of Luther's foul language was *not* edited out of the *Tischreden*, as might be expected if

Luther's scribes and editors were trying to present readers with a sanitized, hagiographical version of Luther's private life. However careful we must be in interpreting Luther's own recollections of the trip as recorded by others, the *Tischreden* are still invaluable sources that any biographer would be grateful to possess if we had them for historically important contemporaries of Luther. They need to be used with caution, of course, but so do all historical sources.

Travel stories are notoriously prone to variation, especially with the passage of time, even when told by the same person. It goes without saying that it would be wildly anachronistic for historians today to expect Luther either to have shared their own modern scholarly and scientific presuppositions or to have followed historiographical methodologies fully developed only centuries after his death, as he remembered and recounted his travel experiences years later. Luther was renowned for his prodigious memory,[149] but even the most retentive and strictly accurate of human minds cannot help but continually reinterpret the events of one's own life, refining some memories, dulling or deleting others, and possibly inventing still others, as the years and decades pass. Memory is a veil that may obscure as much as it reveals.[150] Furthermore, Luther's memory, astonishing as it may be when judged by modern standards, was not in fact perfect. It seems that he was not always entirely sure about important dates in his own life, even ones as unforgettable as the year in which he was excommunicated—or the date of his birth.[151]

As Luther remembered the trip in light of the momentous developments connected with the Reformation movement in the years following, reaching one ecclesiastical crescendo after another throughout the course of his life, it is almost impossible that his initial impressions would not have been colored by his subsequent attitudes. These were almost certainly formed as much by his fierce and ongoing contest with the papacy in later years as by the observations he made as a young man at the time of his visit to Rome. When, for instance, late in life (1540), Luther says that he went to Rome "in order to see the head of wickedness and the seat of the devil" (*ut caput scelerum et sedem Diaboli viderem*),[152] it is most unlikely that this was actually the perception of the city that he had in mind before or even during his visit. Indeed, as we have seen, Luther himself indicates elsewhere that he was motivated by an earnest pilgrim's desire to gain forgiveness of sins in this holiest of cities, not to check out all the evils of the place where the devil resided.

We should bear in mind that Luther himself is the ultimate source for anything and everything that can possibly be known for certain about his trip to Rome. Unfortunately, the period of Luther's life before 1512, when he received his doctorate, is relatively poorly documented compared to his later life after he had become a European celebrity. Contemporary records that might have indicated his presence or activities at places along the way or in Rome proper are either missing or silent. By contrast, later trips he took are amply testified to by contemporary witnesses and documented in a variety of records.[153] Of course, even when using what appears to be Luther's own direct testimony about his trip to Rome, we must be careful to differentiate what he says that he witnessed with his own eyes from what he may simply have read or heard from others.

Certainly, we do possess a number of references to Luther's journey to Rome made by contemporaries. There is no reason, however, to believe that any of them had independent access to direct sources regarding the trip other than Luther himself. These include some who were in close contact with Luther, such as Philipp Melanchthon, who wrote and published an all too brief biographical encomium in 1548;[154] Johannes Mathesius, a guest in Luther's house in 1540, who preached a series of sermons on the life of Luther in the 1560s;[155] and Luther's son Paul, whose own biography was written by Matthäus Dresser after Paul's death in 1593.[156] In addition, we have references to the trip to Rome in the biography of Luther published in 1549 by his indefatigable opponent, Johannes Cochlaeus,[157] as well as in the *Chronik* of Johan Oldekop of Hildesheim, who had originally studied in Wittenberg but who later became a staunch opponent of the Reformation.[158] Neither of these last two authors was particularly close to Luther, and not a single one of his biographers, whether hostile or positively inclined toward Luther, was acquainted with him at the time of his trip to Rome.

Persistent local legends have also arisen over the years as various communities where Luther might have visited have appropriated the story of the famous celebrity's trip to Rome for their own purposes.[159] While some of these stories might be based on long and reliable oral traditions, it is nearly impossible for them to be verified at this point. Others are more easily disproved. In Rome itself, for example, there is a *pasquino* (one of Rome's famous "talking statues") called Il Facchino, which has sometimes been identified as Luther. It is embedded in the outside wall of what is now the Banca di Roma on the Via Lata. The face of the statue is badly mutilated, probably as the result of paving stones being thrown against it by Romans who thought it represented the German reformer. Its soft cap is similar to the academic beret worn by Luther in one of his best-known depictions, a portrait painted in 1529 by his friend Lucas Cranach. Although the statue is sometimes attributed in the popular imagination to Michelangelo, in fact it was created long after Luther's visit to Rome by Jacopo del Conte (in the 1580s). It is thought to be a depiction of a water porter (*aquaiolo*) named Abbondio Rizzi, who is carrying a barrel that also serves as a drinking fountain.[160]

Given the absence of independent corroborating evidence, it would be theoretically possible to argue that the entire trip to Rome was invented from whole cloth by Luther. The motivation for so doing could have been to lend his personal critique of Rome more credibility. Such an idea seems farfetched on its face given how often and with what vivid and particular detail Luther himself refers to the trip.[161] But it is not entirely out of the question. Even his observations about specific experiences could have been derived from the written accounts of other contemporary travelers to Rome or from oral sources. It would also help explain why so many of his observations about Rome are inaccurate and why there are so many inconsistencies in his various accounts of the trip. This said, it is most unlikely that Luther would have gone to all the trouble to concoct a story such as this. The mere possibility that he could have done so, however, should serve as a sobering reminder about how much of what we say about Luther's journey to Rome depends ultimately on Luther's own memory and his veracity.[162]

However difficult it may be to agree on the exact details of Luther's trip, and no matter how many discrepancies we discover in his own account and those of others, at the very least we can be sure that his youthful experiences in Rome, even if significantly reimagined, assumed a great deal of significance to Luther with the passage of time.[163] Over the years, for himself and others, Luther managed to turn what might otherwise have been considered a somewhat routine trip made by an undistinguished monk into one of those momentous formative experiences that has shaped the history of the world ever afterward.

To clarify what Luther found most meaningful about the trip to Rome, we should perhaps first emphasize what Luther did *not* spend much time at all talking about. He made little mention of any physical hardships endured on what must have been a grueling trip to and from the city. If he and his companion averaged thirty to forty kilometers a day (a brisk pace), it would have taken them thirty-five to forty-five days to walk to Rome from Wittenberg by the shortest route today (approximately 1,400 kilometers). Based on how long it took Luther to get from Weimar to Augsburg in 1518, Böhmer estimates that it would have taken him at least forty-two days to walk from Erfurt to Rome (between 1,200 and 1,300 kilometers). In 1505, Nikolaus Besler, a fellow Augustinian, took forty-one days to walk from Munich to Rome (approximately nine hundred kilometers).[164] Of course, it may well have taken Luther and his companion longer, depending on the pace they set and how many detours they allowed themselves. There were many different ways to get from Germany to Rome by foot, and the routes were not always clearly indicated, nor were the pathways themselves always level and straight.

The difficulty of the trip was proverbial.[165] The walking would have been rendered even more difficult by the fact that Luther and his companion would have had to make their way over the Alps and the

Apennines in what could have been inclement weather. If Luther left Wittenberg early enough to arrive in Rome by the end of November, it is possible that he and his traveling companion might have avoided some of the worst weather they would have been sure to encounter if they had crossed the Alps a month or more later, but it is not at all uncommon for heavy snow to fall in the high mountain passes in the autumn months and even in the late summer. Indeed, the winter of 1510/11 was exceptionally harsh in Italy, with much snow in Bologna and unending rain in Rome.[166]

If the distance and weather were not obstacles enough for pilgrims coming from northern Europe to Rome, it was also not uncommon for them to be set upon along the way by murderers, robbers, and kidnappers, who found pilgrims attractive targets because of the money they often carried with them.[167] Some monastic pilgrims to Rome took with them no money, but Luther may have been provided with funds. According to Matthäus Dresser's *Narratio brevis de profectione Martini Lutheri in urbem Romam* (the first of many monographs over the years dedicated to Luther's trip to Rome, published in 1598), he took with him ten golden gulden. Dresser gives a different reason altogether for the trip than is usually provided. Luther went to Rome to try to gain a dispensation permitting Augustinian friars who were extremely weak (*in summa infirmitate*) to eat meat on fast days.[168]

Of all the possible discomforts and catastrophes that might have been experienced on such a trip, Luther mentions only one—namely, an apparent bout of fever from which he and his companion suffered (in Padua, according to Dresser).[169] One night, Luther says, they had left the windows open, and when they awoke the next morning, their heads "were so full of vapors" that they could barely travel one mile the next day and suffered terribly from thirst. Wine made them feel sick, and it would have been fatal (*letalis*) to drink the water.[170] Perhaps, it has been suggested, Luther was suffering from an incipient bout of malaria. Malaria was common enough in those days and often deadly. Pope Leo X is supposed to have died of "terminal malaria," although he may also have been poisoned.[171]

If it was malaria from which he was suffering, Luther's recovery was remarkably swift. His cure was affected, he says, by eating two pomegranates. In Italy, pomegranates usually do not ripen until the fall, so this is one of the bits of evidence that has been used by biographers upon which to base their calculations for the timing of the trip. Pomegranates were often given as gifts to Italian children on the feast day of *Ognissanti* (November 1). However, if stored at cooler temperatures, the fruit can remain edible for several months after harvest, so it is questionable how valuable this particular piece of information may be for dating with precision the time of year when Luther made his trip.

We should also note that Luther paid little attention afterward to what is considered by many tourists today to be some of the most breathtaking scenery in the world, the Alps. Although he does describe the safest mountain pass as "most pleasant" (*amoenissima*), it is only because it was the shortest, not the most spectacular route.[172] The soaring mountains, which he must have had plenty of opportunities to observe, close up and from a distance, elicit from him only a comment on the difficulties they must present for farmers.[173] Luther's silence in this regard is not so very surprising. Most scholars agree that it was only later that the Alps were converted from a cause of fear for travelers into a source of inspiration. The English lexicographer Samuel Johnson still regarded them as annoying "protuberances."[174] Unlike more recent pilgrims for whom an ambitious walking trip is itself as much the point as any particular destination, Luther seems to have had his eyes fixed firmly on his goal. The city of Rome itself is what interested him, much more than anything else, even the beauty of nature, that he may have seen or experienced on the way there or back.

So what happened to him in Rome that was so meaningful for Luther? As he reconstructs and retells his experiences in Rome years later, it is clear that he came to consider it an invaluable exercise in great (and false) expectations dashed. This had been a painful but educational moment for the sensitive, idealistic, and deeply religious young man. Looking back at the trip in a sermon preached decades later, Luther declares that he had gone to Rome as a "fool." He carried onions with him to the city and brought back garlic: "Whoever went to Rome and brought money with him would gain forgiveness for his sins. Like a fool, I, too, carried onions to Rome and brought back garlic."[175] According to Oberman, with this expression Luther means to say that he got cheated in a kind of unfair transnational exchange. He was fooled and received only "shit for shillings."[176]

With his reference to onions and garlic, Luther is likely referring to a popular story like one of the German *Märchen* collected in the nineteenth century by Karl Simrock. Once there were two merchants, the first of whom brought onions to a country where they were a rare commodity and received much money for his highly desirable product as a result. A second merchant, trying to follow up on this success, brought to the same country garlic, which was considered an even rarer commodity there. Since the people of the country had spent all their money on onions, however, the only thing they could give the second merchant in payment were onions, which, of course, they considered more valuable than money.[177] Unlike the second merchant in the story who came home with onions, Luther returned with garlic, but the point seems to be similar. Luther had hoped to get something in Rome—namely, the forgiveness of sins, which was much more valuable than what he and other pilgrims brought there (that is to say, money)—but he returned home after the exchange disappointed.[178]

Regardless of how we interpret the somewhat puzzling reference to onions and garlic, it is clear that later on, Luther regarded the trip to Rome as a decisive turning point in his spiritual development. The former "very crazy papist" (*papista insanissimus*),[179] trying to earn his way into heaven by doing good works and going on a pious pilgrimage to Rome, had become a more knowledgeable and critical Christian. All of this was thanks to his immersion experience in the very heart of the papacy: "I was a great big papist (*maximus papista*), and what's more, I observed their wickedness in Rome and learned and practiced their way of doing things."[180] This means that few could be in such a well-informed position to critique Rome as the spiritually mature Luther. He had been a devoted papist to begin with, and now he had a deep insider's perspective on how the flawed ecclesiastical system actually operated in Rome itself. From Luther's own retrospective point of view, the opening of his eyes to the spiritual degradation of Rome was dramatic, akin to the conversion of Saul on the road to Damascus that "rent such a great hole in the synagogue."[181] At the end of his life, Luther describes himself at this early stage in his spiritual maturation as "such a great Saul," applying to himself the former name of the apostle Paul, a strict Pharisee who had been deeply immersed in the very religious system that he ended up criticizing after he became a follower of Christ.[182]

Luther's own son Paul may have contributed to the dramatization of the decisive impact the trip to Rome supposedly had on his father at the time. He related that Luther once told him and others that while he was making his painful way up the steps of the Scala sancta, the passage from Habakkuk (2:4) quoted in the first chapter of Romans ("The just shall live by faith"; 1:17) suddenly occurred to him.[183] And when Luther got back to Wittenberg, his son declared, the Epistle to the Romans became "his most important foundation" (*sein hochst Fundament*).[184] If Luther's Reformation "breakthrough" (*Durchbruch*) really happened already when he was in Rome instead of somewhat later, it would give the trip even more importance from a biographical perspective. But tempting as it is to credit the testimony of a son, Paul was only thirteen years old when Martin died. And Paul's father does not himself suggest such an early timing for this theological breakthrough. In the autobiographical foreword to the edition of his Latin works in 1545, Martin Luther sounds quite convinced that it was only some years after his trip to Rome (probably 1518–19) that he first realized that the expression "the righteousness of God" in the first chapter of Romans referred to the righteousness that God bestows on humans through faith rather than the righteousness he demands from them in the form of good works.[185] It was at this turning point in his life, Luther declares, that he began to love the expression "the righteousness of God with as great a love as I had previously hated it." The apostle Paul's words were suddenly for him the "sweetest expression," and he felt that the gates of "paradise itself" had been opened to allow him to enter.[186]

It may well be, in fact, that Luther's theological "breakthrough" did not occur at any one single, transformative moment but was rather a cumulative process in which a number of different preliminary experiences played a role.[187] Luther's trip to Rome could certainly have been one of these experiences, if not the precipitating one.[188] That this spiritual process was somewhat unsteady and not nearly as dramatically decisive as the expression "breakthrough" suggests may be gathered from a letter that Luther wrote to Melanchthon in August 1527, in which he declares that he had recently been "in death and hell" and felt as though he had "almost lost Christ completely" and had been driven to "despair and blasphemy against God."[189] If there was indeed a momentous "breakthrough" for Luther a decade or more earlier, it could not have been as final and determinative a single event as it has sometimes been thought to be.

"But we speak of what we have seen" (*Sed quae vidimus, loquimur*). With what is possibly an allusion to a phrase used by the medieval theologian Bernard of Clairvaux,[190] Luther highlights in one of the *Tischreden* of 1536 what he believed to be one of the most helpful benefits he later on derived from his trip to Rome: "Because our Lord God brought me into this awful, hateful business, if someone offered me 100,000 florins not to have seen and heard Rome, I wouldn't take it; I would have to be careful not to do violence to him. But we speak of what we have seen."[191] The experience permitted him to confirm with his own eyes and ears the rumors he had heard about Rome, and for this reason, if for no other, he would not have missed it for anything. In fact, he recommended that anyone who wanted to become a preacher should "go to Rome and observe" the same things he had seen while there.[192] Such a preacher would be able to condemn Rome from the pulpit in a more vivid and powerful way than one who relied only upon hearsay. Elsewhere Luther says, "I couldn't have believed such things, even if someone had told them to me, unless I had seen them with my own eyes."[193] Luther may not have set out for Rome for this purpose, but when he was in the thick of his fierce ecclesiastical controversy with Rome, he was grateful that he could base his critique on his own firsthand observations rather than relying only upon the reports of others. The personal, physical, memorable connection that he made with the city of Rome as a pious pilgrim was something that he would use in the years to come to great effect to bolster his credibility with his followers—as a critic of Rome.

So what exactly were "such things" that Luther saw with his own eyes in Rome? Certainly, one thing that offended Luther deeply was that so many of the spiritual activities in Rome seemed to center on making money. He complained later, "After all, isn't the entire spiritual regimen basically nothing except money, money, money? Everything is aimed at making money."[194] If simony were eliminated, the splendor of the Roman curia "would be completely devastated."[195] Luther was not the first to point out that in the Vulgate's rendering of 1 Timothy 6:10, *Radix omnium malorum avaritia* ("The love of money is the root of all evil"), the first letters of the four Latin words spell *Roma*.[196] Already in 1520, he was complaining that in Rome, "no one considers what is right or wrong, but only what is money or is not money."[197] Of ecclesiastical law, he once declared, "Oh, how much taxing and cheating are the rule here, so that it appears as though every ecclesiastical law was put in place for the sole purpose of contriving ways to get hold of money. Anyone who wants to be a Christian must disentangle himself from this!"[198]

Avaricious Rome did not impress the budding German theologian as a hub of learning and knowledge. Far from being a place where the most intelligent and scholarly Christians of the day would congregate for the purpose of mutual edification and enlightenment, Rome disappointed Luther from an intellectual perspective. Some of the priests did not really know Latin, the indispensable language of the Vulgate and the liturgy.[199] "Under the pope, there was not a single person who knew grammar, dialectic, rhetoric," Luther declares hyperbolically in a sermon of 1532.[200] The cardinals, who were supposed to be the preeminent spiritual leaders of the church, were so busy with "matters of business and power" that they had little time for study, unlike the diligent Luther: "Then I came to Rome only to find the men there most unlearned. Oh, dear Lord God, what were the cardinals supposed to know, given that they were overwhelmed with matters of business and power? In my case, I have plenty of trouble even though I study day in and day out and practice every hour."[201] Even the humanist learning promoted by some of the Renaissance popes did not matter as much in Rome as did material things. In one of the *Tischreden* from the winter of 1542/43, Luther quotes a monk who had humorously described the situation in Rome thus: "At the time of the martyrs, people had a conscience (*conscientia*), but during the time of the popes and the bishops, they erased *con-* from the word *conscientia*, so that only knowledge (*scientia*) remained; now they have lost the syllable *sci-*, and nothing remains but things (*entia*)."[202]

The cardinals of Rome at Luther's time did indeed have many *entia*. Most of them were very well off. Many of the newly built and luxurious palaces in Rome in the early sixteenth century belonged to them. These included the Palazzo Venezia, rebuilt for Cardinal Pietro Barbo (later Pope Paul II) beginning in 1451; the Palazzo dei Penitenzieri near Saint Peter's, built for Cardinal Domenico della Rovere and finished in 1490; and the Cancelleria, built by Bramante for Cardinal Raffaele Riario between 1489 and 1513.[203] Other impressive palaces belonging to wealthy cardinals at the time include the Palazzo Altemps, acquired by Cardinal Francesco Soderini in 1511; the Palazzo Torlonia, residence of the Cardinal Adriano Castellesi, begun in 1496; and the Palazzo Madama, built for the Medici family and completed in 1505.[204]

Luther was also deeply offended by the trivialization in Rome of the very spiritual activities that he took most seriously, including the celebration of the Mass. He found worship in Rome rushed. The more Masses a priest said, the more income he could generate. Luther claims to have witnessed personally seven (or eight) Masses being celebrated within the space of one hour at "one altar of Saint Sebastian."[205] This is probably a reference to the church of S. Pietro in

Vincoli, where relics of the martyr Sebastian were housed in a chapel devoted to the saint, and not to the basilica bearing his name on the Appian Way.[206] Two priests would celebrate two different Masses at the same altar, Luther complained, heedless of the resulting confusion, because "they were most brazenly seeking to make money."[207] Before Luther could even get to the Gospel lesson in a Mass over which he was presiding, the priest next to him had already finished with his and was yelling at him, "*Passa. Passa.* Keep it moving. Get out of there."[208]

Luther also relates in one of his *Tischreden* how in Rome he overheard Carthusian monks laughing at dinner as they told how some priests made light of the solemnities involved in the sacred process of transubstantiation: "Over the bread and the wine they said, 'Bread you are, and bread you will remain' (*Panis es et panis manebis*)."[209] In another version of the same account found in *The Private Mass and the Consecration of Priests* of 1533, the "Carthusians" are *Curtisanen.*[210] These were not courtesans but ecclesiastical courtiers, "members of the papal court."[211] In later life, Luther had little love for either papal courtiers or Carthusians,[212] so it hardly matters whom exactly he overheard mocking the mysteries of the Eucharist. Such blasphemous language regarding the solemn Mass had hurt Luther deeply at the time ("I was a young and very pious monk, and such words caused me pain"), just as he was very offended by the "slapdash" (*rips raps*) fashion in which the Masses in Rome were conducted, "as if they were putting on a juggling show."[213]

The kind of simple piety on the part of visitors to Rome like Luther was noted with scorn by Romans who held a devout Christian "to be nothing more than a fool," especially if he took no money, as Luther did not, for celebrating Mass.[214] At the time of his visit to Rome, he was himself still a relatively new priest, just three or four years removed from his own first celebration of the Mass, an experience that had moved him deeply at the time. Even though he was "very well prepared," when he had approached the altar in Erfurt in 1507, he found himself trembling.[215] He was "utterly stupefied and terror-stricken" in the presence of "the divine majesty."[216] For all the time that Luther was in Rome, by contrast, he heard "not one little word of God."[217] Nor did he believe that anyone could be found in the city able to deliver a single "pious sermon."[218] In one of his own sermons, Luther declares that even though he was now a *doctor Scripturae*, he would still gladly have raced to Rome if he could hope to hear preached there "just one psalm, or one of the Ten Commandments, or one article of faith."[219] As far as the delivery of sermons in Italy was concerned, Luther deplored what he considered to be overly animated preachers: "By running around, contorting themselves, and using all sorts of different gesticulations and sounds, they come across as silly."[220]

Luther's critiques of Rome's ungodliness were by no means unique to him. Many northern humanists had traveled to Rome in the late fifteenth and early sixteenth centuries. These include such influential figures as Peter Luder, Rudolph Agricola, Conrad Celtes, Johann Reuchlin, and Desiderius Erasmus. Many of them returned from their visits filled not only with a deeper appreciation for the achievements of the Italian humanists but also with a more critical view of the Roman church. Five years or so before Luther's trip, Erasmus wrote of his own personal experiences in Rome: "With my own ears I heard the most loathsome blasphemies against Christ and his apostles. Many acquaintances of mine have heard priests of the curia uttering disgusting words so loudly, even during Mass, that all around them could hear it."[221] Ulrich von Hutten went to Italy twice, and in his *Vadiscus*, he observes caustically: "Three things there are which those who go to Rome usually bring back with them: a bad conscience, a ruined stomach, and an empty purse."[222] Ten years after Luther's visit there, Ignatius Loyola was advised against going to Rome because of its "stupendous depravity."[223] In the last year of his reign (1523), Pope Adrian VI admitted, "We know that for years there have been many abominable offenses in spiritual matters and violations of the Commandments committed at this Holy See, yes, that everything has in fact been perverted."[224] Luther notes that Cardinal Pietro Bembo had once called Rome the "sewer of the worst people and of the whole world" (*sentina pessimorum hominum et totius orbis*). In this connection, he quotes a Latin couplet of the Carmelite poet Baptista Spagnuoli Mantuanus: "You who want to live holy lives, depart from Rome. / Everything is permitted here, except for living an upright life."[225] Late in life, Luther quotes Mantuan's "About the Calamities of These Times, or the Seven Capital Sins":

> The house of Peter is decadent, defiled with luxury unrestrained. In this I am disclosing no secrets, I am telling nothing unknown, I crave permission to state matters of common knowledge. This is what the cities and peoples talk about, this is the scandal, the old established scandal throughout all Europe, that is destroying good sound morality: sacred land is given over to debauchees, the holy altar is made over to catamites, and the reverend temples of the gods serve the turn of Ganymede. Why be surprised that their wealth grows and their fallen houses are rebuilt? The effeminate Arab sells balls of scented incense, the Tyrian sells raiment; temples, priests, altars, holy things, wreaths, fires, incense, prayers are on sale to us—heaven is on sale—and God himself.[226]

According to *Retrato de la Loçana andaluza*, a salacious exposé of the underworld in Rome, written by Francisco Delicado and published in 1528, the city had over thirty thousand prostitutes. Indeed, Rome was said to have more of them than there were monks in Venice, philosophers in Greece, or doctors in Florence. *Roma puttana* was practically a bordello.[227] Many of the prostitutes lived close to each other in the Campo Marzio area, not far removed from where Luther would have been if he was staying at either S. Agostino or S. Maria del Popolo. That they moved in humanist circles may be discerned from the fact that many of their names were derived from Greek mythology (e.g., Cassandra, Penthesilea, Polyxena) and Roman history (e.g., Livia, Tiberia, Virgilia).[228]

Luther was also aware of the rumors of scandals that had swirled around previous popes like Alexander VI, who blatantly acknowledged his children by his mistresses and used his office to enrich other members of the Borgia family. It was said that one of his sons gambled away one hundred thousand ducats in one evening and laughed it off because the income from indulgences sold to the Germans would pay for it.[229] The mistress of Cesare Borgia, Fiammetta, had a chapel in S. Agostino and was buried in the church.[230]

Like the earlier reformer Savonarola (executed in 1498 when Luther was a teenager), who was notorious for his harsh attacks on Florentine immorality, Luther was a stern critic of contemporary mores as he observed them in Rome. On his trip to Worms in 1521, Luther was supposedly given a picture of Savonarola by a cleric in Naumburg who must have seen some sort of connection between the two reformers.[231] Of the "lasciviousness" (*scortatio*) in Rome under Julius II, Luther says that it was "so great beyond measure that it is shameful even to mention it. For under Pope Julius, a certain cardinal took a wife and after a year forced her to leave him and after that year took her back again. When the cardinal died, his wife cried, lamenting that she had had a good and decent husband who had been content with one wife."[232] Luther was also highly critical of the homosexuality of many in the Roman clergy. In one of his early letters (1516), he uses *sodomitari* synonymously with *romanari*.[233] Years later, in his Genesis lectures, he comments, "I saw some cardinals in Rome who were revered almost as saints because they contented themselves with the sexual company of women. There, you see, unspeakable acts of wickedness are committed not secretly or in private, but publicly, endorsed by the example and authority of the leaders and the entire city."[234]

Luther was even more concerned about the Roman church leaders' apparent lack of faith and the effect this had on those who looked up to them as spiritual shepherds. The scandalous way in which these ecclesiastical elites led their personal lives was inexcusable, but it was the doctrine and practice of the church that lay at the heart of Luther's most urgent concerns. At least as judged from his later perspective, it is not on account of their sanctified living that human beings are righteous in God's eyes. Indeed, sinners in Wittenberg were just as bad as sinners in Rome: "Our way of living is as bad as it is among the papists."[235] But the gravity of one's moral failings and sins in no way prevents God from forgiving them. Far from it. It is the sinful publican in Jesus's parable (Luke 18:9–14) who admits his faults as he prays in the temple, not the pious and far more upright Pharisee, who goes home justified. In his explanations of the Ninety-Five Theses (1518), Luther prefers the publican in the parable to the Pharisee, whose self-righteous contempt for sinners reminds him of those "unhappy" heretics, the Picards, and their tendency to "exult over Roman stench" instead of "showing compassion."[236]

Regardless of how corrupt the church in Rome may have appeared to a pious pilgrim like Luther, clerical depravity itself would have done nothing in principle to diminish the efficacy of the forgiveness he was supposed to be able to earn there. Like Augustine in his conflict with the Donatists, Luther believed that the validity of a sacrament in no way depended on how sinful or unworthy the officiant might be.

As earnestly as any other pilgrim fresh from the hinterlands, Luther wanted to make a full confession in Rome of all of his sins. But he had already done so twice before, while he was in Erfurt.[237] None of the years in which he might have been in Rome was a Jubilee Year, so the trip to Rome itself did not offer Luther plenary indulgence. Furthermore, there were many indulgences that Luther could have earned in Wittenberg. Frederick the Wise's collection of relics in the Castle Church was growing rapidly. By 1518, it had become one of the largest of such collections in Europe, with over seventeen thousand items. By 1520, there were over nineteen thousand pieces, which, if properly venerated, could earn pious pilgrims nearly two million days off of their stays in purgatory. In nearby Halle, it is estimated that thirty-nine million days of indulgence could be earned by visiting the collection of relics there.[238] According to a Spanish theologian, the average stay in purgatory lasted between one thousand and two thousand years (i.e., 365,000 to 700,000 days), so unless he and his loved ones were unusually sinful, Luther might as well have stayed at home if all he was seeking in Rome was a reduction in time to be spent in purgatory.[239]

There was something about the apostolic foundation of the Roman church itself, not simply the Masses that could be said and indulgences that might be earned in the city, that continued to command Luther's attention after his return home. Whether it was a sudden or gradual process by which he became disillusioned with much of the elaborate physical and spiritual superstructure that had been constructed over the centuries upon that foundation, the deep historical rootedness of the Roman church never lost its appeal for Luther.[240] Even before entering the city, as we have seen, Luther was aware of the early martyrs who had shed their blood there for the faith that he shared with them. In stark contrast with modern Romanists who persecuted reformers like Luther, these earliest Roman Christians were among the persecuted. They had lost their lives *for* the church rather than making their living *from* the church. And in Rome these blessed dead included not only the dubious saints of later pious lore but indisputably historical ones, including the chief of Jesus's disciples, Peter, the "rock" upon which Christ promised to build his church, and the great apostle to the gentiles, Paul. These were the twin patron saints of the city, the Romulus and Remus, if you will, of Christian Rome.[241]

As late as 1532, Luther still believed that Peter had been in Rome, "even though that is not able to be proven from Scripture."[242] This in spite of how skeptical he had by now become about the legends that had grown up around the deaths and remains of other saints.[243] By 1537, to be sure, when someone asked Luther at table why the "papists" did not make more of Paul instead of Peter, we find him pointing out the inconsistencies in the legends associated with Peter's connections with Rome. There is no explicit mention of a stay in or a visit to Rome on the part of Peter in the canonical New Testament:

> Peter has the keys, but Paul has the sword. For them [the Papists], it was more important to have the keys to unlock

the chests than the sword. What they write about Pilate, Caiaphas, and Peter coming to Rome before Caesar are fables. I do not know whether Peter came to Rome because the variations in the historical accounts make me suspicious, and the following gives me pause: Christ died under Tiberius, who reigned for five years after Christ, and they all say that Peter and Paul died under Nero, whose last year was the thirty-fifth year after the death of Christ. Now Saint Peter lived in Jerusalem some eighteen years after Christ, as Paul testifies to the Galatians, then seven years in Antioch, and after that the popular story is that he ruled for twenty-five years in Rome, for in all of the coronations of the popes, some boys go before them, setting off fireworks high in the sky and shouting, "Holy father, *Sic transit gloria mundi*. Remember, O pope, that you will not reign for as many years as Peter." For no pope has ever reigned for twenty-five years. If one now adds up all the years, Peter could not have been crucified under Nero, for that would be fifteen years too short. In sum, the reckoning of the histories is very confused. And Luke writes that Paul was a free man in Rome for an entire year, and he never mentions one word about Saint Peter [being in Rome].[244]

Even as late as 1545, however, we find Luther leaving open the possibility that Peter may have been in Rome, saying that he does not want "to be the judge" of the question, even as he acknowledges that "some learned people want to think that Saint Peter never came to Rome."[245]

Just as significant for Luther as Peter's historic presence in Rome, especially as the years passed, was that of Paul's, whose theology was proving to be so important for Luther's own. The final verses of the Acts of the Apostles present the reader with a picture of Paul dwelling for two entire years in his own residence in Rome, welcoming visitors, "preaching the kingdom of God, and teaching those things which concern the Lord Jesus Christ, with all confidence, no man forbidding him" (Acts 28:30–31). The apostle's letter to the Romans was one of the great building blocks of Luther's theology, an epistle that he considered "daily bread for the soul" and maintained that every Christian should know by heart.[246] Luther never doubted that Paul went to Rome or that he was executed there.

In 1519, nearly a decade after his trip to the city, Luther could still speak of the unique historicity and special divine status of the church of Peter, Paul, and other martyrs in glowing terms: "That the Roman church is venerated before God above all others there can be no doubt, because that is where Saints Peter and Paul, forty-six popes, in addition to many hundred thousands of martyrs, shed their blood and overcame hell and the world so that one can well see how God has a special consideration for these same churches."[247] Even much later, in 1539, nearly three decades after his visit there, Luther had still not forgotten that Rome was once "the most holy city" (*sanctissima*) despite its currently debased status (*nunc pessima facta*).[248]

During the latter part of his life, Luther evinced a growing interest in ecclesiastical history. Despite his increasing and angry impatience with contemporary Roman church officials, at the same time he was devoting more and more of his time to studying the history of their (and his) church. In 1539, he issued his "fundamental and exhaustive" work, *On the Councils and the Church*.[249] Rome, of course, is fundamental from any church historian's perspective. Even if Luther had by now begun to wonder whether Peter was actually buried in Rome, it still continued to be for him the single most important city of the Catholic tradition. No matter how unholy Rome had now become, no matter how unjustified the pope's claim to hegemony over other bishops of the church might be, Luther never suggests that the historical legacy of the eternal city should simply be forgotten or dismissed from consideration. Far from it. Even as new, independent churches began to be established all over Germany and elsewhere in Europe, with their own traditions and (much shorter) histories, Luther continued to think and write about the Roman church continually.

According to Oldekop, while Luther was in Rome, he was so favorably impressed with the city that he actually requested permission from the pope to stay on for ten years in order to study there "in worldly clothing." Because he had gone to Rome "more on account of his own desire and will" and did not have the authorization of his superior, his request was denied.[250] It is true that Oldekop's account in general is regarded as biased and unreliable by most scholars. This former student of Luther was firmly opposed to the Reformation by the time he wrote his *Chronik*. On the other hand, why would any biographer, even a biased one, go to all the trouble of fabricating such a story? Why might Oldekop have thought that an early desire on young Luther's part to stay longer in Italy would be a strike against him? The detail does not seem necessarily negatively biased. Still, Luther himself makes no mention of such a request, nor do any of his other early biographers.

"Who Knows Whether It's True?"

Luther's trip to Rome assumed significance in subsequent centuries in ways he could hardly have foreseen in his own lifetime. The image of a naive German monk scurrying around the streets of the grand, decadent city, amazed and appalled at what he saw and heard, eager to arrive but perhaps also just as eager to leave, is a compelling one, especially for those who imagine a strict dichotomy between Protestants and Catholics, northern and southern Europe, Germany and Italy. The iconic figure of Luther in Rome has often been seen as representing a decisive turning point not only in the history of the Reformation but also in the development of modern empirical sensibilities, the rejection of medieval "superstitions," and the evolution of Germany as an independent and powerful nation-state in its own right.

Perhaps the most iconic "modern" moment of all is the young German's self-described spasm of doubt at the top of the Scala sancta immediately following his painful ascent up the steps. The scene has been memorably filmed in the 1953 movie *Martin Luther*, which was nominated for two Academy Awards, and the 2003 movie *Luther*, starring Joseph Fiennes. When he got to the top of the steps, as we have seen, Luther says that he asked himself, "Who knows whether it's true?" As he goes on to explain to his congregation in Wittenberg years later, "That kind of praying isn't any good" (*Non valet ista oratio*).[251]

If we only consider the young man in doubtful perplexity at this moment, wondering at the top of the hallowed steps "whether it's true," it is not at all surprising that this Luther would be regarded by some as an incipient rebellious genius, a forerunner of the Enlightenment, paving the way for all of those skeptical visitors since—Protestants, agnostics, atheists, anticlerics, and others—who also learned to mistrust and even detest Rome and its fake pieties, its condescending pretentiousness, its fustiness, and above all its interest in profiteering from pilgrims.

In this number we may include Johann Wolfgang von Goethe, who loved pagan Rome and found the erotic freedoms he enjoyed in the city intoxicating even as he detested its Catholic manifestations. Of the time that Goethe spent in Rome in 1786/87, he declared that it was the only time "in his entire life" that he had been happy.[252] He even had a "strange desire" to hear the pope "open his golden mouth" to speak of salvation, but when he attended a celebration of the Feast of All Souls in the palace on the Quirinal, his reaction to watching the pope "gesticulating and muttering like an ordinary priest" was emphatically negative. His aversion, he felt, was an expression of his "Protestant original sin" (*protestantische Erbsünde*).[253] Goethe was raised in a Lutheran family. If there is an Adam ultimately responsible for Goethe's inherited antipapist sensibilities, it is hard to imagine any candidate more likely to be proposed than Luther.

The French novelist Stendhal (Marie-Henri Beyle), who was a frequent visitor to Rome, was keenly aware of the long shadows cast by "that great man" who had struck such fear "in the hearts of the popes," as he describes Luther in his Roman journal, *Promenades dans Rome* (1828).[254] Stendhal may not have prostrated himself as Luther did at the sight of Rome, but he does observe that "it is an immemorial custom . . . to be moved upon arriving in Rome," and he speaks of the deep stirring of his heart upon entering the eternal city.[255] Like Luther, who was struck by the catacombs of Rome, the sensitive Stendhal was deeply affected by his visit to the tombs in Santa Croce in Florence. He even fell into "a sort of ecstasy" there, complete with heart palpitations (the so-called Stendhal syndrome).[256] But Stendhal also knew that not all visitors to Rome shared his passion. He was quite aware of "the bored eyes of most of the foreigners who tramp the streets of Rome," who within a month of arrival in the city "soon have more than their eyes can stand of paintings, statues and great architectural works" and quickly "develop an aversion for Rome."[257] As much as Stendhal himself loved the city and its inhabitants, not least because he appreciated "the Roman revery, which seems so sweet to us and makes us forget all the interests of active life,"[258] he considered Roman Catholicism to be a "religion of terror."[259] "Above all things," he observes, "Rome fears free inquiry, which may lead to Protestantism. Hence the art of thinking has always been discouraged here and, when necessary, persecuted."[260]

Deep ambivalence toward Rome can be detected in other later visitors as well. Sigmund Freud yearned for the city as "ardently" as Aeneas but at the same time "longed to destroy it as passionately as Hannibal."[261] Freud loved Michelangelo's sculpture of Moses in the church of Saint Peter in Chains. He wrote an essay entitled "Moses and Michelangelo" in 1914 after studying the sculpture intensely for "three lonely weeks." Otherwise, he was "deeply neurotic" about gentile Rome. It took years of "determined and unsparing self-analysis" before Freud could finally overcome his resistance to the idea of visiting the city. He "triumphantly entered Rome" only when he was in his midforties, in 1901.[262]

If Freud's phobia about Rome may be attributed to his own cultural and religious affiliations, Protestantism no doubt generated just as much anti-Catholicism among other visitors to the city. Of the pious pilgrims he saw climbing the Scala sancta on their knees some three hundred years after Luther's own ascent, the English novelist Charles Dickens wrote scathingly, "I never in my life, saw anything at once so ridiculous, and so unpleasant, as this sight—ridiculous in the absurd incidents inseparable from it; and unpleasant in its senseless and unmeaning degradation."[263] As William Vance has suggested, for many American elites in the nineteenth century who envisioned Rome in art and literature or actually visited it, the city represented the epitome of the exotic, even sinister Catholic "other."[264] The midwestern American satirist Mark Twain found in the city too many churches and "well-fed priests" for his liking.[265]

It is tempting to project onto the figure of Luther wrapt in doubt at the top of the Holy Steps the same kind of enlightened skepticism we perceive in later Protestants like the Victorian Dickens or anticlerics like Twain. Richard Marius imagines that Luther was plagued by very deep doubts indeed, "swept along" as he was "by one of the great recurring waves of skepticism in human history." These doubts, according to Marius, included fundamental ones: "that God exists at all and that he can or will raise the dead."[266] The question that Marius's youthful Luther asked at the top of the staircase in Rome "seems to have reverberated in his heart throughout his life."[267] In the context of the sermon of 1545 in which Luther recounts this episode, however, it is clear that his expressed doubts were quite limited; they only applied to the ability of the prayers said on the Holy Steps to affect the release of souls from purgatory. Luther explains what he means by "Who knows whether it's true?" with the very next words preached to his congregation: "That kind of praying isn't any good."[268] It is the very specific kind of praying that he had just been doing on the steps (*ista oratio*), repetitive and manipulative, about whose efficacy he was now dubious, not every kind of prayer or prayer in general.[269] It may even be that Luther was simply wondering to himself if the steps he had just climbed were authentic.[270]

In any event, as opposed to sure knowledge, doubt is not entirely incompatible with faith, contra Marius. At the top of the steps, Luther does not say that he now *knows* for certain that "it is not true." He is simply questioning whether anyone does know if it is true. Such doubts often occur to those even with the firmest of faiths. A degree of dubiousness as to the value of climbing these particular steps in order to reduce time spent in purgatory does not necessarily mean the obliteration of religious confidence altogether.

As Oberman observes of Luther's famous question ("Who knows whether it is true?"), it would be a mistake to see this "flash of doubt" as "indicative of the emergence of a 'new skepticism' and the onset of the Enlightenment; his kind of skepticism rather arose from the conviction that God would not allow Himself to be pinned down in this way."[271] No matter how much the visit to Rome may have led to skepticism in Luther's mind, at the time itself or later on, about the legitimacy of relics and indulgences or the veracity of the legends of saints and their miracles, we have no reason to believe that it did anything at all to shake his belief in fundamental Christian doctrines, including repentance and the power of prayer. While Marius opines, "I think Böhmer is incorrect in his contention that Luther's journey to Rome left his Catholicism fundamentally unshaken," he presents little actual evidence to support his own contention.[272]

No one can fully explore the recesses of anyone else's heart or measure the sincerity of religious faith, especially from such a distance as we are removed from Luther, but he does indeed seem to have remained faithful until the end of his life to the chief tenets of the Christian faith despite frequent attacks by the devil and his own conscience. In fact, in the first of his famous Ninety-Five Theses of 1517, Luther offers a ringing endorsement of the importance of genuine repentance as a mainspring for the Christian life: "When our Lord and Master Jesus Christ said, 'Repent, etc.,' he meant that the whole life of the faithful should be one of repentance."[273] After his visit to Rome, Luther certainly developed serious doubts about the legitimacy of the notion of paying for indulgences in order to reduce time in purgatory, but it is clear that in 1517 he was more committed than ever to the principles of repentance and forgiveness of sin.

As for prayer, long after he returned home from Rome, Luther continued to pray daily the same *Pater noster* he had recited on the Holy Steps. "Every morning—and whenever I have time," he wrote in his preface to the *Large Catechism* (published in 1529), "I read and say, word for word, the Ten Commandments, the Creed, the

Lord's Prayer, the Psalms, and such. I must still read and study them daily."[274] Luther also turned the Lord's Prayer into German verse in one of his late chorales (1539), *Vater unser im Himmelreich* (1539), still sung in Lutheran churches to this day.[275]

Nor, in spite of all of the mockery of eucharistic sanctities that he witnessed in Rome, did Luther lose confidence in the reality of Christ's presence in the elements, which he contended for vigorously in the face of opposition from the Swiss theologian Ulrich Zwingli and other reformers who were inclined to interpret the mystery of the Lord's Supper symbolically and not literally.

Eventually, Luther did indeed lose whatever faith he might have once had in the utility of pilgrimages. By 1520, he had begun to express strong reservations about pilgrimages to Rome, although even then he did not consider them always in and of themselves to be "bad," even if they were "ill-advised at this time."[276] Such trips might bring one closer to the actual physical remains of the saints of old, but not necessarily to their spirits. In a sermon preached in 1539, Luther told his congregation,

> We do not have the head of Paul or Peter, etc., but we do have the spirit and soul of both of them, that which they have in their hearts. In Rome they still don't know where either of their heads is. God dealt with their bodies as he did with Moses's. He had to die in the desert so that the Jews wouldn't worship him. In France there are supposed to be six apostles, in Spain four. Trier has Matthew. But we have John, Peter, and Paul alive, just as we have Christ; their spirits and souls live in us and speak with us. Even if I had their bones in a gold coffin, they still would not speak to us.[277]

Even if Luther disparaged the idea of physical pilgrimages to Rome later on, he never lost his interest in what might be considered the ultimate spiritual purpose of such a pilgrimage. He continued to express keen interest in appropriating for himself and his followers "the spirit and soul" of the two great patron saints of the city, especially Paul. In one of his last sermons, preached on January 26, 1546, the day after the Feast of the Conversion of Saul, Luther assured his listeners that "the dear Paul is our apostle." So are the other apostles, of course, but Paul is singled out as "our apostle" because "he came to Rome and abundantly preached and taught the gospel of faith in Christ Jesus there and was beheaded there." In the sermon, Luther makes much of Paul's ministry and death in Rome but also assures his congregation members that they need not go to Rome to see Paul's dead body, since they themselves already possess the "real body and spirit of Paul in his holy epistles."[278]

As represented by some Catholic critics and Protestant admirers of his own time and thereafter, Luther was already at the time of his visit to Rome a budding rebel against ecclesiastical authority—an incipient proto-Protestant, as it were. Cochlaeus says that Luther was chosen by the dissenting monasteries to represent them, noting that "he had a sharp (*acer*) disposition and was bold and fierce when it came to disagreement."[279] Hartmann Grisar suggests that Luther viewed the positive religious benefits that Rome had to offer pilgrims with suspicion even before he visited there. According to this view, the youthful Luther was already predisposed to see the dark side of popular piety, and his experiences in the city did not so much change his views about the uselessness of pilgrimages as confirm them.[280]

Especially if Luther was sent to Rome by order of Staupitz in 1511, not in opposition to him in 1510, it may be more accurate to see him at this early stage of his spiritual development not as an incorrigible rebel, perfectly willing to challenge his monastic superior, but rather as "a true son of his spiritual father Staupitz, and an obedient monk of his order."[281] Our perspective on Luther in Rome changes considerably if we not only fix our gaze on his figure, perplexed and dubious, at the top of the Holy Steps, but also train our eyes on the German pilgrim a few minutes earlier, still on his knees, praying over and over again the *Pater noster* in his slow ascent up the steps. We should remember that this is the same Luther who not many days earlier had dropped to the ground at the mere sight of the sacred city in the distance. This is the same Luther who was still addressing Pope Leo X in 1518 in superlative terms as his "most blessed father," before whom he "prostrated" himself metaphorically, just as he had physically done when he first viewed papal Rome.[282] This young friar may have been in Rome to carry out an assigned mission for his order, but at the same time, he was determined to turn the trip into a true pilgrimage, seeking spiritual sustenance in his quest for salvation. That he would be so very critical of specific spiritual practices that he observed in Rome, then or later, only serves to confirm the seriousness with which he regarded the lofty ideals of genuine repentance and forgiveness that underlay such religious protocols in the first place.

To understand Luther's state of mind at the time aright, it may help to situate him within the long and broad tradition of sacred pilgrimages. Such journeys, of course, loom large in religious traditions other than Christianity. The holy city of Mecca, birthplace of Mohammed, is visited by millions of Muslims annually (the Hajj is one of the five pillars of Islam). At the time of his visit to Rome, young Luther's reverential attitude toward the holy city of his own faith was probably not all that different from that of the typical Islamic pilgrim today.

Luther was by no means the first, of course, to make a trip to Rome for spiritual reasons. Within a century of Constantine's conversion, we find the Spanish poet Prudentius making a trip to "the city of Romulus" and marveling at the sheer quantity of saints' remains that he saw there.[283] Hildebert of Lavardin (d. 1133) made several trips to Rome and was deeply impressed by its ruins. No other city, he wrote, could compare to it: "Nothing is equal to you, Rome, even though you are nearly a complete wreck. But broken as you are, you teach us how great you were when intact."[284]

Luther's pilgrimage to the holy city was also certainly not among the last. Up to the present day, millions of credulous, pious, and expectant pilgrims like the young German friar have made the arduous trip to Rome to catch a glimpse of the man they regard as their spiritual father, to worship reverently in Saint Peter's and other churches, to pray devoutly as they climb the Holy Steps, to feel vividly the link between themselves and all of the blessed dead, including those great apostles Peter and Paul, who have gone before them. And for them, too, the experience has been unforgettable. Rome is truly holy in the eyes of many of these pilgrims.

Consider the emotion-filled nineteenth-century *laudatio Romae* in the Fifth Lesson in the Second Nocturne of the Proper Office of the Saints for July 4:

> This is why I love Rome, although if I would, there are many other things for which I might praise her—her greatness, her antiquity, her beauty, her population, her empire, her wealth, or her victories. But all these I pass by, and I call Rome blessed for this cause that Paul, in his lifetime, loved her children as well, was so kindly toward them, taught openly there, and at length laid down his life among them. They have there his holy body, and this alone maketh that city illustrious more than doth aught else. And just as a great and strong body hath two bright eyes, so are the bodies of these two Holy Apostles in the city of Rome.[285]

The Sixth Lesson goes on to imagine what the city of Rome will see on the last day when "she beholdeth Paul and Peter rising suddenly out of that coffin, to be caught up to meet the Lord."[286] Something like this reverent state of mind may well have been possessed by Luther as he entered the city and began to explore its sacred wonders.

Some visitors to Rome who started out as Protestant skeptics have turned into true admirers of the city later—an interesting reversal of the pattern of Luther's relationship with Rome. When John Henry Newman first visited Rome in 1833, he regarded it "with deep and conflicting thoughts." As Joyce Sugg puts it, "He loved the city, and he feared it too."[287] He was "nervous of the city and its religion, terrified of priests, anxious about the fulfilment of apocalyptic prophecy."[288] Newman himself remembers hearing a "speculative Anglican" saying that a Christian could never view the city "without the bitterest, the most loving and the most melancholy thoughts."[289] Its art and architecture were marvelous in the young man's eyes, but although he was fully aware that Rome was the home of the early apostles, he also saw in the city the grim reminders of a cruel empire and a corrupt church. He considered the Colosseum the Roman equivalent of the tower of Babel.

Eventually, Newman converted to Roman Catholicism, was ordained a priest, and was installed as a cardinal in Rome, much to the consternation of his Protestant friends and family in the British Isles. He was recently canonized (October 13, 2019). Over the course of his subsequent visits to Rome, Newman's views of the city changed considerably. When he was staying at the Propaganda College in 1846 near the Vatican, he wrote that he had been "happy" before at Oriel, "happier" in other locations, but found himself "happiest" in Rome: "It is so wonderful to find myself here, in Propaganda—it is a kind of a dream—and yet so quiet, so safe, so happy—as if I had always been here—as if there had been no violent rupture or vicissitude in my course of life—nay more quiet and happy than before."[290]

Such rapturous responses to Rome are not unknown even in more recent times. The modern city still has the capacity to enthrall the devout visitor. Bishop Richard J. Sklba recollects his early days as a young American student in Rome in the 1950s: "The exposure to Italy of the mid-fifties was truly an entirely new world for me, just having turned nineteen, mid-college, and having been fairly sheltered by my Wisconsin background. The thrill of living in such proximity to the tomb of Peter just a short passeggiato [*sic*] down the hill was an opportunity I could never have imagined! The possibility of encountering the austere figure of Pius XII so regularly was virtually inconceivable until I arrived and even heard his voice."[291] More recently, Cheryl White, who returned to Roman Catholicism after twenty years as an Episcopalian, speaks of looking forward to a general audience in Rome with Pope Francis "with an excitement [she] could hardly contain." The "thrill" of being able to take a photograph of the pope made it, she says, "a day I will never forget."

Despite the fact that before her visit to the excavations (*scavi*) beneath Saint Peter's, White prepared for "the likely flood of emotions," she admits that when she did experience it, "nothing could have prevented me from openly weeping."[292]

Even though they may never become fervent Catholics like Cardinal Newman or Cheryl White, there are still plenty of Protestants today who, as Joshua Kinlaw puts it, "are drawn to Rome, though we define ourselves against it. Strictly speaking, we do not go there on pilgrimage. Yet we have always visited Rome, at once attracted and repulsed. It began in 1510, when Martin Luther took the trip that triggered the Reformation."[293]

When we attempt to imagine the feelings that the young Augustinian friar may actually have had while he was in Rome, we should try to capture their entire possible range. On the one hand, there is no reason at all to question the idea that Luther really did experience a dull throb of doubt as he reached the top of the Holy Steps or even felt the seething pulse of incipient hatred as he left the city behind him and began making his way back home to Germany. His disturbing experiences in the sacred city, too, which he recounts later, need not all be regarded only as retrospective reconstructions with no basis in reality.

On the other hand, it would be a mistake to assume that this young visitor to the city did not also experience something of the same thrilling, almost ecstatic sense of spiritual excitement that others have felt upon visiting this most sacred (to them) of cities. Like other pilgrims, Luther appears to have been overwhelmed by the mere sight of the long-anticipated cityscape of holy Rome laid out below him in the distance. Like other pilgrims, he ran around visiting as many of the churches of Rome as he could during his brief time there. And like other pilgrims to Rome before and since, Luther never afterward forgot or tired of telling about visiting the places where the bodies of so many early saints and martyrs lay buried underground, as he made his own personal and physical connection with the deep Christian past.

Hundreds of years before Luther, Jerome (d. 420) described the powerful feelings he experienced as a boy when he would go down into the catacombs of Rome:

> As you enter, the walls on either side hold the bodies of the dead and everything is so dark that it nearly seems as if that prophecy had been fulfilled: "Let them descend into hell while living" [Ps 55:15]. And the diffused light comes down from above so that you would think that it does not enter through windows but rather through a light shaft, relieving the horror of the shadows. And again, as you cautiously step forward, surrounded by black night, there comes to mind that line of Virgil [*Aeneid* 2.755]: "Horror everywhere terrifies my soul and at the same time the very silence itself."[294]

Hundreds of years after Luther visited the catacombs, Fulton J. Sheen, in the early 1960s, made similar observations about the "sense of awe and wonder which the catacombs inspire in the mind of anyone who has explored them, and no matter how many times one has descended into that chilly silence which is blacker than blackness."[295]

It is the intense passion of the "crazy" pilgrim who experiences a "sense of awe and wonder" in a sacred place that may help account for the depth of Luther's later angry resentment of the city he had once regarded as "holy" and even "most holy." Certainly, the youthful Luther who wondered "whether it's true" may well have inspired more than one skeptical visitor to Rome since his momentous trip, including those who have viewed it as the seat of the antichrist or the epitome of religious hypocrisy. But the throngs of pious pilgrims—there were some four million visitors to the Vatican in 2016—who have been "thrilled" to be in the holy city because of its physical connection with Christianity's historic past may also be seen as following in the footsteps of the pious German friar whose complex relationship with Rome has troubled the Christian world ever since.[296]

2

"I Love Cicero"

THE LATINIST

EVEN THOUGH IT WAS primarily the "holy" city, Christian Rome, that was at the center of Luther's attention during his visit there, he did not ignore the monuments of the ancient pagan city that had remained standing over the years. Later in life, he comments on some of these. Far fewer of the remains of republican and imperial Rome were visible at Luther's time than today, especially after all of the excavations of recent centuries. Nor were they as accessible to visitors then as the Christian sites were. Medieval guidebooks to Rome paid more attention to churches and sacred relics than to ancient ruins.[1] Not every pious pilgrim took particular notice of pagan Roman remnants. The fact that Luther did so while he was in Rome is telling.

Long after Luther returned home, the ancient city and its civilization continued to command his attention. The venerable language of the Romans, Latin, which he himself mastered; the verbal genius of its poets; the virtues of its great leaders; the wisdom of its philosophers; the extent of its civilizing power—all of these positive aspects of Rome continued to resonate with him as long as he lived. The demise of the Roman Empire interested Luther deeply. It was not only a matter of historical inevitability that great empires such as Rome should perish but also a matter of divine judgment. Like Babylon in the Old Testament, Luther's Rome was a great city doomed for destruction. For all of their virtuous qualities, which Luther respected enormously, the ancient Romans were still lost without Christ. And the most visible proof thereof was the fact that the great city Luther visited was now just a shadow of its former self.

Luther's attitude toward the cultural achievements of the ancient Greeks and Romans has often been misunderstood. We should not allow his disapproval of Aristotle's philosophy as applied to Christian theology by the scholastics, his harsh disparagement of Epicurus and "Epicureans," or his privileging of faith over meretricious reason to cause us to overlook the respect with which he regarded some aspects of what we in the English-speaking world today refer to as "the Classics." Nor, as we shall see, should we take entirely seriously his own self-dismissal as something of a "barbarian" when it came to his expertise in the ancient languages and literatures, especially Latin.[2] And even if it is true that Luther was averse to the notion of free will championed by his humanist adversary, Erasmus, his own anthropology was actually closer to that of the humanists of his time (including Erasmus) than to that of many posthumanists or transhumanists today.

There can be little question that despite differences with his fellow humanists, Luther was as interested in classical antiquity as they were. Like them, Luther was intent on returning to authoritative literary sources (*ad fontes*) instead of relying on later traditions, eager to cultivate personally the study of ancient history and languages, and deeply concerned to make sure that young people were well educated in the liberal arts so that they might become useful citizens of their respective communities. Certainly, like other early modern humanists, he could and did write distinguished Latin prose and verse. Luther also found much in ancient Roman morality to admire, and he thought deeply about the lessons that might be learned from Roman history.

It would not be misleading, therefore, to describe Luther as a "Latinist," if by that term we mean not a professional classical scholar but someone with a deep and abiding interest in "the Latin language or Roman culture."[3] To be sure, Luther was not exactly the same kind of humanist as Erasmus, who wrote the most elegant Latin, or his own erudite colleague Melanchthon, who produced scholarly editions of ancient authors.[4] Nor, for that matter, did this "biblical humanist," as Luther has been aptly described, resemble anything like the typical modern classical philologist or archeologist who studies the pagan Greco-Roman past but pays only slight attention to early Christian texts and antiquities.[5] In what follows, I shall suggest that Luther's engagement with pagan Rome was neither simply inevitable nor purely superficial. Whether or not he can be said to have directly (or indirectly) influenced others since who have wandered through the ruins of ancient Rome and pondered the meaning of the decline and fall of its great empire, Luther certainly needs to be included prominently in their number.[6]

"Now It Has Been Ravaged" (*Iam lacerata est*)

When he related his first impressions of the city years later, Luther remembered being struck from afar by how greatly sixteenth-century Rome differed from what he imagined to be its former, grander self. After he caught his first glimpse of Rome and greeted it, as we have seen, his very next thought was to describe its current dilapidated condition as "ravaged" (*lacerata*). In one of his table conversations when he was talking about the former "grandeur" (*pompa*) of Rome and its monuments, he observed that the "city now is clearly a corpse" (*cadaver*).[7] Just a few decades earlier, the Italian humanist Poggio Bracciolini had made a similar observation about the ruins of ancient Rome; they seemed to him "like a gigantic rotted corpse."[8] Centuries later, the metaphor was still in vogue. Rome reminded the Irish novelist James Joyce "of a man who lives by exhibiting his grandmother's corpse."[9]

Luther was struck by how much debris had accumulated in the city over time. He noticed that the foundations of modern buildings were at the level where the roofs of earlier buildings had been. In a sermon of 1535, he told his congregation, "But Rome is a rats' nest (*Rattennest*) and not worthy of being called a city; it is as far under the ground as two men [standing on top of each other]."[10] In another sermon of the same year, he illustrated this point vividly by indicating that ancient Rome lay as deep under the surface as he himself stood in the pulpit above his congregation.[11] Once he observed at table that it was easy to see "how deep the rubble lies towards the Tiber and the bridge."[12] Luther was probably thinking of the bridge known today as Ponte Sant'Angelo, originally built in 134 CE by the emperor Hadrian (its Latin name Pons Aelius reflects Publius Aelius Hadrianus's family name) to facilitate access to his mausoleum on the west side of the Tiber River. It was known as Pons Sancti Petri in the Middle Ages because it was regularly crossed by pilgrims making their way to Saint Peter's Basilica from elsewhere in Rome.[13] There was nothing in this part of the city, according to Luther, but "pure rubble" (*eittel schutt*) extending as deep as the length of two pikes carried by a *Landsknecht* (a German mercenary soldier).[14]

Certainly, there were not nearly as many people in Luther's Rome as there had once been. The Aurelian Walls had at one time enclosed one of the largest urban populations of the ancient world, but the Roman populace in Luther's day had been dramatically reduced to a size that was only a fraction of its former number. During a conversation at table in 1537, Luther held forth on the size of the city of Rome and the number of citizens in the Roman Empire: "The size of Rome, as I have seen it, is as wide as it is from here to the Poltersberg." After that, Luther took time to read "from the historians about the number of Roman citizens: 20 years before Christ's birth there were 4,100,000 citizens, and not much longer thereafter they were 6,900,000 in number." Luther was impressed by that last number, "if it is true" (*si verum est*). Someone else at the table then observed that the city of Rome could only support 50,000 men at the present time.[15] Rome was far smaller in 1510–12 than other Italian cities such as Florence (approximately 100,000 inhabitants) and Venice (approximately 167,000 inhabitants). Shortly before the time of the sack of Rome in 1527, the city had 55,035 inhabitants.[16]

The word *lacerata* suggests that from Luther's perspective, the city that he glimpsed in the distance had been not just neglected but deliberately ravaged. The Latin verb *lacerare* carries with it connotations of physical rather than spiritual ruination, and the physical city of Rome that Luther visited had certainly suffered over the years, whether at the hands of invaders from without or at the hands of residents from within. Beginning as early as the fifth century CE, the splendid marble-clad buildings of old were beginning to be used as though they were stone quarries; in 458, the emperor Majorian passed an edict directed against the dismantling of ancient buildings.[17] Like other such subsequent legislation, it had little effect.

From the distance at which Luther first caught sight of the city, the bell towers of churches would have been visible as well as the tops of some ancient monuments and modern buildings, but actual traces of "ravaging" may have been harder to make out. Certainly, stretched out below him, there would have been large tracts of meadows, vineyards, trees, and other verdure within the ancient city walls, far more than there would have been in Augustus's or Trajan's bustling Rome. Whether Luther could really discern from his vantage point high on Monte Mario the contrast between Rome's ancient splendor and its current diminishment, or whether the sight only confirmed an impression that he had already previously formed in his mind, is hard to know for certain.

On the other hand, some of Luther's observations about the ancient city do seem to be based on firsthand and close-up experiences. During the four weeks he was in Rome, Luther not only took time to visit popular pilgrimage sites but also made a point of wandering around the ruins of "old Rome." He did so despite the enormous risks involved, as we learn from one of the *Tischreden* of 1536: "Then he made mention of the sites of Rome, which he had wandered around for four weeks at very great danger to himself (*in summo periculo*), and he said it was clear that that place, old Rome with its very fine buildings (*optima aedificia*), had been leveled to the ground by the Goths."[18] Especially if Luther was unaccompanied on these expeditions or had only one companion, the German tourist could have been quite vulnerable to thieves and others who might have wished to prey upon him.

The dangers in the city to which Luther alludes may have been just as real in his time as in the thirteenth century, when the Roman Senate passed an edict that forbade the kidnapping of pilgrims, giving us some indication of the severity of the risks faced by visitors to Rome.[19] At least at night, according to Luther, the streets were patrolled by hundreds of police, who stopped people and searched them, but there was still plenty of violence in Rome: "If anyone is caught on the streets, he must stop, and if he has a weapon on him, he is either hanged or drowned and thrown into the Tiber or given a whipping. Still, life is grim and murderous there."[20]

Among the ancient "sites of Rome" that it seems he was determined to view, Luther mentions the Colosseum, still one of the most easily identifiable landmarks of the city today: "There is a round structure in the form of a theater, and in fact it reaches the height of fifteen rows of seats in a circle and holds two hundred thousand people. Its walls and foundation are still extant."[21] Technically speaking, the Colosseum is an amphitheater, not a theater, and its capacity was more limited than Luther imagined; ancient sources calculated that it could hold close to ninety thousand people, but the number was probably closer to fifty thousand. (Luther may have been thinking of the seating capacity of the Circus Maximus, which could indeed accommodate several hundred thousand people.) But even though he did not assign the Flavian amphitheater its proper name, got the term for its architectural form wrong, and overestimated its seating capacity, Luther cannot have been thinking of any other ancient Roman building than the Colosseum.

Begun by the emperor Vespasian in 72 CE and finished by his son Titus eight years later, by Luther's time, the Colosseum had long since ceased to be used to hold the gladiatorial contests and gory animal extravaganzas for which it had been so well known in antiquity.[22] The great arena was essentially abandoned, and eventually people began to set up housing in its archways. In the twelfth century, the Frangipane family took over part of the structure and fortified it. As a well-known site of Christian martyrdoms, the Colosseum had long been considered a consecrated space, and a small chapel was set up there in 1519. On Good Fridays, Santa Maria della Pietà al Colosseo (the amphitheater's Roman Catholic designation) is where the pope has traditionally led the Stations of the Cross. By the end of the sixteenth century, Pope Sixtus V had become interested in converting the entire building into a wool factory. Even as late as the nineteenth century, so much vegetation was still growing in the arena that it was possible for Richard Deakin to identify 420 plants there, some of them exotic, thanks to all of the seeds in excrement left behind by animals brought from as far away as northern Africa and Asia Minor to be slaughtered.[23] Only in the 1870s was the site finally cleared for archeological purposes.[24]

Luther was aware of the seven hills (*septem montes*) traditionally associated with Rome. He must have walked up and down some if not all of them in the course of his visit there. In one of the *Tischreden* of 1532, he points out that much of the population of Rome had long ago moved to those areas of the city such as the Campo Marzio and Trastevere that lay outside the ancient urban area once defined by these seven hills: "And Rome, which once had been famous for its seven hills, is now altogether laid waste, so that no emperor or pope can restore it again after the devastation of the Goths, and it now only exists where once there was countryside, outside the area of those seven hills."[25]

Of the hills of ancient Rome, Luther describes the Capitoline as being in such a state of ruin that nearly no monuments could be seen on it except for one building. No doubt he is referring to the Senatorial Palace (Palazzo Senatorio), constructed beginning in the middle of the twelfth century atop the ancient Tabularium, an imposing records and office building built during the late Republican period of Roman history: "And he spoke about the Capitoline Hill, how it was so ground down that nearly no monuments at all were visible there except for one structure that had been fused together with great boulders and stones that cannot be destroyed. But the Goths are supposed to have hewn a hole into each stone to indicate eternal devastation."[26] There are holes still visible in the southern wall of the Tabularium, as there are in the Colosseum, but their regularity suggests that they were intended to serve as clamp holes. As the clamps themselves were made of metal such as bronze, they were most likely removed for their value, leaving the holes empty.[27] It is unlikely that the Gothic invaders would have taken time to drill holes with such precision simply in order to make some sort of statement about the permanence of the devastation they had wrought upon the eternal city.[28]

Michelangelo's extensive redesign of the northwestern side of the Capitoline Hill was not begun until well after Luther left the city. But Luther was quite impressed by the Tarpeian Rock, a precipitous cliff descending from the southern side of the Capitoline, and he reckoned that it was higher than the Aventine, the Capitoline, and the Quirinal hills. In fact, as measured from sea level, the altitude of the Tarpeian Rock is lower than the three hills to which Luther compares it.[29]

If he was on the Capitoline, Luther would have caught at least a glimpse of the Forum Romanum on the southeastern side of the hill. Perhaps he even descended in order to walk around in it. Of course, it would have looked far different then than it does today. The forum only began to be scientifically explored in the late eighteenth century. Official excavations by the Italian government were undertaken in 1898 and continue to this day. The ancient forum had been used in the Middle Ages by aristocratic Roman families who built defensive towers on top of the ruins. (It was sometimes referred to as "the field of towers," Campo Torrechiano.) Eventually the area began to be used as a meadow (hence its other name, Campo Vaccino, literally "cow field"), where cattle would graze picturesquely among the ruins. Beginning already in the seventeenth century, the juxtaposition of dilapidated antique grandeur and contemporary flora and fauna was a popular subject for many artists, including Claude Lorrain, Giovanni Battista Piranesi, and J. M. W. Turner.[30]

Of the many baths and aqueducts for which ancient Rome was so well known, Luther specifically mentions the baths of the emperor Diocletian and the aqueduct associated with it. The Thermae Diocletiani were the largest of the Roman baths, bigger in capacity even than those of Caracalla, whose ruined remains are still visible today. Begun in 298 CE, Diocletian's baths were finished in 305 or 306, and they continued to be used until 537, when Vitiges, king of the Ostrogoths, cut off the water supply to the city. In the 1560s, Michelangelo made use of the bath's ancient *frigidarium* and *tepidarium* to construct a new basilica on the site, S. Maria degli Angeli e dei Martiri. The Aqua Marcia, the longest of the four great Roman aqueducts, supplied the water for the baths of Diocletian. Luther suggests that it was twenty-five "German miles" in length and that the water came all the way from Naples: "And he spoke about the baths of Diocletian, whose aqueduct ran for twenty-five German miles from Naples to a splendidly built house. The wealth of the world was there, where they did whatever they pleased."[31] The German mile at Luther's time was considerably longer than the American mile. In Saxony in the seventeenth century, the mile was 9,062 meters long. If so, Luther's "twenty-five German miles" would translate to something like 140 American miles. In fact, the Aqua Marcia was between fifty-six and fifty-seven American miles long, and the springs that fed it lay not south of Rome, where Naples is located, but near modern Aniene in the Anio River valley to the east of the city.[32] Parts of the aqueduct are still visible today in the Parco degli Acquedotti to the southeast of the city of Rome.

Of all the ancient buildings in Rome, the Pantheon made the greatest impression on Luther. He mentions it repeatedly.[33] In 1533, he notes, "In Rome they have a round temple; in it the Romans placed statues of all of the gods, except Christ, whom nobody can endure."[34] In 1538, he comments on the significance of its name: "So the Romans also collected false gods from all over the world and built a church that they called the Pantheon—that is, the church of all the gods."[35] As late as 1542 or 1543, he was still talking about the Pantheon: "In Rome there is a temple which I have seen. It has no windows; on top there is a round hole and a vaulted ceiling. It is tall and has only marble columns, which I could hardly reach around with my two arms. On the vaulted ceiling above, all the gods are painted: Jupiter, Neptune, Mars, Venus, as they are now named."[36]

While Luther's description of the Pantheon appears to be based on his own personal observations, he did not remember the structure completely accurately. There is indeed an *oculus* in the windowless

Pantheon, and it did honor more than one deity—hence its traditional Greek name, meaning "all the gods"—but the Olympian deities that Luther mentions by their Roman names were never "painted" (*gemalt*) on the ceiling. No doubt there were statues of some of them originally in the pagan temple. The ancient historian Dio Cassius mentions images of Mars and Venus. A bust that was supposed to be of Cybele was removed from the Pantheon only in 1545.[37] Long before Luther's time, in the seventh century, the building was converted into a Christian church, S. Maria ad Martyres, or as it is popularly known today, S. Maria Rotonda.

Luther knew of Hadrian's mausoleum, which has survived more or less intact because it was converted into a fortress during the Middle Ages, Castel Sant'Angelo.[38] A statue of the archangel Michael stands at the top of what was once the tallest building in Rome. In the later Middle Ages, it was connected by an elevated, fortified corridor (Passetto Borgo) leading to the papal residence (half a mile away), and it was here that Pope Clement fled for refuge during the sack of Rome in 1527. Castel Sant'Angelo was also notorious as a papal prison, where Giordano Bruno was detained for six years. The structure serves as the memorable setting for the last act of Verdi's *Tosca*.

Of other well-known ancient Roman sites that Luther would have been likely to have seen in his peregrinations around the ancient city, such as the columns of Trajan and Marcus Aurelius, the Egyptian obelisks, the arches of Constantine and Titus, the Senate house (Curia Julia) converted into a church (S. Adriano al Foro), the Domus aurea of Nero (rediscovered by accident in the late fifteenth century), or the Mausoleum of Augustus, which had been turned into a fortress (by the Colonna family) and later used as a circus and as a concert hall (until closed in the 1930s by Mussolini), as far as I have been able to discover, Luther makes no specific mention.[39]

Luther's Latin

Latin was the language that the young pilgrim used to salute the holy city that he saw in the distance (*Salve, sancta Roma!*) and to decry its dilapidated condition (*iam lacerata*). German was his native tongue, to be sure—the language that Luther would have spoken at home with his parents and siblings when he was growing up—but he was educated in Latin and continued to use the language actively for a wide variety of purposes throughout his life. Luther was bilingual, altogether fluent in both German and Latin.

Throughout the Middle Ages, despite grammatical alterations, novel vocabulary, and differing pronunciations and orthographies—even as it gave birth to independent vernacular languages like French, Italian, and Spanish—Latin had always continued to be Latin. The language used by pagan Romans like Caesar and Cicero or Christian authors like Augustine and Bernard of Clairvaux was still very much the same as Luther's.[40] If Cicero and Augustine and Luther could have traveled through time to meet with each other, they would have had very few problems at all communicating with each other in Latin.

Language is a complex matter. Far from serving simply as a means of communication, language is also critical for the construction of individual and collective identity. Latin was the language of the Pax Romana. Not only native Romans but the Indigenous peoples of its far-flung empire used it as a lingua franca, a mutually intelligible tongue. Without Latin, the spread of Christianity across the western Roman Empire would not have happened so rapidly. Latin was an important part of the *praeparatio evangelii*. The fact that so many different people with so many different cultural heritages in provinces as far removed from Rome as Britannia and Dacia (modern Romania) could make themselves understood to each other using a common tongue helped promote the values of a singular *Romanitas* in the first place and facilitate the spread of a monotheistic religion and the development of a centralized church later.[41] Even in the early modern period, Latin was still instrumental in helping shape the cultural identity of learned Europeans like Luther and his contemporaries.

Luther's Latinity has not infrequently been overshadowed by his unique contributions to German. "The father of the German language," as he has with some justification been described, proved to be astonishingly adroit with his native tongue, using German with great acumen to advance the Reformation in a way that could never have happened had he written only in Latin. In recognition of his literary talents in German, one of his contemporary admirers described him as "the real German Cicero" (*rechter Teutscher Cicero*).[42] Luther's German translation of the Bible, his catechism, and his chorales were hugely popular and continued to be read, recited, memorized, and sung for centuries after he died. In the nineteenth century, Friedrich Nietzsche could still describe Luther's translation of the Bible as a "masterpiece of German prose," declaring it to be "the best German book."[43] But Luther was deeply interested in languages other than his mother tongue, especially ancient ones. Even after his formal schooling in Latin was long behind him, he continued to study ancient Greek and biblical Hebrew. According to Oldekop's *Chronik*, Luther took Hebrew lessons from a Jewish physician named Jacob while in Rome.[44]

By Luther's time, the question of Latin's proper usage had become a burning issue—not only in Italy but also north of the Alps. Humanists everywhere were resolutely opposed to what they considered the distortion of pristine Latinity during the Middle Ages and insisted on returning to classical grammatical, lexical, and stylistic norms. They scorned the "barbaric" Latinity of the scholastic theologians of the later Middle Ages. Ciceronianism (or a modified Ciceronianism) was all the rage. As an alumnus of the University of Erfurt, one of the hotbeds of humanism in Germany, the young Luther was very much aware of this movement, if not a full-fledged participant in it.[45] The ideals of those who wished to return *ad fontes*, to the ultimate source of "pure" Latinity, seemed laudable to him. While not himself a strict Ciceronian by any means, in a letter of 1537 to the poet Helius Eobanus Hessus, Luther wrote approvingly of neo-Latin prose stylists: "I commend the more those who want to seem Ciceronian and to be praised as such."[46]

Luther loved the Latin language, was steeped in its ancient literature, and was fascinated by the history of pagan Rome. He quoted the classical Roman authors frequently and often from memory. The only books he took with him when he entered the cloister in Erfurt in 1505 were copies of two Latin poets, Virgil and Plautus, not more predictable religious fare such as the sermons of Augustine or Peter Lombard's *Sentences.*[47] His choice of reading material at the time was no accident, any more than his decision to share the fact with others twenty-five years later.

Like Petrarch and other humanists who regarded Virgil and Cicero as the great exemplars of Latin verse and prose excellence, respectively, Luther was especially attracted to these two Roman authors. Their names occur hundreds of times in the indices to the *Weimarer Ausgabe* of Luther's works. Luther even dared to hope that Cicero, who had "worked hard to discover what God was, and even got so far that he determined that there was only one God," would be given some kind of consideration in the next life: "Very well then. God is a fair judge. He will deal well with people such as these, for I believe that even Cicero should not be as severely condemned as Caiaphas. Just as he [Caiaphas] sits in the lowest level of hell, Cicero will be in paradise."[48] Virgil was equally highly regarded by Luther. When asked how he had learned to write his popular German hymns, he credited his success to Virgil, because, as he said, the famous Roman poet was able to so artistically "apply his song and words to the story that he relates."[49] Once at table, Luther recited "some verses from the fourth book of the *Aeneid*" as he mused aloud about how tragically moving Virgil's poetry would have been (*quantos affectus tragicos movisset*) had he "dealt with Roman topics and the times of the Caesars." Luther supposed that it would have taken Virgil "48 books" to have done so.[50] Virgil's *Eclogues, Georgics,* and *Aeneid,* as well as Cicero's letters, continued to be on Luther's mind to the very end of his life.[51]

In addition to Virgil and Cicero, Luther also quoted frequently from Horace, Ovid, and Terence, who were particular favorites of his. The Latin authors Catullus, Ennius, Juvenal, Livy, Lucan, Martial, Plautus, Pliny the Elder and Younger, Quintilian, Sallust, Seneca, Statius, Suetonius, Tacitus, Valerius Flaccus, and Varro are all referenced or quoted in his writings. Some of these authors, no doubt, Luther never read in their entirety, especially after his days in school were over, and others he knew only secondhand, as they were quoted in collections such as Erasmus's *Adagia*. But at one point later in his life, it seems that Luther not only purchased a copy of Lucan's *Pharsalia* but also read the historical epic critically and then discussed it at table: "I don't know whether he is a poet or a historian. For this is how they are to be distinguished: A historian says what is true, while an orator or one who is well spoken says what is like the truth. But a poet writes what is neither true nor like the truth." Luther goes on to discuss Aristotle's views on poetry as he compares poets with painters, who make their subjects look much more beautiful (*viel schöner*) than they really are.[52]

Luther used Latin, in both its oral and written forms, with an easy facility that few professional Latinists today could ever dream of rivaling. He was probably only seven years old when he was enrolled in the Latin school in Mansfeld.[53] As he furthered his education in other schools and at the university, his instruction would have continued to be entirely in Latin. After he entered the monastery in Erfurt in 1501, Latin was the language Luther would have used exclusively for collective prayer and worship. By the time he left there, he probably would have memorized much, if not all, of the Vulgate.[54] Throughout his career, he wrote many of his theological treatises and prefaces in Latin. As a professor at the University of Wittenberg, he delivered his lectures, including his monumental series on Genesis, primarily in Latin. He wrote many of his letters in Latin and seems to have used an interesting combination of Latin and German (*Mischsprache*) at the table. Of the more than eight hundred of Luther's writings listed in Kurt Aland's *Hilfsbuch zum Lutherstudium*, it has been calculated that "around 240 of these works [almost 30 percent] employ exclusively or, at least, extensively the Latin language."[55] In 1543, Luther declared modestly that he was nothing more than a "German preacher and uneducated teacher" who had written little in the Latin language.[56] This is misleading. It is true that Luther wrote more and more often in German in later life, but he still continued to use Latin well into his final years.[57]

Luther was quite aware of how language works. As an exegete, he often used the technical terminology traditionally employed to describe the specifics of grammar (gender, pronouns, articles, tenses, active verbs, substantives, etc.). He was well aware of the difference between the moods of verbs, such as indicative, subjunctive, and optative.[58] Luther remarks on the differences among the dative, genitive, and accusative cases of nouns in his early lectures on the Psalms.[59] In a letter of 1537, he plays on the declension of the noun *Christus* in Latin: *Christi sumus in nominativo et genitivo* ("we are Christs and Christ's, in the nominative and the genitive case").[60]

Luther was also well versed in the principles of rhetoric, a key element of Roman education. He used the traditional figures taught by the ancient rhetors and was familiar with their Greek and Latin nomenclature as well as the divisions of discourse. He admired Quintilian, whose authoritative treatment of Latin rhetoric influenced him deeply. "I really do prefer him to nearly all authors," he writes in a 1519 letter.[61] In his treatise *On the Bondage of the Will* directed against Erasmus, he imagines Quintilian speaking (an example of the sophisticated rhetorical device of prosopopoeia) about how best to write about rhetoric: "In my judgment, those foolish and superfluous things we say about *inventio, dispositio, elocutio, memoria*, and *pronuntiatio* should be left out." The only thing necessary to say is that "eloquence is experience in speaking well." Luther is sure that Erasmus would laugh at such a reductionist trivialization of the complex art of rhetoric, especially when expressed by a Latin author like Quintilian, who published a massive work (twelve books) on the subject (*Institutio oratoria*).[62] Luther put his knowledge of figural language to use in theological controversies, as, for instance, in his dispute with other reformers regarding the Lord's Supper.[63]

Luther greatly admired Cicero's rhetorical teachings and personal eloquence.[64] Cicero's emphasis on the importance of *ethos* for the purposes of persuasion impressed the preacher in him: "There is no better way of moving others than to be moved yourself in the first place."[65] He especially appreciated the Roman orator's understanding of the value of decorum, the ability to de-emphasize "what is inappropriate" and to make the most of "what is appropriate." This is particularly striking when we consider how often Luther's own language, in his own lifetime and thereafter, has been judged to be "inappropriate." This "indispensable precept" (*necessarium praeceptum*) was why Luther could say, "I love Cicero" (*Darüm hab ich Ciceronem lieb*).[66]

This formulation of affection in modern German, as in *Ich habe dich lieb*, does not usually express such a strong emotional bond as the more direct expression, *Ich liebe dich*. One might use the former expression in reference to a family member such as a brother or sister while reserving the latter for a romantic relationship. Luther is certainly not suggesting that he loves Cicero in this latter sense. At the same time, it is noteworthy that Luther uses the word "love" at all in this context instead of a word such as "respect" or "admire," let us say, to describe his appreciation of the Roman rhetor's fine sense of decorum. At the very least, we can say that Luther's affection for Cicero went far beyond the ordinary regard one *littérateur* might have for another who served as his role model. That Luther would express his appreciation for Cicero in such emotional terms (and would wish to share heaven with him for all eternity) strongly suggests that he felt a deep sense of intellectual and even spiritual kinship with the ancient Roman that went far beyond wanting to adorn his own prose with impressive quotations or to show off his erudition to his humanist contemporaries.

Luther's admiration for the Roman comic playwright Terence is expressed in language that is even more unambiguously personal, this time in Latin: *Ego Terencium ideo amo* ("This is why I love Terence"). He goes on to explain, "Because I see that it is rhetorically effective to make a comedy out of someone sleeping with a maiden and then to imagine what his father would have to say about that, and a slave, and a circle of friends. So, comedy can be made out of anything."[67] Luther felt that this Roman playwright of the second century BCE was well suited for the instruction of young people in the sixteenth century. The relatively simple Latin of Terence's situational comedies not only could be used to help schoolboys improve their language skills but could also help introduce them to the different roles people must play in life, such as servants and masters, adolescents and their elders, men and women. Terence was no monk, ignorant of everyday life and concerns, "but he saw how it goes with people" (*wie es den leuten gehet*).[68] Even if there were objectionable, even "obscene" passages in Terence's comedies, Luther insisted that these Latin plays were no less appropriate for young people to read without censorship than the Bible itself, which "contains amatory things everywhere."[69]

Luther himself could and did write a fairly sophisticated form of Latin prose when he chose to do so. In an early (1519) letter that he penned to Erasmus, for instance, we find him employing an impressive range of rhetorical figures, including alliteration, assonance, epiphora, metaphor, polyptoton, and tricolon, all within the space of just three sentences:

> *Toties ego tecum fabulor, et tu mecum, Erasme, decus nostrum et spes nostra, nec dum mutuo nos cognoscimus, nonne monstri hoc simillimum? imo non monstrum, sed plane quotidianum opus. Quis enim est, cuius penetralia non penitus occupet Erasmus, quem non doceat Erasmus, in quo non regnet Erasmus?*[70]

Is it not a very odd thing that I speak so often with you and you with me, Erasmus, our glory and our hope, even though we have never gotten to know each other? Actually, it is not odd at all but rather something that obviously happens every day. For who is there whose inner depths Erasmus does not occupy, whom Erasmus does not instruct, in whom Erasmus does not reign supreme?

No doubt, Luther used Latin prose because it was, in many instances, a more practical and efficient form of communication than German, especially when he was writing letters or treatises that would be read by those outside of the German-speaking world. But the fact that he also wrote Latin verse suggests that Luther must have valued the ancient language for more than utilitarian reasons. It seems that he enjoyed Latin for its own sake; there is really no adequate reason otherwise to explain why he would expend all the time and effort it takes to produce Latin verse. Almost thirty Latin poems attributed to Luther have come down to us. To be sure, these did not circulate as widely as his German hymns did, and it is unlikely that he imagined that they ever would. Instead, they were probably meant to be shared among Luther's learned friends and colleagues, who would be in a position to appreciate their author's facility with the Latin language.

According to Melanchthon, Luther excelled in writing verses in Latin as a schoolboy.[71] But Latin verse composition was not just a juvenile diversion for Luther, as it has been for others. Two of his most ambitious poems, written in hendecasyllables in imitation of Martial's *Epigram* 10.47, were produced quite late in Luther's life (1545).[72] Nor are all of his Latin poems lighthearted or nugatory. Two of his briefest compositions are quite serious: an epitaph for his beloved daughter Magdalena, who died when she was just twelve, and a verse paraphrase of one of his favorite Psalm verses (118:17), which was set to music by a popular Swiss composer of the time, Ludwig Senfl.[73]

Perhaps the most ambitious of all of Luther's Latin verse compositions is "On the Fountain of the Wittenberg Oreads" (*De Fonte Oreadum Witebergensium*), a poem he wrote sometime after 1544, in elegant elegiac distichs:

> *Qui mare, qui fontes, qui flumina cuncta creavit,*
> *Me quoque iussit aquae particulam esse suae.*
> *Corpore sum parvo, scatebris exilibus ortus,*

Magni, me, sed opus, glorior esse Dei.
Negligor incultus, dispersis undique venis,
   Et squalere sinor, per loca foeda luto.
Rustica, more suo, me spernunt, turba coloni,
   Fons, quibus, haud dignus, qui colar, esse putor.
Forsan, si propior melioribus urbibus essem,
   Fontibus urbanis cultior ipse forem.
Non movet agrestis tamen haec iniuria vulgi,
   Dimoveor nullis a bonitate malis.
Servo meas undas puras, nitidasque ministro,
   Gratis, ingratis, omnibus, aequus agor,
Servio namque Deo largo, pincerna benignus,
   Gratuito munus largior inde meum.
Non moror; argenti nihil, aut habeas nihil auri,
   Hausturus gratis, dives inopsque veni.
Sic Deus ingrato dedit, et facit, omnia mundo,
   Cuius ad exemplum me iuvat esse bonum.[74]

The one who created sea, springs, and all rivers has also ordered me to be a small bit of his own water. My size is small, and I arise from diminutive springs, but I glory in the fact that I was made by a God who is great. Untended, I am neglected, and my streams run all over the place, and I am allowed to grow filthy in places befouled with mud. In their usual way, the country people, farmers, fail to appreciate me. They think me a spring not worth cultivating. Perhaps, if I were nearer to cities that were more refined, I would be better tended than the city springs. But this insult on the part of the farming folk does not move me. Evil deeds do not dissuade me from doing good. I keep my water pure and serve it up crystal clear to grateful and ungrateful alike; I deal fairly with everyone. For like a kind butler, I serve a generous God, and I bestow the bounty I get from him at no cost. I don't delay. Even if you have neither silver nor gold, come, rich and poor alike, and drink for free! That is how God gave everything, and still does, to an ungrateful world, and it pleases me to follow his good example.

This is a highly sophisticated piece of Latin poetry. Even as Luther works within the long tradition of verse dedicated to fountains or inscribed upon them, such as Horace's famous *Fons Bandusiae* (Odes 3.13) or, closer to his own time, Giovanni Pontano's poetic praise of the spring Casi, he is also quite innovative as a poet. His fountain does much more than simply offer its refreshing physical gifts to hot and thirsty travelers; it speaks, as poetic fountains sometimes do. And what it has to say is distinctively "Lutheran." In the second to the last distich, the Wittenberg fountain articulates the familiar doctrine of justification by grace, *sola gratia*. Even though the spring may be sullied by the farmers' fields through which it flows, it continues to produce good, free water for all who want it, at no charge. Luther draws heavily here upon the language and imagery of biblical passages such as Isaiah 55:1 and John 4:3–15, even as the formal characteristics of the poem remain classical and depend very little upon biblical poetics (e.g., parallelism).[75]

If the Oreads, the famed mountain nymphs of Greek mythology mentioned in the title of Luther's poem, could be imagined as inhabiting the hilly landscape outside of Wittenberg, it may not be too fanciful to suggest that it was the classical Muses who animated and inspired the traditional liberal arts within the city proper.[76] Certainly, the academic disciplines to which the Muses corresponded, such as poetry and history, were highly regarded at Luther's and Melanchthon's university. Luther's elevated status as *Doctor in Biblia* and dean of the theological faculty (from 1535 to 1546) put him in a unique position to help guide the university's intellectual direction in general in close cooperation with Melanchthon, the so-called *praeceptor Germaniae*, who played more of a hands-on role than Luther in setting up and overseeing curricula at Wittenberg and elsewhere. Luther's support of the liberal arts was not merely a matter of paying them lip service. He put his principles into practice, opposing, for example, the idea of giving lectures in surgery at the university on the grounds that as a discipline it was more practical than theoretical and therefore not well suited for academic study.[77]

Like Melanchthon, Luther disagreed emphatically with more radical reformers who pointed out that Jesus's original followers (like Jesus himself) had no formal education and went so far as to suggest that Latin was unnecessary or even deleterious for the soul's salvation. More than one of Luther's Ninety-Five Theses begins with the phrase "Christians must be taught" (*docendi sunt Christiani*). "I am convinced," he wrote later, "that without experience in literature, pure theology cannot stand upright, just as heretofore it has totally collapsed when literary studies toppled and fell."[78] For Luther, knowledge of the liberal arts (*bonarum artium cognitio*) was one of the fundamental elements in a theologian's education.[79]

Nor was he swayed at all by the arguments of those who considered liberal education to be impractical. In his preface to Justus Menius's *Oeconomia Christiana* of 1529, he inveighs against parents who consider education from a purely mercenary point of view: "If my son learns enough so that he can make money, then he has learned enough." Without a liberal education, Luther maintains, Germans would "remain completely savage animals and pigs, of no use in the world except to gorge themselves and to guzzle."[80]

Central to the liberal arts curriculum at the University of Wittenberg and other Lutheran institutions of learning was the Latin language and its literature. At the foundational levels of education, the ancient poets and orators, "regardless of whether they were pagan or Christian, Greek or Latin," had to be studied, because it is from these authors that "one must learn grammar."[81] Latin was also useful for more advanced students to engage with rhetoric, one of the three essential components (along with grammar and dialectic) of the medieval Trivium. In *To the Christian Nobility of the German Nation*, Luther recommends preserving Cicero's rhetorical writings in the curriculum, as students could make good use of them to become proficient at "speaking well and preaching."[82]

Before he himself had children of his own, Luther wrote of the importance of language study for their intellectual development: "If I had children and could do what I wanted with them, I would make sure that they studied not only languages and history but also singing, music, and all of mathematics."[83] Later on in his life (1542), after he did have children, he wrote to Marcus Crodel, rector of the school in Torgau, "For I do indeed give birth to theologians, but I also would like to produce grammarians and musicians."[84]

Just knowing German was not enough. In Luther's 1524 appeal to the councilmen of Germany, he attacks those who question why one should have to learn "Latin, Greek, and Hebrew and the other liberal arts" instead of German, which theoretically should suffice for one's salvation.[85] In *The Adoration of the Sacrament* (1523), Luther makes a fervent appeal to the Bohemian Brethren: "I would ask that you not despise languages so much but, because you are certainly able to do so, that you have your preachers and talented boys without exception learn Latin, Greek, and Hebrew well."[86]

Another reason to be able to read Latin, besides its importance for grammar and rhetoric, was the fact that the ancient Roman authors could still teach so many relevant moral lessons. Luther found these pagan exemplars beyond criticism when it came to their "industry and diligence."[87] Of Cicero's *De officiis*, Luther declares, "There is nothing better to be set before young people in order for them to learn how to lead an honorable life and pursue the sweetness and humanity of morals."[88] Luther believed that God had preserved the "heathen books" of the ancient moralists for a reason: they were not all that different from the church's "prophets, apostles, theologians, or preachers." Even though most of them were quite unaware of Christianity, the old Roman teachers of virtue were God's gift to the "heathen and the godless," to be respected as nearly on a par with the pre-Christian prophets of the Old Testament.[89]

Roman History

Like other sixteenth-century humanists, Luther was deeply interested in history in general and Roman history in particular. And as Lewis Spitz and others have observed, his interest only increased in the last decades of his life.[90] While he did not himself write a discrete history that might try to account, say, for the rise and fall of the Roman Empire, Luther did compile his own *Computation of the Years of the World*, first published in 1541 and again in 1545. Luther's *Supputatio annorum mundi* has been nicely reproduced in the *Weimarer Ausgabe*, where it occupies 150 pages. It consists of brief historical notes on either side of a central ladder-like column representing years.[91] Luther's interest in Roman history is not confined to such obvious (for a student of the Bible) items as the reign of Herod the Great, the tax collectors of the New Testament (*publicani*), the procurator Pontius Pilate, the destruction of Jerusalem by Titus, or the persecution of Christians under some Roman emperors, all of which intersect with biblical history or the history of the early church.[92] He also makes countless references to ancient Rome and the pagan Romans before the advent of Christianity or apart from it.

The sheer quantity and pervasiveness of the classical references and allusions in Luther's works are impressive. The fact that they occur over the course of his career and in a wide variety of contexts suggests that many, if not all of them, must have been the product of Luther's own personal knowledge and interests in the first place. Exactly how many others may have been added or expanded on by editors as they prepared notes of his lectures, sermons, and conversations for publication is difficult to ascertain with certainty, as Jaroslav Pelikan observes in regard to the Genesis lectures.[93] It should be pointed out that Luther was closely involved in the oversight and approval of the publication of works bearing his name.[94] The Luther depicted in Andrew Pettegree's *Brand Luther* "spent his life in and out of print shops" and was almost obsessive about all aspects of the publication of his works.[95] It is likely that he knew about most or even all of the editorial amplifications in works that he authorized to be published.[96]

It has been suggested that Luther's references to the ancient poets should be viewed primarily as a function of his appreciation of them as sources for verbal "decoration," mostly useful because they could help adorn his own works. According to this view, a Latin poet like Virgil served Luther as little more than a kind of "rhetorical tool."[97] Such an observation fails to do justice to Luther's appropriation of not only the language but also the ideas of the *Aeneid*. Nor does it account for his creative application of the poetry of Virgil to his own life. Already in late antiquity, the epic tale of Aeneas's wanderings and struggles had begun to serve readers like Donatus and Fulgentius as a source for allegorical and moralizing interpretations with far-reaching applications to human life in general. It is possible to read Augustine's *Confessions*, his famous recounting of the struggles and travels of his own early life, as though it were "a version of the story of Aeneas."[98] Luther never wrote anything like the *Confessions*, but at various stages of his controversy with Rome, he did draw on Virgil's epic poem, like so many other readers of the *Aeneid* before him, to find correspondences with personages and events in his own life.

One example is Luther's parody of the first seven lines of the *Aeneid* with which he began his treatise *Against the Armed Man Cochlaeus*. After the Diet of Worms in 1521, Johannes Cochlaeus was miffed when Luther refused to debate with him. A year or so later, Cochlaeus appended the words "Arms are fitting for men" (*Viros arma decent*) to the end of a treatise attacking Luther's theology of the sacraments. Luther responded in February 1523 with his own treatise against Cochlaeus that begins as follows:

> *Arma virumque cano, Mogani qui nuper ab oris*
> *Leucoream fato stolidus Saxonaque venit*
> *Littora, multum ille et furiis vexatus et oestro*
> *Vi scelerum, memorem rasorum cladis ob iram*
> *Multa quoque et Satana passus, quo perderet urbem*

> *Inferretque malum studiis, genus unde malorum*
> *Errorumque patres atque alti gloria Papae.*[99]

I sing of arms and the man who recently came from the region of the Main River to Wittenberg and the Saxon shore, fatally stupid, tormented much by the furies and the frenzied power of wicked deeds, on account of his angry remembrance of the collapse of the monks, having also suffered much at the hands of Satan. He came in order to destroy the city and bring misfortune to its endeavors, whence come evils, the fathers of errors, and the glory of the exalted pope.

Luther does much more here than make a passing allusion to Cochlaeus's Virgilian reference to "arms" and "men" as he takes up the literary challenge. Instead, he appropriates the epic poet's familiar opening lines and makes them his own. Luther becomes a sixteenth-century Virgil, singing in the first person of "arms and the man": *Arma virumque cano.* In this case, the "man" is not Aeneas, who brought the gods of Troy to Rome, but Cochlaeus. Unlike Aeneas, Cochlaeus comes to "the city" not with the purpose of establishing it like Aeneas (*dum conderet urbem*) but in order to destroy it (*perderet*). With the word "city," Luther is referring in the first place to his own Wittenberg (where Cochlaeus's treatise against him, if not Cochlaeus himself, had arrived), but in this context, *urbs* also suggests to the reader's mind *the* city—namely, "Rome." Cochlaeus is causing damage to Wittenberg *and* Rome. If there is a defender of either city, it must be Luther himself, determined to rescue both Wittenberg and Rome from evil, error, and the power of the pope.[100] (For Luther, as for many before and since, Rome was simply "*the* city." In his time, one did not even need to use its proper name to refer to it but could instead simply capitalize the Latin word for "city," *Urbs.*)[101]

The following is another example of Luther's creative appropriation of Virgil. Sometime after the 1539 death of Duke George of Albertine Saxony, a persistent opponent of the Reformation, Luther applied to the demise of his powerful adversary the language of the very last line (12.952) of the *Aeneid*: "and his life fled indignantly with a groan under the shades" (*vitaque cum gemitu fugit indignata sub umbras*). Like Turnus, Aeneas's opponent in the second half of the *Aeneid*, who passed groaning from this life to the next after he was bested by his Trojan adversary, the deceased George is now in the underworld, "under the shades, living his life indignantly with a groan" (*est in inferno vitamque cum gemitu vivit indignatus sub umbras*).[102] By couching his conflict with Duke George in such familiar Virgilian language, Luther is implicitly casting himself as the great progenitor of the Romans, Aeneas, who turns out to be victorious at the end of the *Aeneid* over his archenemy, Turnus.

Similarly, in a 1541 letter to Melanchthon, Luther refers to the object of his polemical treatise *Against Hanswurst*, Duke Henry V of Braunschweig-Lüneburg, as a diabolical "Mezentius," the exiled Etruscan king who joined Turnus and the Rutulians in fighting against the Trojan refugees.[103] Mezentius was killed by Aeneas in Book X of the *Aeneid*. If Henry is Mezentius, it follows that Luther must be his victorious adversary, Aeneas. As in the previous instances of Virgilian appropriation, Luther here uses the epic language of deadly competition between Aeneas and the forces that would oppose his progress not simply to "adorn" his own words but to lend weight to the significance of his great cause, to emphasize the seriousness of the opposition to it (Turnus and Mezentius are formidable warriors), and to underscore the difficulties of his own situation and the ultimate success of his efforts.

These interactions with the *Aeneid* do far more than serve as learned window dressing. Luther is not just another neo-Latin poet living safely in the world of words with little interest or engagement in actual current events. Especially early in his career, many of the situations in which he found himself embroiled were exceedingly dangerous and required him to demonstrate real courage if he was to go forward. Virgil's *pius Aeneas*, obeying the will of Fate and Jupiter in the face of great opposition, was more than just another literary figure for Luther; he was a heroic prototype, a role model, a source of inspiration. So was Julius Caesar. In a letter of 1520, Luther adopts for himself the words that Caesar famously used upon crossing the Rubicon River in 49 BCE as he made his dangerous journey with his army toward Rome: *Iacta alea est.* Luther applies the familiar Latin words to his own problematic situation vis-à-vis the great city: "The die has indeed been cast for me (*iacta mihi alea*), and I scorn Roman fury and favor."[104] The classical allusion is not just for show. Luther *is* Caesar, 1,500 years later, casting his leery eye in a southerly direction on whatever dangers in Rome might await *him* as he considers the irrevocable steps he has taken to provoke his powerful enemies in the city.

Luther's knowledge of the cultural legacy of the classical world has struck one modern scholar of the question as not "unusually profound."[105] This is especially true if one compares Luther with his learned colleague Melanchthon. It is not true, however, if he is compared with other contemporary reformers who distrusted and discouraged classical learning, like his former colleague at the University of Wittenberg, Andreas Bodenstein von Karlstadt.[106] Luther's knowledge of Roman history, from its foundation in 753 BCE to the demise of the western half of the empire in the fifth century CE, needs to be properly contextualized. If it is true that Luther was no Melanchthon, the learned philologist, we should quickly add that he was also no Karsthans, the iconic peasant armed with a hoe and a hearty distrust of humanistic erudition.[107] In modern terms, we might say that he was not a professional classical scholar, but he was also not a typical American undergraduate who has never taken an ancient history course. The following compilation is representative of references to Roman history found in Luther's writings but is by no means complete.

Of the early kings of Rome, Luther knew of Romulus, "the father of the Romans," who killed his brother Remus "so that he could rule alone and name the city of Rome after himself."[108] There is a reference in *Supputatio annorum mundi* to the date of the foundation of Rome (the thirty-sixth year of the reign of King Uzziah).[109] It was Romulus's plan to increase the population of his young city by making it a place of asylum for all, including criminals.[110] Luther was familiar with the name of Numa, the second king of Rome who helped establish laws for the new kingdom. Despite Numa's many laudable virtues, Luther held him responsible for misleading the Romans into idolatry.[111] He also knew the Livian stories (from the first book of *Ab urbe condita*) surrounding the Sabine women and the virtuous Lucretia.[112] He may have known of Brennus, leader of the Gauls when they invaded Rome circa 390 BCE,[113] and he was familiar with Camillus, the Roman consul and dictator who defeated them.[114] Luther referred more than once to the king of Epirus, Pyrrhus, who invaded Italy from Greece and attacked Rome several times in the third century BCE, following the advice of an oracle.[115] More than once, too, Luther pondered the meaning of the great conflict between the Romans and the Carthaginians—in particular, the Second Punic War, when Hannibal was successful in traversing the Alps only to be frustrated by the delaying tactics of the Roman general Quintus Fabius Maximus Verrucosus, nicknamed Cunctator, "the delayer."[116] He knew of the Parthians and their capture of the legionary battle standards at the battle of Carrhae in 53 BCE, when the wealthy triumvir Crassus met his grisly end.[117]

Luther often wrote or spoke of the fateful events leading up to the collapse of the Roman Republic in the first century BCE and the chief protagonists. These included Marius, elected consul seven times; the aristocratic dictator Sulla; and the general Pompey, who dishonored the temple in Jerusalem in 63 BCE by entering the Holy of Holies.[118] Luther frequently brought up the name of the "brave and victorious" Julius Caesar,[119] whom he associated with the powerful, wise, and responsible Hector of Homer's *Iliad*.[120] He knew of the mutinous aristocrat Catiline[121] and, of course, Cicero, who famously exposed the former's conspiracy in the same year that Pompey entered Jerusalem. He described Caesar's assassin Brutus as one of "the very wise and understanding people,"[122] and he was also familiar with Caesar's successors, Mark Antony and Octavian (Augustus). Luther included the latter in the ranks of those whom he called "miracle men," who were able to govern not only others but themselves.[123]

In his *Supputatio annorum mundi*, Luther lists the names of many of the Roman emperors along with pertinent dates and brief details. Elsewhere, Luther comments on a number of them specifically. Of the Julio-Claudian emperors following Augustus, Luther mentions the first-century emperors Tiberius, Caligula, and Nero. He considered Tiberius (as described by Suetonius) to be cruel, but "an angel" if his "filthiness" were compared with that of the pope.[124] In his exposition of the 101st Psalm, Luther includes the Flavian emperor Vespasian in the company of other successful leaders like Cyrus, Themistocles, Alexander the Great, and Augustus.[125] He was familiar with Vespasian's sons: Titus, who credited "divine will rather than his army" for helping him take the city of Jerusalem in 70 CE,[126] and Domitian, who succeeded his brother and was supposed to have persecuted Christians.[127]

Of the later emperors, Luther considered Trajan and Hadrian, two of the "good emperors" of the second century CE, and Diocletian, who divided the empire in the late third century CE in order to ensure its more efficient administration, to be among the "wisest" of Rome's rulers. They received praise from their subjects for their competent governance, despite the fact that "they persecuted the gospel."[128] Luther was by no means the first Christian to respect Trajan for his moral integrity, despite the fact that the emperor considered Christianity a *religio illicita* (see his letter to Pliny the Younger, *Ep.* 10.97). In Christian lore, Gregory the Great is supposed to have been so impressed by Trajan's legendary sense of justice that he baptized his soul retroactively. Dante honors the example of the emperor's humility in the tenth canto of the *Purgatorio*.[129]

On the other hand, Luther was quite critical of later emperors such as Commodus and Heliogabalus. Commodus was "truly inconvenient" (*vere incommodus*) and "another Nero," while Heliogabalus was more of "a beast than a human."[130] (Luther did appreciate the impatient severity with which Alexander Severus, the successor of Heliogabalus, was supposed to have treated sycophants.[131]) In his *Supputatio annorum mundi*, Luther includes the thousand-year anniversary celebration of the foundation of Rome in 248 CE during the reign of Philip the Arab.[132] Not surprisingly, Luther's praise for Constantine, "the wise, gentle, and patient leader"[133] who presided over the Council of Nicaea in 325, is unqualified: "The praiseworthy Caesar Constantine had now become a Christian and given the Christians peace against the tyrants and persecutors with so very serious a faith and such sincere intentions that he even deposed and removed from the kingdom his brother-in-law Licinius, to whom he had given his own sister, Constantia, and whom he had appointed as his fellow Caesar."[134]

Luther also appears to have been familiar with some of the finer points of ancient Roman public life. He knew that as the Romans began to expand their state, they assigned cities and settlements (*coloniae*) differing political privileges.[135] He was familiar with the offices of *consul*, *iudex*, *praefectus*, *carnifex*, and *lictor* (and the *fasces* that the *lictor* carried as an indication of his authority and power to punish malefactors), as well as the *apparitores*, the public servants (e.g., scribes and messengers) who attended Roman magistrates and the *speculatores*, or military scouts or spies.[136]

Luther was aware of and highly critical of the polytheism of the Romans, with their "hundreds of gods."[137] He was familiar with the ancient use of *omina* to predict the future and, of course, the practice of astrology, still taken seriously in his own time.[138] Of the Roman deities, he mentions specifically Apollo, Bacchus, Diana, the Fates, Fortuna, Juno, Mars, Mercury, Neptune, Priapus, Quirinus (the deified Romulus), and Venus.[139] He often refers to the Roman king of the gods, Jupiter or Jove.[140] In a letter of 1537 to Wolfgang Capito, Luther compares himself to Jupiter's father, the titan Saturn who devoured his own children, as he declares that he would prefer to eat all of his books rather than see them collected and republished (with the possible exception of *On the Bondage of the Will* and his catechism).[141] He knew of the priestesses of Vesta, the Vestal Virgins, whose duty it was to keep the sacred fire lit day and night, lest Rome perish,[142] as well as the *flamines*, priests of the pontifical college.[143] He used terms such as *Tartarus* and *Orcus* when referring to the underworld, the home of the Furies.[144] Luther compared the household gods of the ancient Romans—the *lares*, or "good and evil geniuses," as he describes them—to the angels of the Bible.[145]

He knew about such varied aspects of Roman life as their fondness for fattened dormice[146] and the gladiatorial games[147] as well as some of the particulars of Roman dress (including the purple *toga picta*), the distinctive torques worn around the neck by the Gauls from which the Torquati were supposed to have derived their name,[148] the wearing of gold by Roman women (but not Roman men),[149] and the fact that Roman sons would cover their heads when mourning.[150] Luther also comments on the use of wreaths in Roman triumphs.[151] In one of his *Tischreden* of 1538, Luther suggests that the pope has continued the tradition of the ancient triumph: "Nonetheless it [Rome] has retained something in the way of a ceremonial procession (*pompa*), in that the pope celebrates a triumph with heavily ornamented horses leading the way, and he carries the sacrament on an ornamented horse."[152] In an introductory note found at the beginning of an early sermon (1519) on the first Sunday of Advent, the shouts of the crowd welcoming Jesus to Jerusalem are compared to the *acclamatio* of the Roman citizenry on such occasions: *Io triumphe*.[153]

Unlike many professional historians today, to be sure, Luther saw all of human history, including that of Rome, as taking place under the aegis of God's gracious blessing and his stern judgment. Luther was not at all uncomfortable with making sweeping moral pronouncements or trying to find ways in which the lessons of the Roman past—in particular its paradigmatic examples of human virtue and vice—could be applied to the present. Indeed, this was one of the main reasons to study ancient history. In his preface to Galeatius Capella's *History*, published in 1538, Luther makes this clear:

> It is the highly esteemed Roman Varro who says that the very best way to teach is to provide for words an example or illustration, for these help one to understand the discourse more clearly and to retain it much more easily. Otherwise, if one listens to what is said without an example, no matter

how correct and good it may be, it just does not move the heart as much, and also it is not so clear and easily retained. That is why histories are such a very precious thing. For whatever philosophers, wise men, and all of reason can teach or imagine that could be useful for living an honorable life, this is what histories provide in such a powerful way, using examples and stories, presenting them right in front of our eyes, as though we were there, watching everything happen that the words had previously conveyed to our ears in instruction.[154]

Luther concludes by drawing a moral point: "Almost all forms of law, art, good counsel, warning, threatening, terror, comfort, edification, instruction, foresight, wisdom, prudence, together with all virtues, etc., come pouring out of stories and histories as from a fountain of living water."[155] Indeed, it was precisely in view of their "excellent virtues" that "God gave the Romans their empire" in the first place, according to Luther (and Augustine before him; see *De civitate Dei* 5.12).[156] And "virtue" is what helped perpetuate the Roman *res publica*. As the early Latin poet Ennius once said, "The Roman state stands because of its ancient morals and its men."[157]

The four cardinal virtues highlighted in Cicero's *De officiis* (1.15) are courage, wisdom, moderation (or temperance), and justice. The English word "virtue" comes from the Latin word *virtus*, which has at its etymological root the idea of "manliness." Central to that concept is the quality of bravery (*fortitudo*), so important for a warrior state such as Rome. It was because they were "endowed with conspicuous and truly heroic virtues" that Luther respected such "great and outstanding men" among the Romans as "Marcus Fabius, Attilius Regulus, Cicero, Pomponius Atticus, and many others."[158] These Roman "heroes" were willing to risk their own happiness and even their lives not in order to aggrandize themselves but to accomplish outstanding things for the well-being of the state.

By "Marcus Fabius" Luther probably means not the little-known consul of that name (who served in 245 BCE) but rather the much better known Quintus Fabius Maximus (Cunctator) discussed above. Most likely Luther has confused the first name (*praenomen*) of the general famed for his delaying tactics with that of Marcus Fabius Quintilianus, the rhetor of the first century CE whose works, as we have seen, Luther admired greatly. Marcus Atilius Regulus was the self-sacrificing general during the First Punic War who, in order to keep his word, voluntarily returned to Carthage, where he was tortured and died (cf. Horace, *Carm.* 3.5). Luther's respect for Cicero's heroism is interesting, because the Roman orator was not famous for his military accomplishments, nor was he always brave. Nevertheless, at the end of his life, Cicero did discover his backbone, stood up to his dangerous foe Mark Antony, and literally lost his head for so doing. Luther observes admiringly of Cicero that he "bravely (*fortiter*) endured death in a just and good cause."[159] Cicero's friend, the banker Atticus, was not known for his military exploits either, but Luther considered him heroic, too, because of his truthfulness and constancy.[160] Both qualities can lead one into situations where heroism is required. "Brave" as these Roman heroes may have been, none could equal the martial courage of the "victorious" Julius Caesar.[161] He lost very few if any of the fifty-two battles he waged, in which his armies killed over one million men.[162] Although Augustus was not nearly as renowned a military commander as Julius Caesar had been, Luther includes him in his exposition of Psalm 101, in which he discusses what it means for a nation to have an exceptional leader who is "a fine hero."[163]

The Roman heroes possessed not only courage but wisdom (*prudentia*). They were "outstanding in wisdom and more famous than other gentiles for their serious discipline."[164] Christians had no particular monopoly on wisdom; in fact, the truth was quite the opposite. As Jesus himself once declared, "The children of this world are in their generation wiser than the children of light" (Luke 16:8). "When it comes to native wit, learning, or industry," Luther asks Erasmus, "what Christian is there who could be compared to Cicero alone, to say nothing of the Greeks?"[165] This wisdom is not abstract or theoretical knowledge, at which Aristotle excelled, but knowledge put to work. Luther far preferred Cicero to Aristotle when it came to such practical wisdom.[166] Aristotle may have been a more profound and far-reaching thinker, but the "very hardworking" Cicero was the wiser of the two.[167] There is more philosophy in one book of Cicero, Luther opined, than in all the works of Aristotle.[168] It was not simply by dint of their military power but with the timely application of wisdom (*non viribus sed sapientia*) that the Romans were able to conquer the world.[169] Augustus was willing to give up his power, but his ultimate decision not to do so turned out to be a wise one for himself and the state.[170] Roman wisdom applied not only to civic affairs and foreign policy but also to the way in which individuals lived with their most immediate neighbors. "The wise Roman" Cato put it well: "One should make every effort to behave in such a way that our neighbors love us and are kindly disposed toward us."[171]

The virtue of moderation or temperance, as applied not only at the personal level—say, in terms of living simply and avoiding overindulgence in food and drink and luxuries (*frugalitas*)—but also to the collective actions of the state, was an important part of Rome's amazing success story. The selfless Roman heroes in the first books of Livy's *Ab urbe condita* were fierce warriors, of course, and the Roman military machine was unmatched for its ruthless efficiency, but the best of the Romans knew when to use military force and when not to. It was not enough simply to crush one's enemy in battle, as Hannibal, the great opponent of Rome, was well aware. Friendship can be as effective as force when it comes to sustaining an empire. Luther quotes from one of Terence's comedies in this regard: "Whoever thinks that a realm that has to be preserved by the use of force is more permanent than one that remains united thanks to friendship, I hold to be completely wrong."[172] In his lectures on Deuteronomy, Luther quotes the sage advice Anchises gives to Aeneas in Virgil's *Aeneid* 6.853 about showing mercy to those who have been subdued but beating down the proud in war: *Parcere subiectis et debellare superbos*.[173] In the same context, he observes, "And Augustus always preferred peace to war and said that war should not be waged unless absolutely necessary. Accordingly, he said that war is like a golden fishhook, where the expense is greater than the gain; no single catch can make up for the hook if it is lost."[174]

Cicero and other "best men" among the gentiles sought not only wisdom but "justice," according to their lights.[175] Justice is the virtue, one could say, for which all the others exist. It is the reason for the existence of laws, which are designed to support and enforce justice. The Romans were famous for their laws, and Roman law still possessed enormous importance in Luther's Europe.[176] Luther refers to "the law of the Romans" (*Romanorum Ius*) when he describes Paul's right as a Roman citizen to a trial before execution (Acts 25) in a sermon he preached on John 19.[177] In his exposition of Psalm 101, Luther commends the "fine old jurists" in general and Ulpian of Tyre in particular. Ulpian served as praetorian prefect for Alexander Severus, and his legal writings constitute a considerable portion of the *Pandects* (or *Digest*), compiled by order of Justinian.[178] When thinking of justice in a broader sense, as it applies not only to the family but also to the state, Luther admired Roman exemplars of virtue precisely because they tried to do good things for the collective whole. This was one of the main reasons Cicero impressed Luther so. Far more than "the leisured ass," Aristotle, "who had plenty of money and time on his hands," Cicero was "full of cares and civic burdens" and labored diligently on behalf of his fellow citizens.[179] Even though Cicero and Scipio were themselves hardly paragons of virtue, nonetheless they were "called just" insofar as they vigorously punished crimes against the republic.[180] Luther compares effective Roman emperors such as Augustus and Vespasian favorably with biblical leaders like Samson, David, and Jehoiada.[181] He considers the "worldly governance" of Augustus and Trajan to be exemplary.[182] These competent leaders of "the heathen and the godless" were "their Davids and Solomons."[183] Such rulers are never capricious or rapacious but judicious, heeding the advice of Tiberius: "It is the property of a good shepherd to shear, not to skin his sheep."[184]

Just states are those that understand the value of harmony (*concordia*) for their own continued prosperity. In his lectures on Deuteronomy, Luther quotes Sallust's *Bellum Iugurthinum* 10.6 ("through concord small states become great; through discord the greatest states are undone") as he gives an unusual etymology for the Latin word *civitas* ("state"), suggesting that it is derived from the words *cives* ("citizens") and *unitas* ("unity").[185] Luther commended the Romans for making distinctions in their laws between citizens and noncitizens and between colonies and the city of Rome itself, "lest all things become confused and equal." Even though such distinctions might seem to have the appearance of unfairness, a state needs to be founded on a set of just principles that distinguish between maid-servants and senators if it is to enjoy "public peace" (*pax publica*).[186]

Vices can be as pedagogically useful as virtues. When it comes to teaching young people about the best ways in which members of a society can live safely and productively together, negative examples might be even more effective than positive ones. For Luther, Aesop's fables were helpful conduits for the inculcation of such valuable life lessons, especially for children and servants. Luther quoted them frequently and in 1530 even set out to prepare his own edition of the fables for practical use in the Lutheran home.[187] He associated many of them with vices such as foolishness, pride, and envy. For instance, to the famous fable of the dog with the bone who sees its reflection in the water, imagines that there is a second bone, and loses the bone already in his mouth in the process of trying to get one that is not, Luther gave the simple but telling title "Greed."

Luther was by no means uncritical of Rome's heroes. They were most often unsuccessful in the end. Even though Roman leaders like Cicero and Brutus were considered to be "extraordinarily wise and understanding" and "luminaries in the areas of natural law and reason," nonetheless they were unable to achieve all of the good for the state that they had planned.[188] After the catastrophic failure of his efforts to achieve his dream of concord, Cicero had to admit bitterly that his highly touted wisdom had proved useless.[189] Clearly, great virtues in and of themselves were insufficient to ensure the smooth administration of a state such as Rome—to say nothing of an individual's political survival.

Rome also had its fair share of rulers who lacked even the most rudimentary virtues. Unlike Caesar, who was loved by the people and renowned for his generosity and clemency, some later Roman rulers were immeasurably cruel and had little interest in treating the populace well. The emperor Caligula is supposed to have said, "Let them hate provided that they fear" (*Oderint dum metuant*).[190] Luther suggests that his own ecclesiastical enemies would have preferred that he and other reformers had only one neck so that, like Caligula, they could decapitate all of them with one stroke of the sword.[191] Caligula wanted to be worshipped "as a god" and "to be adored in the midst of the gods in Rome,"[192] but he was killed after ruling for only a short time, two years.[193] The Roman people eventually turned against Nero, too, but things in Rome were no better after he died than before.[194] When emperors like Heliogabalus and Commodus first came to power, they raised high hopes among everyone, but such hopes did not last long.[195]

What motivated even the best of the Romans, men like Caesar and Cicero, really? Luther was not naive about the underlying motives they might have had for doing great things for their commonwealth. No matter how much they talked about their altruistic reasons for providing their services to the republic, their ambition was inspired by "nothing other than their desire for glory."[196] And like the unsatisfied dog in the Aesopic fable, these pagan examples of heroic virtue were never able to find contentment. No matter how much they had, they always wanted to have more, until at last they ended up with nothing. Julius Caesar achieved ultimate power but was not satisfied even with this. In the end he "perished miserably."[197] In a sermon of 1524, Luther told his congregation that Caesar had a dream in which he slept with his mother, a dream that Luther suggests might have meant that Caesar "would bring his fatherland beneath himself and do harm to it."[198] How very different all of this striving for power and glory is from the kingdom of heaven, where the greatest is least and where the meek inherit the earth! The prince of peace arrived in Jerusalem in the utmost humility, "riding on a borrowed donkey"

(Matt 21:2–3), unlike Julius Caesar in Rome, "with his worldly splendor, battle gear, silver, and gold."[199] The Romans may have been great, but because they did not have God or even know him, Luther was sure that they could not have been truly happy.[200] Even the remarkable integrity of the unbribable Gaius Fabricius Luscinus does not count as righteousness before God if it is without faith.[201]

Despite all of its great heroic leaders and their obvious virtues, the Roman Empire eventually fell. In the end, it was no more stable and enduring than "a water bubble" (*bulla aquatica*).[202] At first, Rome appeared impressive enough, but it turned out to be exceedingly fragile. Augustus hoped that his fundamental work would establish the state on a permanent basis, "but those who followed him soon overthrew it all."[203] Like Alexander the Great, the leaders of Rome intended to establish "an eternal empire," but it failed like all of the empires that preceded it.[204] At least for a while, Rome was "the sword of the Lord" (*gladius Domini*), but eventually "Christ laughed at its power and wisdom," and the great empire fell at last.[205]

Luther often pondered the question of Rome's decline and fall and speculated as to its cause. One explanation was that it was the empire's very successes, ironically enough, that led to its demise. There is an inevitable cycle to such things. Pompey had collected a great deal of money for the Roman treasury,[206] but shortly thereafter, Julius Caesar used it to pay his soldiers.[207] Good times must be followed by bad. Augustus built a beautiful city, but within a few decades, Nero had burned it down. At the beginning of his reign, according to Luther, Octavian had found Rome a city of "wood," but he left it a splendid city of "gold."[208] These are not the building materials that are usually mentioned in connection with Augustus's renovations of Rome. According to Suetonius (*Divus Augustus* 28.3), Augustus found Rome a city of brick and left it a city of marble. Elsewhere, Luther does describe the city as made of brick (*latericia*).[209] But wood was often used for construction in ancient Rome, especially for temporary theaters, before the first stone theater (of Pompey) was built in 55 BCE, and one of the standard epithets for the later city of Rome is "golden" (see, e.g., Prudentius, *Apotheosis* 385). Whether

Augustus used gold or marble to transform the appearance of a Rome originally built of wood or brick, it did not take long before Nero and other destructive rulers ruined the impressive city that the first emperor had created. This reminded Luther of the proverb "One builds, but the other destroys." Augustus strove to "adorn" the city, but "the shit Nero" (*Nero stercus*) destroyed it.[210]

In his early lectures on the Psalter, Luther attributes to Hannibal the idea that a "great republic" could not long stand "without an external enemy."[211] It would grow lazy and corrupt if it was not required to remain constantly vigilant. This idea is more often associated with the Roman senator Scipio Nasica, who frequently argued with Cato the Elder about whether Rome should continue to have an external enemy (or destroy its great rival Carthage) after the Second Punic War. The latter was in the habit of ending practically every speech in the Senate, no matter the topic at hand, with the same predictable conclusion: "Furthermore, I think that Carthage should be destroyed."[212] Cato's counsel eventually won the day. The Romans laid waste to the North African city in 146 BCE. In his explanations of the Ninety-Five Theses, Luther cites the famous argument as it might be applied to heretics and errorists in the church.[213]

Above all, in Rome's tragic history, Luther saw the will of God being done. Just as God had acted in the Old Testament when he destroyed kings like Jeroboam, Ahab, and Ahaziah, so too the mighty Lord raised up and then removed Roman rulers such as Julius Caesar, Nero, and Domitian.[214] The one who sits in the heavens laughs at Rome and other gentile nations (Ps 2:4); even "the most celebrated" cities in the history of the world are now "so devastated that nobody can restore them to their ancient grandeur."[215] For Luther, Rome's decline and fall was a function of its failure to accept Christianity.[216] Precisely because of its opposition to the church of Christ, "it collapsed and was thoroughly burned and sacked three times" (*drey mal*).[217]

The first of these times was in 410, when Alaric's Visigothic troops took the city. They largely spared Christians and Christian buildings and only stayed in Rome for a few days. They could have done far more damage to the city than they did, but the effect on Romans was dramatic. For some eight hundred years, their invincible city had withstood all attempts at invasion. Centuries earlier, in 390 BCE, the Gauls had succeeded in occupying much of the city and would have taken the citadel on the Capitoline itself, according to legend, were it not for some insomniac geese. But that had been the last successful invasion of the city of Rome. The emotional impact of the Goths' first sacking of the city on contemporary Romans can hardly be overestimated. In tones of despair, Jerome complained that the city that itself had taken the whole world captive was now itself taken (*Ep.* 127).[218] In a sermon on John 8:28, Luther mentions Augustine's *City of God*, written after 410 to address complaints registered by the Romans that they were worse off now than when they were pagans. Luther knew the work well.[219] His own perspectives on the demise of Rome and its causes are deeply indebted in general to Augustine's panoramic view of the subject. The Romans who did not believe the gospel at the time of Paul and Peter eventually had no choice but to believe "after Rome lay ruined, destroyed by the Goths and the Wends."[220]

The sacking of the city in 410 was soon followed by a second one, carried out by the Vandals (Luther's "Wends") under Genseric in 455. These invaders stayed longer in Rome than the Visigoths and carried away even more booty. Several years earlier, the city of Rome had been spared by the Huns. One of the most fearsome challengers to Rome's hegemony, Attila, the leader of the Huns, who had "terrified not only the Roman Empire but also the entire world" with his army of five hundred thousand men,[221] got as far into Italy as the southern edge of Lake Garda, but he was dissuaded from proceeding on to Rome in 452 by an embassy that included Pope Leo I.[222]

It is not entirely clear whether Luther thought there was a total of three or four sackings of Rome by the Goths. In *Against the Papacy in Rome, Founded by the Devil*, Luther says that Rome was conquered and destroyed four times (*viermal*) by the Goths and the Vandals within the space of one hundred years.[223] In 472, Ricimer, a German general who served as *magister militum* in the western empire, successfully besieged the city. It is possible that Luther considered this to be the "third" sacking of Rome.[224] There was an even later sacking of the city in 548, when "Rome was destroyed by the Goths through Totila," king of the Ostrogoths, but this happened well over a century after the first of these catastrophic events in 410.[225]

The blame for such catastrophes, according to Luther, should be assigned not so much to a capricious God as to the deficiencies of sinful humanity. Human sinfulness is not confined only to the ancient Romans but is also a factor in the demise of all nations. Luther applies this sobering history lesson to his own contemporary Germans. In contemplating the failure of Europe's attempts to defend itself against the Turks, he explains that "our sins have aroused the anger of God against us." God has armed the Turks "with anger and cruelty" and at the same time has instilled fear in the Germans so that "we have forgotten our virtue and have degenerated in comparison with our ancestors."[226] Luther's Germans will find that God has the same fate waiting for them as met the Romans: "He used the Romans to shoot the obstinate Jews, the Goths and the Wends to shoot the Romans, the Persians to shoot the Chaldeans, and the Turks to shoot the Greeks. He will also find a cannonball (*kugel*) for us Germans, to hit us and not miss, for we have pushed things too far and still refuse to quit."[227]

"Ruin Porn"

Luther was neither the first nor the last visitor to Rome to have his attention drawn to its famous ancient ruins, to contemplate their former greatness, and to be fascinated by the abundant evidence of ruin and decay in the city.[228] Nor were his moralizing reflections on the significance of the remains of pagan Rome unique to him by any means. It may be helpful, therefore, to contextualize his reactions to the "ravaged" city by considering other responses registered by visitors to ancient Rome over the centuries.

Many of them, like Luther, have sought to draw moral lessons from the obvious evidence before their eyes of the downfall of this venerable city and civilization. Others, artists especially, have been prompted by aesthetic urges, including a nostalgic fascination with Rome's faded grandeur. Still others, especially in modern times, are motivated by purely scholarly interests. Luther's fascination with the ancient city had relatively little to do with either aesthetic considerations or the preservationist instincts of present-day antiquarians, but that does not mean his interests in Rome were necessarily any less intense. Certainly, his memories of the "ravaged" city lingered in his mind long after his trip to Rome had become a distant dream from his youthful past.

Even more remarkable perhaps than the eventual ruination of Rome is that the Romans themselves worried about it obsessively for so many years before it actually happened. As he observed the destruction of the city of Carthage at the end of the Third Punic War, Scipio Aemilianus is said to have wept as he thought about the rise and fall of other nations, quoting the lines from Homer's *Iliad* (6.448–49): "A day will come when sacred Troy, and Priam, and the people ruled by Priam of the good ash spear, will perish." When asked by the historian Polybius why he had cited the ancient Greek poet's words, Scipio indicated that he was thinking about the fate of his own city, Rome, in light of the volatility of history.[229] All of this melancholic worry centuries before the last Roman emperor in the west was removed from office! And Scipio was not the only ancient Roman who dreamed of an empire without end but also had nightmares about an empire that would end very soon.

Luther shared the fascination of Scipio and other Romans with the end of Troy and other great civilizations, including their own. Even though he considered Germany to be superior in many ways, he was convinced that it would end up like Homer's Troy, in ruins. Luther uses Virgil's words (*Aeneid* 2.325: *Fuimus Troes, fuit Ilium et ingens*) to predict the demise of his own land: "Germany has always been the best land and nation, but what happened to Troy will happen to Germany, so that people will say, 'It's over. We Trojans are finished; huge Ilium lies in ruins'" (*Es ist aus. Fuimus Troes, iacet Ilium ingens*).[230]

Even before the Goths sacked Rome in the fifth century CE, the status of the city had been declining. The emperor Diocletian had transferred the capital of the western half of his empire from Rome to Milan in 286 CE. In 402 CE, the capital was moved to Ravenna. Jerome was already describing the "golden Capitoline" as "desolate" (*squalatum*) in a letter written around that time (*Ep.* 107). All of the temples of Rome were covered "with mold and spider-webs."[231] By the time the Goths had finished with all of their sackings of the city, the situation seemed as dire to Pope Gregory the Great as one of the most dramatic moments in the waning days of the Roman Republic, the Catilinarian conspiracy. In one of his letters (*Ep.* 5.37), Gregory makes use of Cicero's famous words of expostulation, *O tempora! O mores!* addressed to the Senate (and Catiline) as the pope laments the fact that "barbarians" had now destroyed so much of Rome. Ruins were everywhere.[232] (Centuries later, Luther lamented the calamities of his own times using the same Ciceronian language: *O tempora! O Sathan!*[233]) In the eighth century, Alcuin of York can still refer to Rome as "the head of the world" (*caput mundi*), but of the "golden" city that was once "the adornment of the world," he declares, nothing now remains "but harsh ruins."[234] In 846, the Saracens made a raid on the city, landing at Ostia and proceeding to Rome. They succeeded in devastating the basilicas of Paul and Peter, both of which lay outside of the Aurelian Walls, but they were unable to breach the walls themselves. Some two hundred years later, many of the buildings of ancient Rome, including structures on the Capitoline and Palatine hills, were burned by Norman invaders under the leadership of Robert Guiscard, who came to the rescue of Pope Gregory VII in 1084.

By the early modern period, more and more visitors to the city had begun to take a lively interest in its pagan remains. Like Luther, they often drew edifying Christian lessons from them. The fourteenth-century Petrarch loved Rome and visited it five times, walking through the ruins and meditating on the greatness of the city and its passing. To the cardinal Giovanni Colonna he wrote, "It is scarcely to be believed how great in me is the desire to contemplate that city which, though a desert, is the effigy of antique Rome."[235] Elsewhere, he marveled at how much of ancient Rome, including its enormous baths and great palaces, had been destroyed. Human glory is fleeting, this influential Italian humanist concluded, and nothing, not even the eternal city, lasts forever, except for God.[236] As Poggio sat on the Capitoline Hill and looked out over the Forum overgrown with vegetation stretched out below him, he conceived of his "elegant" but "moral" treatise on the fickleness of fortune (*De varietate fortunae*).[237] To Francesco Albertini, author of a popular guidebook to Rome published in 1510, is attributed the memorable phrase *Nam quanta Roma fuit ipsa ruina docet* ("For how great Rome was, its ruined state itself teaches us").[238]

In the early modern period, we see the beginnings of serious scholarship devoted to the study of ancient Rome. As early as the fourteenth century, Cola di Rienzo, the "tribune of freedom, peace, and justice" and the "liberator of the Holy Roman Republic," was interested in deciphering ancient inscriptions in the city.[239] The celebrated painter Raphael, who was named superintendent of antiquities in Rome in 1516, wrote a firm letter to Pope Leo X protesting against the plundering of the ancient ruins for modern building purposes.[240] The pioneering art historian Johann Joachim Winckelmann moved from Germany to live permanently in Rome, where he was eventually named prefect of antiquities beginning in 1763. In his day, much of the plundering of Rome was being done by Rome-worshipping tourists from Britain and elsewhere who carted off fragments of the antique past to display in their museums and gardens at home. "Were our amphitheatre portable, the English would carry it off" was a complaint that could be heard in Rome in the eighteenth century.[241]

It was while he was in the ancient city in 1764 that Edward Gibbon conceived of *The Decline and Fall of the Roman Empire*. Twelve years later, the first volume was published, and the final (sixth) volume was finished only in 1789. Gibbon decided to write his *opus magnum*, famous for its "marmoreally imposing" prose, as he sat "musing on the Capitol" (like Poggio before him), "while the bare-footed fryars were chanting their litanies in the temple of Jupiter."[242] The Franciscan cloister of Ara Coeli, whose brothers Gibbon heard chanting, was demolished in the late nineteenth century in order to make room for the Altare della Patria (also known as the Vittoriano), a huge monument of white marble built to honor Vittorio Emanuele II and completed in 1935.[243] The stark contrast between what Gibbon may have been looking at (the pagan Roman forum that lay below him) and the sounds that he was hearing at the same time (Gregorian chants) may well have served as the catalyst for his massive study.

Like Luther, Gibbon believed that Christianity was responsible ultimately for the Roman Empire's downfall, but he did not see human sin and divine judgment at work in the process in the same way that Luther and others did. It was the pacific teachings and practice of the early Christians that contributed to the loss of the heroic virtues that had for so long helped the Romans to prevail against their "barbarian" neighbors. By contrast, a contemporary of Gibbon's, the evangelical hymn writer William Cowper, expressly connects imperial Rome's demise with its bloodthirsty "guilt" in *Boadicea: An Ode* (1782): "Rome shall perish—write that word / In the blood that she has spilt. / Perish hopeless and abhorr'd / Deep in ruin as in guilt."[244]

A virulent strain of anti-Catholicism is evident in the writings of Protestants like William Beckford, who did an Italian tour in 1780 and, while visiting the Colosseum, experienced "a vehement desire" to "pulverize the whole circle of saints' nests and chapels which disgrace the area." He complained of "the vile effect of this holy trumpery" and with all of his heart wished to kick it into the Tiber River. What would Vespasian have thought of the Flavian amphitheater, Beckford asks, if he could have seen it filled not with gladiators but with lazy abbots "such as would have made a lion's mouth water, fatter, I dare say, than any saint in the whole martyrology and ten times more tantalizing?"[245]

It was neither purely scholarly motivations nor anti-Catholic sensibilities that inspired English Romantic poets to wax eloquent about the ruins of Rome.[246] Their relationship with the city was motivated primarily by emotional and aesthetic considerations. The sight of the ruins of the great but long past civilization inspired nostalgic thoughts in Lord Byron, who referred to Rome as "the Niobe of nations." Unlike other cities that look to the future, Rome is all about the past, weeping endlessly for her lost children like the mythical Niobe, who was finally turned into a stone dripping with water. The city stands "childless and crownless, in her voiceless woe; / An empty urn within her wither'd hands / Whose holy dust was scatter'd long ago" (*Childe Harold*, Canto 4, stanza 79).[247] Percy Bysshe Shelley strikes a similarly melancholy chord in his lament for the death of John Keats (*Adonais* 49):

> Go thou to Rome,—at once the Paradise,
> The grave, the city, and the wilderness;
> And where its wrecks like shattered mountains rise,
> And flowering weeds, and fragrant copses dress
> The bones of Desolation's nakedness
> Pass, till the spirit of the spot shall lead
> Thy footsteps to a slope of green access
> Where, like an infant's smile, over the dead
> A light of laughing flowers along the grass is spread.[248]

Shelley's Rome, not unlike Luther's, is not so much a city as a "grave," filled with "the bones of Desolation's nakedness." Shelley's own ashes were buried in the Protestant Cemetery in Rome (as was the body of Keats) along with the remains of other *acattolici*. The house where Keats lived near the Spanish Steps has now been turned into a museum.

While himself not a poet but rather an Anglican schoolmaster, Thomas Arnold wrote a three-volume history of Rome (left unfinished at his death in 1842) and confessed himself "bewitched" by Rome and the "inexplicable solemnity and beauty of her ruined condition."[249] The seductive attraction of the ruins of Rome is captured well by Charles Dickens in his *Pictures from Italy* (1846) as he describes a walk he took out on the Appian Way: "Except where the distant Apennines bound the view upon the left, the whole wide prospect is one field of ruin. Broken aqueducts, left in the most picturesque and beautiful clusters of arches; broken temples; broken tombs. A desert of decay, sombre and desolate beyond all expression; and with a history in every stone that strews the ground."[250] The "desert of decay" that other, more practical observers today might see as prime real estate opportunities, Dickens and other nineteenth-century visitors to Rome regarded as "picturesque and beautiful." Indeed, the modern developments of the city at the expense of its ruins, while essential for Rome's current success as a metropolitan center, have served as a source of considerable regret to many an inveterate nostalgist.

The American writer Henry James, who set one of his later novels, *The Golden Bowl*, in "inexhaustible" Rome and wrote a most moving description of the Protestant Cemetery in *The Italian Hours*, was deeply disturbed by the clearing and excavating of the Colosseum and the Roman Forum. He missed the multitudes of flowers that had been mowed down in the interest of archeological scholarship. Ruins had their own strange, salutary purpose for James. In *Portrait of a Lady* (1880–81), he writes that as viewed against "a world of ruins," the ruin of one person's happiness "seemed a less unnatural catastrophe." A visit to Rome made it possible for her melancholic guests to rest their "weariness upon things that had crumbled for centuries and yet were still upright," to drop their "secret sadness into the silence of lonely places, where its very modern quality detached itself and grew objective."[251]

For many other Americans (besides the expatriate Henry James), the very fact that Rome was so old represented a kind of un-American alterity. Unlike youthful America in the nineteenth century, eager to embrace the frontier and the future, Rome mostly looked backward instead of forward. As William Vance observes, "Rome, a city with no future, was antithetical to what America was and (in all ways except the aesthetic) to dreams of what it might become."[252] In his "Song of the Exposition" (1871), Walt Whitman urges the "Muse" to leave off inspiring outdated epic poems dealing with tired subjects like Troy and Aeneas and to move to America, where "a better, fresher, busier sphere, a wide, untried domain awaits."[253] Not all of Whitman's compatriots were as optimistic as he about America. When Henry Adams compared his own Boston with Rome, he found them both to be ruined, but the former more so than the latter: "I went to Boston the other day, and stood in Beacon Street, and wept over its shrunken ruins. One or two squares of houses are all that remain; the world about is mere adipose tissue hanging on the old skeleton. I thought of Rome and the Capitol. Honestly it was not unlike, but Boston was the more ruin of the two."[254]

After World War I, thanks to Mussolini's ambitious political and architectural agenda, there was a risk that the city "of visual poetry," with its "galaxies of enormous whiskered ruins half obscured by a profusion of picturesque houses," would be transformed permanently into a gigantic civic propaganda piece for Fascism.[255] But the modernization of Rome that Mussolini and others envisioned never really took hold. After *il Duce* was executed in 1945, most tourists still came to the historic city not in order to marvel at its Fascist architecture (e.g., the Colosseo Quadrato in EUR) or to enjoy its new urban amenities, such as the metro system (begun in 1955), but to be overwhelmed by its antiquity. The Swiss psychologist Carl Jung had something of a "Rome complex" and found himself unable to deal with the city's deep historicity. He never actually managed to visit Rome, although he did make plans to go in his old age (1949), only to be "stricken with a faint while [he] was buying tickets." For Jung, visiting such an intensely historical city as Rome was a far more complicated matter than traveling to Paris or London. He imagined that any sensitive human being who walked around Rome would have to be affected deeply "at every step by the spirit that broods there."[256] More recently, Bob Dylan, an American musician, less exquisitely sensitive perhaps than Jung, was relatively unfazed by the "ancient footprints" he found everywhere in the "streets of Rome," which he describes as "filled with rubble" in his 1971 song "When I Paint My Masterpiece."[257]

None of this should be taken to mean that Lord Byron, Henry James, or others who visited Rome in the centuries following Luther's visit there were necessarily influenced by Luther and his experiences in the city in any sort of direct fashion. All that I want to observe here is that there has been a long stream of other visitors to Rome over the centuries who have been moved as deeply as Luther, in various ways, by its historic remains. Like Luther, many of them have also been distinctly unimpressed by the contemporary city. The main appeal of the eternal city is not its future but its palpable past, Rome's "rubble." Luther must certainly be considered one of the best known and most influential of all of the visitors to Rome who have tried to assess and articulate what the ruination of this great city and civilization so long ago might mean to them at the present time.

3

"The Kingdom Ours Remaineth"
THE CITIZEN

THIS CHAPTER EXPLORES THE question of Luther's identity as a citizen, especially his status as a subject of the Holy Roman Empire. This is not, to be sure, the political affiliation associated with his name that usually comes first to mind. Luther most often identified himself as a German in the midst of his own "dear" Germans. His native tongue was that of "the Saxon chancery."[1] His most immediate set of political loyalties was to the electoral princes of Ernestine Saxony. At the time of the Diet of Worms, the elector was Prince Frederick III, known as "the Wise," whose castle in Torgau was roughly fifty kilometers from Luther's Wittenberg. Over the subsequent centuries, Luther has been claimed by many Germans themselves as one of their most influential early representatives. The Romantic poet Heinrich Heine pronounced Luther to be "the most German man of German history."[2]

But as has been true of so many others in his own time and since, Luther had more than one political identity. Underlying his own local affiliations, his attachment to Saxony and Wittenberg, his "Germanness," if you will, was another set of affinities, deeper if not as immediately obvious, which we may with some justification call his sixteenth-century *Romanitas*. It would not have been at all difficult for Luther to make a connection, however tenuous, between his own status as a subject of the Holy Roman Empire in good standing, which he was from his birth in 1483 until 1521 (over half of his life), and that of the heroes of ancient Rome whom he so often describes in admiring terms.

In a discussion at table with Dr. Heinrich Schneidewein, an old friend who had just returned from a trip to Italy, Luther spoke about the continuity of the Roman Empire thus: "The Roman Empire began to prosper at the time of the apostles. In fact, 750 years ago it was handed over to the Germans under Charles the Great. He had three sons to whom he gave the divided empire: Germany to one, France to another, Italy to the third. But the emperor continued to be German throughout."[3] As seen from Luther's perspective, the empire ruled by Nero when the apostle Paul was in the city of Rome was the same one that had been "handed over to the Germans" at the time of the Frankish ruler Charlemagne, who in turn had planned to leave this empire to his sons, Charles, Louis, and Carloman (or Pepin). Hundreds of years later, Luther's own Charles V, who was born in Flanders and spent far more time in the Lowlands and Spain than he ever did in what is now Italy, was the ruler of this same Roman Empire.[4] Despite the obvious historical discontinuities, Luther was still able to discern a connection between the ancient empire at the time of the apostles and his own contemporary "German" Roman Empire.

In what follows, we shall explore the question of Luther's awareness of the Holy Roman Empire—its history and current status—and consider how he regarded his own relationship with the institution and its representatives. The highly formulaic quality of the deferential language he uses in his letters and elsewhere when addressing or referring to the emperor and other civil authorities does not necessarily mean that these words were never seriously intended. After all, Luther was not always respectful of all of them. He felt free to label and libel Duke Henry of Braunschweig as *Hanswurst*, the name of a buffoonish character who was a figure of ridicule in popular German comedy of the time.[5]

The respectful terminology "our Lord Caesar," which he uses in the first sentence of *Against the Papacy in Rome, Founded by the Devil* to refer to Charles V, stands in stark contrast to his punning description of Pope Paul III as "all hellish father" (instead of "all holy father") in the same sentence.[6] Charles V was Luther's emperor, and even though it turned out that he was unalterably opposed to Luther and the Reformation, his imperial authority was sacrosanct to Luther. Long after his own condemnation at Worms, Luther joined other reformers in hoping against hope that Charles might somehow end up supporting their cause against the papacy. After all, it was by no means inevitable that this or any other Holy Roman emperor would have had to oppose a protest movement against the Roman papacy. Certainly, Charles's predecessors in his imperial office did not always (or even often) endorse the claims of the pope or defend the supreme pontiff's decisions.

Luther's attitude toward Charles V and the Holy Roman Empire was of a piece with his respect in general for the traditional authority of secular magistrates, including those connected with local regimes in Germany, many of whom enthusiastically supported his cause. In his appeal for a free council in 1520, Luther describes not only "the Roman emperor, Charles," but also "electors, princes, counts, lords, knights, nobles, councilors," in support of the idea of a general council, as "most illustrious, highborn, wellborn, noble, puissant, wise, prudent."[7]

As a political thinker, Luther was quite conservative in many ways—this despite his frequent depiction in popular culture as something of a rebel. In *Luther*, Eric Till's cinematic production of 2003, "rebel" is the first word in the subtitle (*Rebel, Genius, Liberator*). Luther is described as rebellious even by such reputable scholars as Heinz Schilling; the subtitle of his biography of Martin Luther is *Rebel in an Age of Upheaval*. However "rebellious" he may have seemed to be during his tumultuous times, especially early on, Luther turned out to be anything but a political revolutionary. Indeed, he was a consistent advocate for civic and social stability. Even with regard to his efforts to effect changes within the church, the common appellation "reformer" may be too extreme to describe accurately his motivations and methods.[8] At best, we can join Martin Brecht in calling him a "cautious" (*behutsamer*) reformer.[9]

It is true that later intellectual developments such as the insistence on individual liberties that rest upon "inalienable" human rights may owe something to the lone monk who stood before the emperor in Worms and bravely spoke of his reluctance to go against his conscience (*contra conscientiam agere*).[10] But right up to the end of his life, Luther continued to believe strongly in the bondage of the individual human will, the real power of both God and the devil at work in this world as well as the next, and the God-given responsibility of civil authorities to enforce law and order. In fact, Luther's Reformation could well be described, as it has been, as a "magisterial" one, insofar as its leaders, including Luther himself, were quite ready to cooperate with local and regional magistrates, especially when it came to the administration of the new churches and schools in their regions.[11] In this respect, Luther was quite different from contemporary and subsequent reformers who strove for greater ecclesiastical influence in civic affairs or even dreamed of creating theocratic utopias not only in Europe but in new realms that lay on the other side of the Atlantic Ocean.

Despite the civic obligations that Luther continued to insist that he and every other Christian owed to their communities, finally it was neither an empire, nor a state, nor a city to which he gave his ultimate allegiance but the body of Christ, present in every place where the word of God is taught in its truth and purity and the sacraments rightly administered. In this sense (and in this sense only) should we understand the reference to a "kingdom" in the last line of his most famous chorale, "A Mighty Fortress Is Our God": "And take they our life, / Goods, fame, child and wife, / Let these all be gone, / They yet have nothing won; / The kingdom ours remaineth."[12]

Luther and the Holy Roman Empire

"That body which called itself and still does call itself the Holy Roman Empire was never in any way holy, nor Roman, nor an empire."[13] Voltaire's witty remark in his 1756 *Essai sur l'histoire générale et sur les mœurs et l'esprit des nations* about the contradictions inherent in the Holy Roman Empire plays up the marked differences that by his time existed between the name and the reality of this aging institution. Many of his eighteenth-century contemporaries would have found it easy to agree with the judgment of the famous French *philosophe* on all three counts, especially in light of the increasing power of European nation-states such as England and France, with their own imperial ambitions. At its prime, the Holy Roman Empire was a far-flung conglomeration of hundreds of cities, duchies, principalities, and ecclesiastical holdings, a large number of them in what is now Germany and Italy, but its extent and power had been severely diminished by the time it was finally dissolved in 1806, just a few decades after Voltaire's death (1778). Still, it would be quite anachronistic to assume that Voltaire's cynical quip would have made much sense to Luther. Whether or not the Holy Roman Empire at Luther's time was in reality all that its name claimed, it is safe to say that Luther did indeed believe that it was more "holy" and more "Roman" and more of an "empire" than Voltaire did.

Let us start with the last term first. The Latin words from which the English words "empire" and "emperor" are derived are *imperium* and *imperator*, respectively. During the time of the Roman Republic, the term *imperator* was usually applied to military commanders. The *imperium* that they wielded was based on the authority they had over their troops. The first *Imperator Caesar* was Julius Caesar, followed by Octavian, whose authority applied not only to the city of Rome and Italy (*imperium consulare*) but also to the provinces (*imperium maius*). The title of *imperator* began to be applied as a regular rule to the autocratic rulers of the Roman Empire beginning in "the year of the four emperors" (69 CE). Roman rulers continued to be named *imperatores* for hundreds of years thereafter. The term persisted in the western part of the empire until 476 CE, when "Imperator Caesar Flavius Romulus Augustulus" (his full title) stepped down as ruler. The "barbarian" chieftain Odoacer, who forced him to do so, bore the title not of "Roman emperor" but of "king of Italy" (*rex Italiae*).

There still continued to be a Roman emperor for many centuries after 476 CE, but his court was not in Rome but in Byzantium (renamed Constantinople), the city that Constantine had chosen to serve as the capital of his empire in the fourth century. During the sixth century, the forces of the powerful Byzantine emperor Justinian defeated Gothic tribes in North Africa, Italy, and southern Spain, and these former constituent territories were reincorporated into his Roman Empire for a time.[14] But in subsequent years, especially following the Great Schism of 1054, the influence of the Byzantine emperor in western Europe was diminished. The eastern half of the Roman Empire continued to exist for almost another millennium, until Istanbul was taken by the Turks in 1453, just thirty years before Luther was born.

In the western part of Europe, the Roman Empire was revived only with the rise of the Merovingian and the Carolingian dynasties. The king of the Franks, Charlemagne, who had defeated the Lombards, was crowned by the pope in Rome and denominated *imperator* and *augustus* on Christmas Day 800.[15] The imperial nomenclature is significant because it makes it clear that Charlemagne was considered not only a successful regional ruler in northern Europe but the successor of the Roman emperors. He was "the renewer of the empire of the Romans" (*renovator imperii Romanorum*). Charlemagne's full imperial title (with variations) was "Charles, the most serene Augustus, crowned by God, the great peaceful emperor who governs the Roman Empire" (*Carolus serenissimus augustus deo coronatus magnus pacificus imperator Romanum gubernans imperium*).[16] Even after his death, visitors to Aachen would have been able to read this "nobleman of the Romans" (*patricius Romanorum*) described on his tomb slab as "the great and orthodox emperor" (*magnus atque orthodoxus imperator*).[17] Charlemagne was certainly no mere figurehead, an emperor in name only, but a powerful ruler who exerted very real control over an extensive territory.

Powerful, too, were Otto I (the Great), during whose reign in the tenth century the Holy Roman Empire was formally reconstituted, and the great Hohenstaufen emperors Frederick Barbarossa and his grandson, Frederick II. Barbarossa especially was larger than life.[18] After his death, a legend arose that he was not dead but sleeping in a cave (somewhere in Thuringia or Bavaria) and that he would someday awaken and lead Germany to great imperial success, perhaps even to do battle with the antichrist. The same was said of Frederick II.

It is true, to be sure, that there were some Holy Roman emperors who were seen as little more than figureheads. Frederick III, the last emperor to be crowned in Rome, enjoyed a very long reign in the second half of the fifteenth century, but he was regarded by many of his contemporaries as "stingy, unforgiving, and oafish." What may have been patient tenacity on his part was often taken for laziness or indifference, and he was ridiculed as "chief nightcap" (*Erzschlafmütze*).[19]

But at the peak of its power and prestige during the reign of the Hohenstaufens, no one could possibly have considered the Holy Roman Empire to be inconsequential. It encompassed not only Germany but Bohemia, Burgundy, and large parts of northern Italy. Even as late as Luther's time, the realm of the Habsburg Charles V included much of the traditional territory associated with the empire. (In addition, he was king of Spain and its growing transatlantic holdings.) Luther considered the contemporary empire to be an ongoing and viable political entity: "It still has its estates, laws, members, and offices and to some extent still functions."[20] Certainly, "imperial law" (*das Keiserliche Recht*) was very much in effect in Luther's Germany.[21]

Luther's empire was also still a "Roman" empire to some extent. It is true that none of the emperors were Roman by birth, and very few of them ever lived in Rome, but when Charlemagne was crowned emperor, it was in Rome that the coronation happened (in Saint Peter's Basilica). He did not normally wear "foreign clothes" (*peregrina indumenta*), but for this occasion, Charlemagne was dressed in Mediterranean sandals and a tunic instead of his usual boots and warm trousers, even though it was late December.[22] Otto the Great was not only called *Imperator Augustus* but also given the title so often bestowed upon Roman heroes of antiquity, "father of the fatherland" (*pater patriae*), after his liberation of Lechfeld from the Magyars in 955. The church of S. Bartolomeo on the Isola Tiberina in Rome was his foundation. Otto the Second, "our German Roman emperor," as Luther calls him, is buried in Saint Peter's in Rome.[23] He was called "the Red" because of his bloody murder of the heads of Roman families at a banquet to which he had invited them. There was a tradition that Otto the Third built a palace for himself on the Aventine Hill.[24] Frederick II Hohenstaufen, whose intellectual abilities were so astonishing (he spoke six languages) that he was dubbed "the wonder of the world" (*stupor mundi*), appears on coins of the time wearing a laurel crown and dressed in a Roman toga. He spent much of his reign not in Germany but in Italy. By the time he was three years old, he had already been named king of Sicily.[25]

Hundreds of years after the reign of Frederick II, Luther was still calling his own emperor, Charles V, the "Roman Caesar."[26] The word *Kaiser* is simply the German form of the cognomen of Gaius Julius Caesar, the great-uncle and adoptive father of Octavian, later known as Caesar Augustus. Originally a family nickname (it possibly meant "hairy" in Latin), the word *Caesar* began to be applied to later rulers of the Roman Empire with no familial connection to the *Julii Caesares*. In the last part of the first century, for example, the title of the emperor Titus, of the *gens Flavia*, was "Titus Flavius Caesar Vespasianus." Even following Diocletian's division of the empire into two halves in the late third century, each half was under the control of an Augustus and a Caesar.[27] In the first two decades of the twentieth century, the titles *Kaiser* and *Tsar* were still being used as royal appellations in Germany and Russia.

None of this is to suggest that Luther was not fully aware that the Holy Roman Empire was anything but a straightforward continuation of the empire of ancient Rome. The Caesar "today," Luther declares in his *Operationes in Psalmos* (1519–21), is no more "Roman" than the Jews are "servants of the Christians and subject to Caesar."[28] In his preface to the book of Revelation, Luther points out that the current empire was only a dim reflection of the earlier one: "The pope reestablished the Roman Empire after it had fallen and brought it from the Greeks and conveyed it from the Greeks to the Germans. Even so, it is an image of the Roman Empire rather than the actual body of the empire as it once existed."[29] The Roman Empire proper had long ago disappeared. It was the image only of the Roman Empire that had been transferred to the "German Caesars,"[30] but images are not unimportant.

The other adjective used to describe this peculiar empire, "holy," did not begin to be used regularly until somewhat later, in the 1200s. No doubt the close connection with the papacy, beginning already with Charlemagne's coronation in Saint Peter's by Pope Leo III, helped substantiate the empire's claim to holiness. Ideally, the pope was to govern all spiritual matters in cooperation with the emperor, who was responsible for secular governance. Which of these took precedence over the other, however, was not always easy to determine, since the division between their two spheres of power was never as clear as one might wish, and the issue became hotly contested throughout much of the later Middle Ages. One of the most memorable moments in the so-called Investiture Controversy was in January 1077, when Henry IV was forced to wait for three days in chilly Canossa before meeting with Hildebrand (Pope Gregory VII) in order to beseech him to lift the interdict that had been imposed on his realm.[31] Relationships between pope and emperor had deteriorated to such an extent by the time of Frederick II that the emperor was excommunicated multiple times and was even denounced by one of the popes (Gregory IX) as the antichrist. Pope Boniface VIII is supposed to have once exclaimed, "I am Caesar—I am Emperor."[32] In his bull *Unam sanctam* (1302), he declared that the papacy was ultimately responsible for both of the "two swords" (cf. Luke 22:38)— that is, spiritual and secular authority. How thoroughly some of his "subjects" rejected Boniface's absolute claims to authority and resented his lust for worldly power may be gathered from Dante's damning references to him in the *Inferno* (19.49–63).

More than once, Luther refers to the Holy Roman Empire as "holy" (*sacrum*).[33] His emperor, Charles V, who succeeded his grandfather Maximilian in 1519 and was crowned in Bologna by the pope in

1530 (the last emperor to be so honored), had divine authority in Luther's eyes. Such a conviction on the part of Luther and his contemporaries was not only anchored in tradition but supported by biblical passages such as Romans 13:1–7 and 1 Peter 2:13–20. It is true that the ground beneath the time-honored principle of the "divine right" of rulers was beginning to shake, but it crumbled apart completely only well after Luther's time.

Roughly fifty years before Luther's birth, the Italian humanist Lorenzo Valla had decisively proved the so-called Donation of Constantine to be a forgery. The "Donation" was one of the most important documents substantiating the authoritative claims of the papacy vis-à-vis the empire. According to it, the first Christian emperor was supposed to have bestowed upon Pope Sylvester sovereignty over the western part of the Roman Empire out of gratitude for being cured of leprosy. Valla argued convincingly on the basis of glaring anachronisms and the poor quality of the Latin that the document could not be a product of the fourth century but must be a much later forgery. His discovery was momentous because it seriously undermined the claims of the papacy to be superior to the empire and its rulers.

Luther was fully aware of Valla's research and its significance, thanks to the edition of Ulrich von Hutten that he had come across as early as 1520. Some seventeen years later, Luther published an annotated translation of the text of the "Donation of Constantine" in an effort to "attack the lies of the papal church and its abomination" and to "defend the truth against the devil himself and his damned school of fools." Luther refers to the "inferior" (*böse*) Latinity of the text of the "Donation," but he is also careful to make it clear that his critique of the document was not intended to contravene in any way "God and his holy church."[34]

If the Investiture Controversy pitted pope against emperor, the historic tension between the two potentates also reflected the hard feelings that often existed between Germans and Italians, who made up the majority of the peoples living in the cities and states that formed the Holy Roman Empire. Like many of his fellow countrymen, Luther had deep prejudices not only about Rome in particular but also about Italy. The Italians, Luther once opined to his dinner companions, believed that the only real crime was personal poverty: "In short, in Italy there is no shame except in being poor. Murder and theft they do punish, but just a little and because they have to. Otherwise no sin is considered too much for anyone."[35] The Italians were "the most deceitful and tricky people" as far as Luther was concerned. Still, he did not suggest that they should be avoided by Germans entirely on this account. Instead, he recommended that after they were properly educated, "young people should visit Italy and experience their trickiness and foolishness so that they would know how to protect themselves against them."[36]

Luther was convinced that Germany sent more money to Rome in his own day than ever before, with very little to show for it other than "scorn and insults."[37] The Romans considered everybody else, especially the Germans, to be nothing more than silly "geese and ducks," at whose expense "they can eat and be nourished so very well in the name of God, to whom they pay as little heed as they would to a scarecrow."[38] Luther sensed that the general attitude in Rome was to try to suck up as much money from "German fools" as possible.[39] Northern pilgrims coming to Rome like the young Luther were much more pious than the native Romans: "If somebody in Rome says, 'He's a *Bon christian*,' that means he's a real fool."[40] It was precisely on this account that "good Christian" pilgrims in Rome were so likely to be fleeced. The Italians mocked the Germans because the latter actually believed the Bible: "The Italians make fun of us because we believe everything in the Bible. The pope says that Christ was a bastard, because he was born of a virgin, but a virgin who gives birth is a whore. That's how much they believe the Bible. And they say that if we were to trust in God, we would be the most miserable of people and could never be happy again; it is best instead to put on a happy face and not believe everything."[41]

Some Italians considered Germans to be no better than barbaric "beasts," possessed of little culture and lacking civilized manners.[42] Gianantonio Campano, the court poet of Pope Pius II, was supposed to have mooned the Germans as he crossed the Alpine frontier upon his return back to southern civilization after his visit to the land of "beasts and barbarians whom he did not consider good enough to gulp down the pope's shit."[43] The scatological insults went both ways, naturally. There are graphic sixteenth-century depictions of German farmers baring their backsides and farting in the pope's direction.[44] While not uncritical of his fellow Germans' lack of culture and education, Luther was convinced that they were beginning to make great strides forward, thanks to the Reformation, especially as the ancient languages and literatures came to the forefront and people began to think more critically (*sapere*).[45]

Not all of Luther's experiences with Italians were necessarily negative. Frau Ursula Cotta, with whom Luther is supposed (according to local tradition) to have had a happy stay while a young student at the parish school connected with the church of Saint George in Eisenach, was married to a prominent citizen named Konrad (or Kunz) Cotta, who came "from a noble Italian family who had acquired wealth by commerce."[46] Favorable, too, are Luther's comments in one of the *Tischreden* of 1538 about the Italian hospitals in Florence and their staff. The details he provides (e.g., the cleanliness of the linens) suggest that he himself may have been cared for personally while passing through the city, although he does not expressly say so:

> They are regally constructed and provided with the best food and drink, diligent attendants, and very learned physicians. The beds and linens are very clean, and the beds are painted. As soon as the sick patient is brought in, they take off all his clothes, which are kept safe for him in good faith in the presence of a notary, and then he is dressed in a white gown and laid in a nicely painted bed with clean sheets. Soon, two doctors are brought in. Attendants come bringing food and drink in glass vessels that are very clean; they don't touch the food even with one little finger but serve it on a tray. The most noble matrons, completely veiled, come

to assist. Without revealing their identity, they attend to the poor for a few days and then return home again. I witnessed with what great care they preserved the practice of hospitality in Florence. It was also true of the foundling asylum, where infants are very well sheltered, fed, and taught. They are dressed in uniforms and cared for in the most fatherly of fashions.[47]

The main hospital in Florence at Luther's time was the Spedale di S. Maria Nuova, not far from the Duomo, founded by the father of Dante's Beatrice. The hospital for foundlings, the Spedale degli Innocenti, was built during the Cinquecento. The building was designed by Filippo Brunelleschi and decorated by Andrea della Robbia.[48]

Luther also praised the landscape of Italy, with its abundant vineyards and olive trees, especially the fertile Po River valley. It was a "most delightful region" (*regio jucundissima*).[49] He noticed that the Italians did not drink as heavily as their northern neighbors. While he may well have gained some familiarity with the regional cuisines of Italy while traveling there, he makes little mention of food other than to remark on what must have been for him exotic details of their diet, such as their fondness for frogs and turtles.[50] It is unlikely, but not impossible, that his comments about taking onions with him to Rome and returning with garlic (see the discussion in chapter 1) have something to do with the respective culinary merits of garlic and onion.

Luther was struck by the Italians' frequent use of gestures and their well-tailored clothing; he himself mended his own trousers.[51] In comparison with his own German neighbors, he found the Italians more hospitable and courteous. In commenting on how Rebecca offered Eleazar, Isaac's servant, something to drink when he arrived at a well in her town (Gen 24:15–28), Luther observes,

> Such examples of virtue are rare among us. For we live here not with humans but with pigs, who neither know nor learn anything about either faith or honorable conduct. So we

need patience on account of the glory of God who placed us here. But Rebecca learned humanity, civility, and sweetness of manners from her parents, so she respectfully offers a drink to the servant and says, "Drink, sir." Among other more civilized peoples, you still find such refinement. The Italians say, "*Mi ser si* (my sir, yes)." Germans who are a little more cultivated and civilized say, "Dear friend, dear chap." You will hear nothing similar to that in this barbaric land.[52]

On the other hand, Luther was critical of a number of customs in Italy—for example, the way in which they danced, which he thought too lewd. Once, years after he returned from Rome, when he caught sight of German girls and boys dancing together, he approved of the evident joy that they took in the exercise and contrasted their dancing with the way in which Italians danced: "But as much as the Italians want to be chaste when dancing, nonetheless they are lascivious in their movements. They do not embrace each other or even touch hands but instead use a little washcloth to hold on to each other. Still the dancing movements are very lascivious. The Italian are very jealous. Woe to anyone who speaks to a wife who is not his own!"[53] He also objected to the fact that women in Italy needed to be veiled and took issue with the Italians' willingness to relieve themselves in public ("like dogs").[54]

While he certainly would have been able to use Latin in his communication with fellow clerics in Italy, Luther never learned to understand the Italian language itself or its many dialects. Even though a common spiritual bond might help Christians who spoke different languages to transcend linguistic barriers, Luther recognized that the failure to understand another's language could lead to miscommunication and worse: "I do not understand a speaker of Italian, nor does he understand me, and so almost inevitably occasions for anger and hostility arise between us. But if we both know Christ, we embrace each other's members as though they were our own and kiss each other fondly."[55]

Charles V and the Sack of Rome

In 1521, more than seven centuries after Charles the Great's reign had ended, we find Luther addressing his own emperor Charles, the fifth to be so named, using some of the same traditional and exalted imperial terminology: "To the most serene and unconquerable Lord Charles V, chosen to be emperor of the Romans, Caesar Augustus, king of the Spaniards and of both Sicily and Jerusalem, etc., archduke of Austria, Duke of Burgundy, etc., his [i.e., Luther's] most merciful lord."[56] The formulaic language describing Charles, loaded as it is with polite superlatives, is in marked contrast with the self-deprecating language Luther uses to refer to himself in a letter written the previous year to the same emperor. In it, Luther describes himself as a "pauper" who lies "prostrate before the feet" of his "Royal Majesty." He is "most unworthy" to bring his case before "the most worthy" emperor.[57]

While such language of extreme exaltation and submission was standard epistolary etiquette at the time, it also reflects a premodern reality that may be difficult for those today who are used to more egalitarian principles to appreciate fully. Social hierarchy was very much the norm at the time, and Luther's superlatives were not only for show; they were intended to acknowledge the reality of the exalted status of this God-ordained ruler in his own and others' minds.

Even though it was not yet clear in 1521 that the young Charles would be a "most unconquerable emperor" (*invictissimus imperator*), he turned out to be tireless as a ruler, winning a number of signal victories in the course of his long reign. He was not, in fact, always victorious, but he could and did defeat formidable foes. Following the Diet of Worms, Charles joined forces with Leo X against the combined forces of the French and the Venetians and was victorious, liberating the city of Milan and even capturing Francis I himself in 1525 at the Battle of Pavia. His efforts to keep the ascendant Turks at bay were somewhat successful (they were turned back from the gates of Vienna in 1529), although their threat to eastern Europe was not entirely removed until much later, after the sea battle of Lepanto in 1571 and their failure to take Vienna in 1683. In 1547, the year after Luther's death, Charles V's troops prevailed against the forces of the Schmalkaldic League at the Battle of Mühlberg (some seventy kilometers south of Wittenberg), and the Landgrave Philip of Hesse and the Saxon elector John Frederick were both captured.

In his capacity as Holy Roman emperor, Charles V not only had military power but could also convene diets to condemn heretics, which is exactly what he did in order to deal with Luther in 1521 at Worms. In a letter to Charles of the previous August, Luther had appealed to his "imperial majesty," citing the example of Athanasius over whose controversy with Arius the emperor Constantine presided at the Council of Nicaea. Perhaps he also had in mind the apostle Paul's famous appeal to Caesar (Acts 25:11), after which he was sent to Rome.[58] In a letter written from Worms, Luther describes his trial in classical Roman terms: Charles is *Caesar*, and his imperial retinue is the *senatus Romanus*.[59]

Luther's appeal to the emperor was not a mere formality, and the negative judgment of Charles in May 1521 was not a foregone conclusion. While the emperor could have been *clementissimus* in judging Luther's case had he so chosen, as it turned out he was anything but "most merciful." In the imperial edict, Luther was declared a heretic and an enemy of the state, and his writings were ordered to be burned. Charles declared himself ready "to mobilize everything against Luther, my kingdoms and dominions, my friends, my body, my blood and my soul."[60] The emperor's order was never able to be enforced fully, thanks to Luther's powerful patron, Frederick the Wise, who had Luther whisked away after the diet to the Wartburg, a secluded fortress near Eisenach.

At least indirectly, Charles was involved in one of the greatest catastrophes for the city of Rome in the sixteenth century. In 1527, led by Charles III, Duke of Bourbon, a large company of German mercenaries (*Landsknechte*) and other troops, who had not been paid for their services, entered the city on May 6 and proceeded to sack it thoroughly. It was only the loyalty of his Swiss guards that enabled Pope Clement VII to escape to Castel Sant'Angelo. Luther describes the sack of Rome in one of the *Tischreden* thus: "Rome was captured by the Duke of Bourbon with a modest army. Even though the Romans and the pope himself were safe in a very well-fortified place, even in a church, the pope barely escaped with his life; the fog was so dense that the enemy could easily scale the wall. They plundered the properties of the cardinals, captured the pope, and set him free after receiving a ransom of three hundred thousand ducats. Outstanding libraries were destroyed; office buildings were turned into horse stables. Many Romans at this time died most miserably."[61]

Even though their invasion of the city was not sanctioned by Charles or approved by Luther, some of the soldiers themselves clearly felt that they were acting on behalf of both of them. Still testifying to their attitude are graffiti that can be seen on Raphael's fresco, *La disputà del sacramento*, in the room known as the Stanza della Segnatura in the Vatican Museum. Although faint and hard to discern today, the word *LUTHERUS* scratched on the fresco is still visible, as well as the acrostic *VKIMP*, short for *Vivat Karolus Imperator* ("Long Live Emperor Charles").[62] The commander of the German *Landsknechte* had been Georg von Frundsberg, Charles V's general and hero of the Battle of Pavia. Said to be a supporter of Luther and to have declared that he was going to Rome in order to hang the pope, perhaps with a rope interwoven with gold that he was carrying with him,[63] Frundsberg himself did not make it to Rome. He suffered a stroke in March in northern Italy and eventually returned to Germany to die there.

Luther did believe that the sack of Rome was part of God's judgment on the city: "This is how Christ reigns, so that the emperor who persecutes Luther for the pope (*pro papa Lutherum*) is compelled to devastate the pope for Luther (*pro Luthero papam*)."[64] The irony of the situation is emphasized by an artful antimetabole. But Luther also observes in a letter of November 1527 to Justus Jonas in all seriousness that he "would not want Rome to be burned down (*exustam*), for that would be a bad omen." Instead, he expresses his wish that the city could be made livable again and the church built up "before we die."[65]

In this connection, it is useful to consider a Latin poem of Luther's aimed at Pope Clement written sometime after the sack of Rome, *In Clementem Papam VII*. The reference to a flood (*diluvium*) suggests that it should be dated around the time of the great flood of 1530:[66]

> *Quum mala tot nostram vexent, te principe, Romam,*
> *Diluvium, caedes, flamma, rapina, lues,*
> *Non ego clementem te, nec clementia dicam*
> *Numina, sed furiam te furiasque deos.*
> *Ergo tuum nomen, si vis me dicere, dicam:*
> *Diluvium es Romae, flamma, rapina, lues.*[67]

Since so many evils afflict our Rome while you are its leader: flood, murder, fire, rapine, plague, I would say that you and your divinities are not clement. You are a fury, and your gods are furies. Therefore, I will say your proper name, if you want me to say it: you are the flood, the fire, the rapine, and the plague of Rome.

The poem refers to a catastrophic situation in the city of Rome, using language (such as *rapina*) that would be appropriately associated with such a devastating event as *il sacco di Roma*. Indeed, the occupation of the city ended only after the churches and monasteries and palazzi of Rome had been so thoroughly looted that by February 1528, there was virtually nothing left to loot. As Luther noted, not even libraries were safe from destruction.[68] Thousands of Roman citizens were killed over the months—so many, in fact, that the corpses left to rot in the streets led to a plague (*lues*) that afflicted not only Roman citizens themselves but also the invaders. By the end of the sacking of Rome, the population of the city had shrunk considerably.[69]

Luther's poem places the blame for Rome's problems not on the imperial troops of Charles V who caused the actual destruction of Rome but on the pope who nearly lost his life during the sack of the city. The responsibility for the flood, the fires, the rapine, and the plague that had so devastated the city is laid squarely at the pope's door, even though Clement certainly could not be considered the direct cause for the sacking of the city.[70] Insofar, however, as he is the *princeps* of Rome (the first line of the poem assigns him the same title that Augustus preferred to use to describe his own role as "first citizen"), he bears ultimate responsibility. Luther was not alone in this assignment of blame. Alfonso de Valdés, a Spanish humanist in the employ of Charles V, also used the sack of the city to criticize Pope Clement in his harsh dialogue, *Lactantius*. He declared the sack of Rome a matter of divine judgment and condemned the ungodliness of its inhabitants.[71]

Scholars have expressed some doubt as to whether Luther himself wrote this poem. One of the reasons for uncertainty is that the autograph is no longer in existence. But the scholar who discovered the poem that he claims was written in Luther's own hand was a highly reputable researcher. Gottlieb Christian Friedrich Mohnike studied at the universities of Greifswald and Jena and over time became a well-known and respected philologist. He published extensively in the area of what we would today call Scandinavian studies (including an edition of the Faereyinga saga) and produced scholarship on Greek and Latin literature, as well as writing a study devoted to the end of Luther's life.[72] There is no reason to think that such an accomplished scholar would not have recognized Luther's handwriting. Nor is it at all likely that he would have simply fabricated the story of this discovery out of whole cloth. For all of its other faults, German scholarship of the nineteenth century is not characterized by an inclination to forgery.[73]

If Luther had not written other Latin poems or if the tone of this poem did not mesh well with what we know about Luther's poetic voice from other uncontested works, the case against his authorship might be stronger. But the playful, mocking tone; the repetition of words; and the kind of elaborate punning we find in this poem are everywhere apparent in Luther's other Latin poetry. We also know that Luther felt a keen antipathy toward Pope Clement, whose leadership had been so inclement for the city of Rome. He calls him "that ecclesiastical enemy of Christ" (*istum Ecclesiasticum hostem Christi*) in a letter of 1529.[74] One of Luther's favorite hexameter lines, which he often quoted and even called his own *Epitaphium*,[75] may refer specifically to this pope: "Alive I was your plague; dying I will be your death, pope" (*Pestis eram vivens, moriens ero mors tua, papa*).[76] Even more devastating for the pope than the actual plague that swept over Clement's disease-ridden city in 1527 is the metaphorical plague that is Luther. Even if the reformer were to die first, Luther had already struck the papacy a lethal blow. The line was added by Melanchthon to what is probably Luther's last portrait, done by his valet, Reifenstein.[77]

An interesting objection that has been raised against Luther's authorship of this poem is that the author refers to Rome as "ours." Luther, that fierce German adversary of the pope, it has been opined, "would hardly have called Rome *nostram*."[78] This is clearly an invalid argument, a case of the logical fallacy known as *petitio principii*. The conclusion of the argument is only as valid as the premise is in the first place. The line of reasoning would seem to be the following: Luther could not have written a poem in which Rome is described as "ours" because he would never have identified himself in such a way with the home of his archenemy, the pope. It is true, to be sure, that Luther often referred to Rome in the third person. He recollects that Leo "excommunicated me from *his* church" (*ab ecclesia sua*).[79] But Luther was also perfectly capable of using the first-person pronominal adjective to describe his relationship with papist adversaries. In his preface to the Wittenberg edition of his German writings (1539), he calls the partisans of the pope "my papists": "For I myself, insofar as I am also mouse droppings mixed up with the pepper, must thank my papists very heartily . . . that they have turned me into a pretty good theologian, which otherwise I would never have become."[80] Clearly, Luther does not mean to suggest here that he would enjoy collegial friendship, or a familial relationship, or spiritual fellowship with his papists. The use of the first person in this context is surely ironic. Still, Luther does seem to be genuinely appreciative of *"my* papists," insofar as he welcomes "affliction" (*tentatio*) in general and recognizes the positive effect certain negative experiences (*Anfechtungen*) may have upon one's spiritual maturation.

The words "our Rome" in this context do not appear to be used ironically. Luther did identify himself in many ways with Rome, even long after his excommunication. Here he may very well be thinking that the city of Rome, the headquarters of the Catholic Church, did rightly belong to reformers of that church, like himself, who had been trying to restore its doctrine to its original scriptural purity, freed from medieval accretions, and thus return the chief city of their faith to its former "holy" status. So Luther may be entirely serious when he calls Rome "our" city, especially if he is remembering the great sense of awe with which years earlier he had visited the place where so many martyrs had shed their blood. In this historical sense, the once holy city might indeed be said to belong not just to its current inhabitants but to "us," to Luther.

Three years after the sack of Rome, Luther was willing for Melanchthon and others to present Charles V with a statement of Lutheran beliefs at another diet, this time in Augsburg, where points of commonality and difference with Roman Catholic doctrine were to be submitted for imperial review. Luther followed the proceedings with great interest but only from afar, just across the border in Coburg, since he did not have the same assurance of safe conduct to travel into the city of Augsburg that he had been given earlier for his trip to and from Worms. The emperor formally rejected the Lutherans' confession in November 1530 on the basis of the *Confutatio* authored by Johann Eck and others.

In light of his own condemnation at Worms nine years earlier, it is interesting to see how willing Luther still was to give Charles respect and to insist on obedience to him in subsequent years. After all, it was this emperor who had commanded his subjects in 1521 not to take Luther "into your houses, not to receive him at court, to give him neither food nor drink, not to hide him, to afford him no help, following, support, or encouragement, either clandestinely or publicly, through words or works." Instead, Luther's fellow citizens were instructed to "seize him and overpower him" and after his capture to send him to Charles "under tightest security."[81] After Charles's dogged defense of papal doctrinal positions at Augsburg, it certainly became abundantly clear to Luther and everyone else that this emperor would never be on the Protestants' side in the prolonged controversy with the pope, despite their hopes to the contrary.

Still, in a sermon he preached on November 20, 1530, we find Luther calling the emperor "dear Charles" (*der liebe Carolus*).[82] In his *Warning to His Dear Germans* a year later, Luther declares in all apparent seriousness that the emperor has earned "the respect and love of the entire world."[83] Even near the end of his life, we find Luther still referring to Charles as "*our* Lord Caesar" (*Carolus Quintus unser Herr Keiser*).[84] Regardless of how disappointed Luther may have been in Charles's response to the Lutherans' confession at Augsburg, he was still Luther's emperor. And he continued to pray for Charles constantly not only in his earlier letters[85] but even in ones written as late as 1544 and 1545.[86]

On the other hand, in a letter written in 1531 to Lazarus Spengler, the town clerk of Nuremberg, Luther contemplates the question of when resistance to imperial authority, which ordinarily is to be obeyed (*Caesari est obediendum*), is justified.[87] If the emperor were to go to battle against the gospel on behalf of the pope, Luther did finally agree that he would have to be opposed despite his divine authority. But it was very difficult for him to come to the conclusion that Protestant princes had the right to resist Charles with force, and it was only with the greatest reluctance that he supported martial Protestant princes such as Philip of Hesse and other members of the Schmalkaldic League, a military alliance established in 1531 in opposition to the emperor.[88]

Later in life especially, Luther could be quite condemnatory of Charles, although he continues to excuse the emperor somewhat, suggesting that he is being used by the pope and bishops, as he does in a letter of 1539.[89] In a letter written a year later, he says that the emperor "was, is, and will be the servant of the servants of the devil."[90] In another letter of 1545, he calls him "wicked" (*nequam*).[91] In a poem written in Latin and German, he predicts that Charles will always return from battle with "his Mars unconquered," except when he takes up arms "against heaven" (*in coelum*), in which case he will be vanquished.[92]

Luther's fullest analysis of Charles's character as a leader occurs in one of the *Tischreden* of 1540 in which Luther discusses both Charles and Ferdinand, his brother. The latter ruled Habsburg Austria. Luther was in favor of acknowledging him as "king of the Romans" for the purpose of negotiating a religious peace begun in March 1532.[93] Ferdinand eventually succeeded his brother as Holy Roman emperor in 1556. Luther characterizes the two brothers thus:

> Charles is a melancholy and sensual man and not heroic. He does not understand our cause, nor would he even were he to hear someone read our books to him. If he were Scipio or Alexander or Pyrrhus, he would break through the pontifical net and win over the Germans for himself. He begins many things but completes few of them. He captured Tunis but now has lost it. He captured Gaul but let it go. And the same goes for Rome. He does not carry through. He backs down easily in his negotiations. Great minds don't do this. What shall I say? Germany lacks a head. Philipp has said that we are a blinded Polyphemus. It is a great burden to lack a leader. Ferdinand is a monk. He prays his seven hours a day but neglects his duties in caring for the state. That's the way Faber [bishop of Vienna] wants it; Ferdinand is absolutely required to listen to him. He too does not understand our cause, nor does he read or hear about it. The papist priests make sure that he does not read or hear about it, thanks to the confessional sessions. They know our theology is surely going to win in the end. And I believe that if the king did understand, he would proceed

> with confidence and drive the pope from Germany. Error
> and weakness are not such serious maladies as open blas-
> phemy as is the case with Maguntinus [Albrecht of Mainz]
> and Duke George.[94]

It is significant that despite his criticisms of Charles as "melancholy"
and "not heroic," Luther is more forgiving of the non-German
emperor, "a sheep among the wolves,"[95] and Ferdinand than he is of
Albrecht, longtime archbishop of Mainz (1514–45), or Duke George,
the former ruler of nearby Albertine Saxony. The reason he gives
for his relative forbearance of the imperial rulers is that Albrecht
and George actually knew the truth and were not merely misled by
others as Charles and his brother had been.

Luther's guarded, intermittent confidence in this "most merciful" emperor does not appear to have been entirely ill founded, at
least in the long run. Charles had long been in favor of calling a
council to deal with the Protestant problem, despite papal objections. Only after the sack of Rome did the idea finally meet with
approval from Pope Clement, but he died in 1534 before the council
could ever meet.[96] Beginning in 1545, a general council was at last
convened in Trent by Pope Paul III to deal with the issues raised by
Luther and other reformers. That year, Luther calculated, was "the
twenty-fourth year since the first *Reichstag* was held at Worms under
this *Kaiser Carolus* when I personally stood before the Caesar and the
entire *Reich*."[97] After some interruptions, the momentous Council of
Trent was finally concluded in 1563, but only after both Luther and
Charles were dead.

After Luther's death, it is said that Charles declined to exhume
and burn his body when his imperial troops took the city of Wittenberg in 1547. His reason was supposedly his disinclination to wage
war against the dead rather than the living.[98] In 1555, the emperor
agreed to a peace treaty with members of the Schmalkaldic League
(the Peace of Augsburg), which provided for the toleration of Lutheranism within the boundaries of the Holy Roman Empire. Shortly

thereafter he retired to a monastery in Extremadura in Spain, where he died in 1558. Charles's last word was supposedly "Jesus."

The Two Kingdoms

One of the keys to understanding Luther's attitude toward the Holy Roman Empire and Charles V can be discovered in his distinctive understanding of the relationship between the church and the world, the doctrine of "the two kingdoms."[99] Unlike the pope, whose claim to legitimacy as the successor of Peter and whose authority over the church at large Luther eventually called into serious question, Charles V was the rightful worldly leader in Luther's eyes, put in place by God as the Holy Roman emperor. Luther was not at all inclined to deny the emperor the right to exercise his lawful claim to power (*gladius*), whereas the pope, he felt, "ought not to be a magistrate or a tyrant."[100]

In many ways, even long after he left the monastery, Luther never ceased to be an Augustinian.[101] Augustine's ideas about the differences between what he called "the city of God" and "the city of man" most certainly exerted an influence on Luther's political thinking. The latter is the city associated with the firstborn son of Adam and Eve. Like Romulus, Cain was a fratricide, and he was also the first human to build a city (Gen 4:17). The city of God, on the other hand, is linked with Cain's younger brother, Abel, who was murdered by his brother and built no city at all on earth. In the eleventh chapter of the Epistle to the Hebrews, Abel is listed among the heroes of faith who confessed "that they were strangers and pilgrims on the earth" and who sought a better country (Heb 11:13–16). For that reason, the writer of the epistle declares, God has "prepared for them a city" (Heb 11:16) of which he himself is the "builder and maker" (Heb 11:10). With Jesus's "kingdom of heaven" and Paul's "Jerusalem which is above" (Gal 4:26) no doubt also in mind, Augustine elaborates on this point:

Thus for all of humanity, when these two cities first began to advance, in the process of procreating and dying, the one born first [Cain] was a citizen of this world, but the one who came after him [Abel] was a stranger in the world and was attached to the city of God, predestined by grace and chosen by grace, a stranger below by grace and a citizen above by grace. . . . For the city of the saints is above, although it gives birth to citizens here in whom it sojourns until the time of its reign arrives. Then they will all be gathered together as they rise up in their bodies, and the promised kingdom will be given to them, where with their prince, the king of the ages, they will rule for time without end.[102]

Luther makes a similar distinction in equally memorable terms between two kingdoms: one of God's left hand and the other of his right. The kingdom of his left hand is subject to "temporal law and governance," which God takes seriously but does not himself rule directly, while the kingdom of his "right hand" is the realm of grace, where God "himself rules" and does not "install parents, magistrates, lictors," but he himself "preaches the gospel to the poor."[103] For Luther, this was a binary vision of political and spiritual reality, although, to be clear, it was not one in which the forces of light and darkness are engaged in a struggle where each side is evenly matched and has an equal chance of winning. Both of Luther's kingdoms belong ultimately to God.

At the time of Nero, as Luther explains it, the spiritual kingdom was ruled by Christ "through the agency of his apostles Peter and Paul against the devil," while the secular kingdom was ruled by the Roman emperor "against Christ."[104] Even though the kingdom of God's left hand is governed by diabolical minions like Nero, the devil is not completely free to operate as he wills even in this sphere. He himself is a creation of God, an angel, albeit a rebellious one. The devil serves not only as a counterforce to God but as his servant as well, doing his best to work his own baleful will but through it all, despite his worst intentions, carrying out God's overarching plan for the world. How else is it possible to understand Job's multiple sufferings at the hands of Satan, all with God's permission? When Paul prays to be delivered from his diabolical affliction, it is God who declines to remove it (2 Cor 12:7–9). The "thorn in the flesh" is a "messenger of Satan," to be sure, but Satan is still operating ultimately under God's supervisory aegis.

This fallen world, riddled with sin, is one that the holy God cannot administer, as Luther puts it rather arrestingly in one of his *Tischreden*: "God does not know how to govern the world, because the world does not want to have God nor allow him to govern it, but prefers Satan, who does indeed know how to govern the world. But God has this going for him, namely, that he can turn the world and the kingdom of Satan in the world into rubble and dust, if they make things too bad."[105] How could a perfect God possibly govern a world so permeated with imperfection? Only the "prince of this world," as Luther calls the devil in "A Mighty Fortress," can do that. So Luther's emperor, temporarily in charge of the kingdom of God's left hand, could be considered to be both the minister of God and his devilish opponent at one and the same time.

It is not so surprising then that Luther could condemn the wickedness of worldly rulers and at the same time admire the wisdom and strength that these divinely ordained authorities demonstrated in maintaining law and order in the respective realms they ruled. When he was in Siena, Luther heard people repeat a saying attributed to Emperor Frederick: "He who does not know how to dissemble, does not know how to rule" (*Qui nescit dissimulare, nescit imperare*).[106] What really mattered to the people of Siena was whether their ruler could get things done expeditiously on their behalf and not whether he was always truthful. Luther reports this Machiavellian sentiment in his interpretation of the 101st Psalm without a word of disapproval.

When there are problems in the kingdom of God's left hand, they need to be resolved with force if necessary by those worldly authorities who have been elected or appointed to do so, however personally ungodly they may be. For Luther, like the apostle Paul, "the powers that be are ordained of God" (Rom 13:1) and should ordinarily be acknowledged as such, obeyed, and respected. This divine authority would include, in Paul's time, the governing power and responsibility assigned to the pagan Roman emperors, even those as terrible as Caligula and Nero. The apostle, whom early church fathers believed was put to death at the command of the emperor Nero, describes the secular authority to which Christians must subject themselves in his letter to the Christian congregation in Rome thus: "But if thou do that which is evil, be afraid; for he beareth not the sword in vain: for he is the minister of God, a revenger to execute wrath upon him that doeth evil" (Rom 13:4–5).

When heresies that begin in the kingdom of God's right hand start to have an impact on law and order in the kingdom of his left hand, the distinctions become blurrier. All the same, secular authorities still need to perform their duties of governance within their spheres of authority. Centuries earlier, Augustine had used the biblical parable of the wedding feast, in which the man in charge of the wedding tells his servants to round up reluctant guests and "compel them to come in" (Luke 14:23), in order to justify using military force against the Donatist Circumcellions when they were locked in a violent controversy with Catholics in North Africa.[107] While Luther appreciated the fact that faith cannot be coerced,[108] like Augustine he acknowledged the authority of secular magistrates to serve as God's agents on earth and to use deadly force against not only enemies of their states but also their own subjects in certain situations.

Unlike some other contemporary reformers of the church, Luther had very little appetite for upsetting the power structures of his day. He valued order and stability and respected the hierarchies that had evolved over time to enforce laws, no matter how patchy and temporary such governance systems might be. Of course, Luther was eager and determined to speak out boldly about much-needed changes in the kingdom of God's right hand. The gospel had become obscured by some of the very doctrines and practices in the church that were originally meant to promote it. Substantial spiritual and theological changes were indeed necessary, therefore, in the kingdom of the right hand, and it could be hoped that they would affect positively the kingdom of the other hand. But Luther's kind of reformation did not directly involve a radical restructuring of secular society and its systems of governance.

As the years went by, Luther became more and more firmly opposed to the ideas and policies of more radical reformers like Thomas Müntzer, who supported the peasants in their violent revolt against the landowners of Germany and ended up dying in the process (he was executed outside the town of Mühlhausen in 1525). In the mid-1530s, Luther writes,

> Therefore, I am not pleased with Mister Smart Aleck, who wants to be in charge of secular regulations, or with all those who want to make things better. Occasionally I do think that the government and the jurists could well make use of a Luther too. But I worry that they might get a Müntzer instead. Because God does not regard secular governance as highly as he does his own eternal governance of the church, for this reason I cannot and will not hope that they get a Luther. Since there is now no hope of getting another system of governance in the Roman Empire, as Daniel also indicates [Dan 2:40], it is inadvisable to change it. Instead, let whoever can do so darn and patch it while we live and let him punish misuse and put bandages and ointment on the pustules. But if someone is going to ruthlessly tear out the pustules, nobody will feel the pain and suffer damage more than these "wise" surgeons [lit. "barbers"] who would rather tear out those things which cause pain than heal them. Very well, Germany is perhaps ripe and—and I worry about this—worthy of strong punishment. May God be gracious to us! I know very well that I am not (praise God) like Müntzer.[109]

Just as Luther made it abundantly clear that he himself was not a Müntzer, nor a Zwingli, the Swiss reformer who died on the battlefield (in 1531 during the Second War of Kappel), he also wanted to make sure that his own peace-loving followers were distinguished from those who were willing to pursue violent means to gain their ends. In his *Warning to His Dear Germans*, Luther writes, "So with this treatise I want to demonstrate before God and the whole world that we who are labeled as Lutherans give no counsel or permission, and yes also no cause, for that [violence]. But rather in every way possible and without ceasing we have prayed and called for peace." When wars or uprisings did occur, nobody would be able to blame them on Luther and his teachings: "For up until now we have indeed taught and lived in a quiet way, have drawn no sword, and have not burned, murdered, or robbed anyone." By contrast, Luther continues, "Müntzer and his revolutionaries have not acted in this way, but act now as the papists do. They do not want to have (or to offer) peace, they interfere in things violently, and they allow no means or work to be effective."[110]

Till the end of his life, Luther continued to be an obedient (if somewhat outspoken) citizen of Ernestine Saxony, a principality ruled by one of the most influential powerbrokers in the entire empire. Frederick the Wise was one of only seven rulers given the authority to elect a Holy Roman emperor. He was supposedly Leo X's choice to fill the position upon Emperor Maximilian's death in 1519. Although it seems that Frederick and Luther never actually met in person, Luther was grateful to the elector for his protection and regularly refers to him using the most deferential language. Years after Frederick's death, Luther observes that his ruler had been dedicated to "ruling and maintaining his household as a wise leader in peace, even as he was considered to be the light of the world (*lux mundi*) in the Roman Empire at his time."[111] After Frederick's death in 1525, Luther worked closely with John the Steadfast (d. 1532), who succeeded his older brother, and then with John's son, John Frederick the Magnanimous (d. 1554). Their laudatory epithets suggest that the three Saxon rulers were appreciated by others besides Luther. These complimentary names seem especially significant when one compares them with the less distinctive adjective assigned to George, the duke of neighboring Albertine Saxony, known simply as "the Bearded," or the negative soubriquet associated with Ivan, the first czar of Russia, "the Terrible."[112] Even though he did not always agree with their decisions, Luther treated Frederick's successors with the same respect he had given their brother and uncle. A letter Luther wrote in 1545 to John Frederick begins with the kind of polite terminology he regularly used to address his Saxon superiors: "Thoroughly enlightened, nobly born leader, most gracious lord."[113]

Luther also took a lively interest in the governance of areas beyond electoral Saxony where the Lutheran Reformation had taken hold. He used his considerable persuasive powers to great effect, writing to council members of cities urging them to set up schools and shaming them for not supporting them properly. During the peasant revolt of 1525, even though he had initially pressed the cause of nonviolence with his *Admonition to Peace*, after seeing the destruction wrought in Thuringia, he urged the princes of Germany to suppress vigorously the peasant revolt. In *Against the Robbing and Murdering Hordes of Peasants*, he urges, "Therefore, dear lords, free here, save here, help here. Spare the poor people, but stab, slaughter, strangle wherever you can. If you die so doing, good for you, because you will never be able to have a more blessed death."[114] Later, against the Jews, too, he called for extreme measures (e.g., burning synagogues) to be carried out by the authorities in his notorious treatise written in 1543, *On the Jews and Their Lies.*

Luther's colleague Melanchthon was also quite willing to cooperate with secular officials of all sorts, especially as he set about establishing schools and participating in theological dialogues. After Luther's death, however, another of his followers, Matthias Flacius, took quite a different tack. Even as Melanchthon worked with Maurice of Saxony to try to work out a political solution to the ongoing theological controversy (the Leipzig Interim of 1548), Flacius was expressing his vehement opposition to any sort of compromise position. Christians had the right and responsibility *not* to cooperate with such negotiated efforts to resolve religious controversies, even those involving matters that would have been considered *adiaphora* had they not been mandated.[115] His uncompromising position in this regard anticipates those adopted by the Puritans in England and elsewhere.[116]

Luther's doctrine of "the two kingdoms" may have contributed at least indirectly to the later concept of the separation of church and state, including its articulation in the First Amendment to the Constitution of the United States several centuries thereafter. On a less positive note, it has been suggested that his willingness as a churchman to support magistrates as they carried out their duties in the secular sphere may also have helped set the ideological stage for the cooperation of the German Lutheran church with the Nazi regime during the 1930s and 1940s.[117] Many clergymen and theologians of the time went along with the Nazi agenda or kept silent even when it became clear that there would be horrific consequences for Jews and others. A few Lutheran pastors like Dietrich Bonhoeffer were willing to become martyrs in the cause of resistance to the Nazi regime, but they were very much exceptions to the general rule, as the majority of the Lutheran clergy cooperated with the government rather than resisting it.

Luther was criticized by some of his contemporaries for himself acting like a pope, making unilateral executive decisions, especially later in life. Simon Lemnius, a former protégé of Melanchthon at the University of Wittenberg who eventually became disaffected and turned against his teachers, directed his lewd drama *Monachopornomachia* against Luther, calling him "the archbishop of Wittenberg and primate of all of Saxony" and accusing him of subjecting "all of your Wittenberg to yourself."[118] The burgermeister of Zwickau referred to Luther in all apparent seriousness as the "German Pope" in 1531.[119]

Despite Luther's own aversion to church law and lawyers, some sort of regulation was needed for the establishment and governance of the new churches in Germany, and it was often and perhaps inevitably Luther to whom his followers looked for guidance and leadership. How reluctant he was to be involved in such matters, especially when they had legal ramifications, may be discerned from remarks such as the following, which he made in a sermon on excommunication preached in 1539: "We do not seek control (*dominium*). We do not want it, nor are we able to exercise it."[120] Martin Brecht points out that despite his considerable personal *gravitas*, which he was unafraid to exercise, Luther "did not understand himself to be *the* bishop, or even *a* bishop in Electoral Saxony."[121] As much as possible, Luther tried to ensure that duly appointed "visitors" would take on that role and carry out those responsibilities. He declined to serve as the "*de facto* chief censor" of the Reformation: "Now, I have no intention—and may God guard me against it—of taking upon myself to be judge or ruler over other preachers, lest I start my own papacy."[122] Luther was grateful that the Wittenberg Consistory, which was established in 1539 as a judicial arm of the church, took over many administrative responsibilities, such as those involving marriage matters, with which he had become increasingly burdened.[123] Nor, at least according to Melanchthon's funeral eulogy, did Luther have any special interest in appropriating for himself "personal power."[124] In household matters, he regularly deferred to his wife's judgment. In letters from the last years of his life, we find him addressing her variously as "mistress of the house," "preacher," "brewer," "gardener," "judge at the pig market," "highly learned," "holy lady," and even "most holy Mrs. Doctor."[125] Katerina von Bora was Luther's "empress" (*keyserin*).[126]

In more recent times, Luther has often been condemned by Marxist historians and others as a "toady of princes."[127] As we have seen, he cultivated close working relationships with local magistrates such as the Ernestine electors, with whom he frequently communicated and to whom he freely gave advice and guidance, especially in matters where the interests of church and state overlapped. Often this was through the agency of Georg Spalatin, the secretary of Frederick the Wise and advisor to his successors. This is not to say, however, that the electors always did what Luther wanted them to do or that Luther always approved of their decisions or conduct. He openly expressed his concerns about how much John Frederick drank, although he did acknowledge that the prince could hold his liquor better than some.[128]

There was no strictly defined "wall of separation" dividing the two kingdoms in Luther's mind. He was very much engaged in the worldly kingdom in which God had placed him, and he had little patience at all with those who would try to escape the world in order to seek greater holiness removed from it. When as a young man Luther decided to become a monk, it is no accident that he chose to join the Augustinian hermits in Erfurt. Unlike the cenobitic Benedictines, who established monasteries that were sometimes located at a considerable distance from towns or cities and often became quite rich and powerful institutions in their own right, the Augustinians were a mendicant order of friars (like the Dominicans and Franciscans), who deliberately chose to live by begging in the context of a larger civic community. Luther, the former Augustinian, was not interested in separating the new Lutheran churches entirely from the world. He warmly embraced the usefulness of Aesop's fables for teaching "Lutheran" children to beware of "two-footed wolves and lions" and to stay safe in the world but not try to escape from it.[129]

Important as civic engagement was for Luther, it did not mean that his ultimate allegiance as a Christian was owed to anything less than "the communion of saints," the *communio sanctorum* of the Apostles' Creed.[130] It mattered little where such communities of faith might be located on earth. This side of heaven, the kingdom of God's right hand could never be physically confined to any one place, not even Jerusalem or Rome (cf. John 4:20–24).[131] In a sermon preached in 1537, Luther declares emphatically, "I am concerned not about the Roman church but the apostolic church."[132] This is the true church, which is not coterminous with any single city or church or denomination but is faithful to the gospel of the resurrected Jesus first preached by the apostles. As such, Luther declares in 1519, it is "nowhere and everywhere":

> And so the church today is nowhere and everywhere. In the same way, thanks to the guidance of the Holy Spirit, this modesty has been preserved for the church in Jerusalem so that it has never striven with other churches about its

primacy and dignity, as the churches at Rome and Constantinople have striven with each other in a perpetual and scandalous contest. This, despite the fact that the church at Jerusalem ought to be given precedence over others by every right (if primacy were to be sought), not only because Christ himself was its pontifex, appointed king by God his father, but also because the entire church began there, and all churches were born there, and it alone is truly the mother of churches, and the disciples were like her priests.... Not that I condemn the monarchical rule of the Roman church, but I do detest the fact that it is extorted with force and aggression as though it were appropriated by a divine precept when it should be established through mutual consensus of the faithful and the bond of charity so that it would be the monarchical rule not of a dominating power but of a ministering love. I condemn the arrogance, but I commend the thing itself. Gold is not bad, but avarice is.[133]

As Luther became convinced from his study of church history,[134] there had been many true Christians outside of Rome's sphere who had never in any way belonged to the Roman church, such as those who found themselves connected with other metropolitan centers of early Christianity: Jerusalem, Antioch, and Alexandria. The bishops in those cities legitimately commanded the respect and obedience of believers in their domain without expanding their claims in such absolutist terms as the papacy had done. It was not surprising that Luther and other reformers should object so strongly to the idea that Christians who did not submit to the authority of the Roman pope were illegitimate, because after all, they themselves were now included in that number.

This kingdom of God's right hand was not as "invisible" for Luther as it has sometimes been supposed to be. He himself preferred the adjective "hidden."[135] Unlike other reformers who understood Christ's body and blood to be present in the Eucharist only symbolically, Luther insisted that Christ was truly present in the Lord's Supper in a physical and not just a spiritual sense. Against objections that Christ could not be present at one and the same time in all the churches where Mass was being celebrated on earth because he was seated at the right hand of God in heaven and could not be in more than one place at a time, Luther appealed to the doctrine of divine ubiquity. Because Christ is not only true man but also true God, for whom the ordinary rules of nature do not apply, his body and blood are mysteriously and truly present in every Eucharist. Wherever two or three are gathered in his name, he is there in the midst of them (Matt 18:20). The word of God, as it is read from the Bible and preached from the pulpit (*viva vox evangelii*), is actually Christ himself, the word of God made flesh (John 1:1). There is a famous painting produced by Lucas Cranach the Elder for the predella of the altarpiece of the Stadtkirche in Wittenberg that depicts Luther in the pulpit preaching to his congregation with a large crucifix positioned between the preacher and his listeners. Like his New Testament model, the apostle Paul, Luther is literally preaching "Christ crucified" (1 Cor 1:23).

Luther believed that this true church could be found even in the mendacious city of Rome. As he puts it in the *Smalcald Articles*, "For (thank God), a seven-year-old child knows what the church is, namely, the holy believers and the lambs who hear their shepherd's voice."[136] Insofar as there are holy "lambs" in Rome who hearken to their good shepherd, the true apostolic church is there too. Even later in life, Luther was careful to distinguish the true body of Christ in Rome from its current misleaders, especially the pope and the curia, who claimed to be in charge of the church but were no longer serving properly as shepherds of the flock of Christ.[137] In a sermon preached later in life, Luther makes a pointed distinction between the "Roman church" proper, which he says has God's word and baptism (the latter perhaps a jab at the Anabaptists) and he still regards as "holy," and the Roman curia and the papacy that currently controls it: "I hold the Roman church in esteem. It is pious. It has God's word and baptism. It is holy. But as for the Roman court, the pope who is the bishop in the court is the devil's bishop and the devil himself; yes, he's the crap which the devil has shat on the church, because he acts in no other way than what may serve the interests of the audacity and lust of his worldly court so that he can become Caesar and king (*keiser und konig*) and flush money out of the chests."[138]

The kingdom of God did not pivot around Luther's own town any more than it did around Rome. As suggested above, Luther had little interest in radical utopian dreams that might be applied to Wittenberg. The kind of consistently proper civic behavior, regulated and enforced by legislation, that turned Geneva into a Calvinist city or Salem, Massachusetts, into a Puritan monoculture was not something that Luther could ever endorse. The idea of a unique "city that is set on an hill" (Matt 5:14), a model for other human communities, was popular with Calvinist immigrants in New England.[139] The ideal new city in America was meant to replace and even surpass all previous cities, including Rome, just as America itself was to become a new Roman Empire, serving as a visible manifestation of an invisible divine will, offering an obvious validation of this new nation's own future expansion. There are over twenty communities in the United States with the name of Rome in their title, and to this day Americans continue to measure the durability of the Pax Americana against the example of the Roman Empire.[140] By contrast, Luther never intended for Wittenberg to become such a model political entity, just as his hope for Germany itself was not "the achievement of national glory, but rather repentance and reform."[141]

As Wittenberg grew larger and more prosperous as a result of Luther's Reformation (and as he grew more familiar with it), his own town increasingly had come to resemble the deeply flawed Rome Luther had visited so many years earlier. "Lutheran" Wittenberg was not a community inhabited by angelic, sinless beings, an earthly foreshadowing of heavenly perfection, but rather an unruly conglomeration of saints and sinners. Drunkenness and other vices were not only prevalent in private but on full public display. Stinginess, hatred, and envy had become so rampant by the end of Luther's ministry there that in June of 1545, he asked rhetorically from the pulpit, "What are we preaching? It would be better if we would quit." All was lost for Wittenberg if it produced so little in the way of fruits of faith after so many years of the proclamation of the gospel there.[142] In fact, Luther was so disturbed by the failure of its citizens to live sanctified lives that he actually left Wittenberg the year before his death, declaring to his wife in a letter that he planned never to return (his heart had "become cold") and advising her to sell their property.[143]

The only claim that Luther's "dumpy" town[144] might have had to be considered special or holy had nothing to do with the exemplary conduct of its citizens or its growth in prosperity and prestige but the fact that God's word in its truth and purity had streamed forth from Wittenberg in recent years, creating "many souls for heaven."[145] Ironically, Luther's own disappointment in the town that he made famous does not characterize the attitude of many latter-day Lutherans who have succeeded in turning it into a tourist destination. It is estimated that the five hundredth anniversary of the posting of the Ninety-Five Theses saw as many as two million tourists (or pilgrims, if you will) descend upon Wittenberg in 2017.[146]

Like many others in his day, Luther believed that the worldly kingdom of God's left hand was going to end very soon. His hopes for any sort of amelioration of life on earth were tempered by his sense of living in the "end times." There would soon be a new heaven and a new earth, he believed, just as the New Testament promises (Rev 21:1). The long-lived institutions associated with the city, referred to as *Urbs aeterna* as early as the reign of Hadrian, would surely pass away.[147] But the same could not be said of the eternal kingdom of God's right hand. The last clause of Luther's explanation of the second petition of the Lord's Prayer in his *Small Catechism* ("Thy kingdom come") emphasizes one of the key characteristics of the kingdom ruled directly by God: its subjects will live godly lives "here in time and there in eternity" (*hie zeitlich und dort ewiglich*).[148] The only "kingdom without end," to use the language of the Nicene Creed (*cuius regni non erit finis*), is the kingdom of God's right hand, not the Roman Empire (in its "holy" or pagan version).

The power struggles that characterize the kingdom of God's left hand are, consequently, only of a temporary nature. The burning political issues that seem so important at the moment will shortly be of no concern at all. The Christian must live for the time being in both kingdoms in as godly and prudent a way as possible, but the only kingdom that ultimately matters *sub specie aeternitatis* is the kingdom of heaven. Indeed, the Christian could be rightly said to be a citizen not of this world but of heaven, as Luther says in his explication of Philippians 3:20: "We are not called citizens of earth any longer, therefore, but whoever is a baptized Christian here is a native citizen of heaven through baptism. So we should conduct ourselves and walk as those who belong there and are at home there, and we should comfort ourselves now because God has thus accepted us and wants to establish us there." The life that the Christian lives in this world, Luther continues, will be eschatologically oriented: "But we are waiting for the Savior who will bring down to us from heaven eternal righteousness, life, honor, and glory."[149]

The strongly eschatological sentiment that characterizes much of Luther's theology can be difficult for those Christians today who focus more on the here and now than the hereafter to appreciate fully. Liberal churches and denominations are known for their interest in issues related to social justice, while conservative Christian bodies often advocate for the stability of the traditional family or promote the advantages that religion can provide in terms of material prosperity. Despite his commitment to education, law, and government, Luther did not believe that the primary or exclusive purpose of the gospel was to make people better behaved in this life or to improve the world. These are incidental benefits that should accrue because individual hearts have been transformed by the gospel, but they are not the ultimate point of the gospel.

Luther's sense that he was living in the end times was closely connected with his growing suspicion (and finally settled opinion) that the Roman church was being governed by the antichrist prophesied in the Scriptures. If he stayed in the Augustinian monastery in Orvieto on his way to or from Rome (some 120 kilometers to the north of the city),[150] Luther might have seen the chapel in the cathedral there with its graphic depictions of the antichrist (the devil at his side is whispering in his ear) and the end of the world, painted by Luca Signorelli just a few years before. Luther's own identification of the pope as the antichrist was a sure eschatological sign. His clear proclamation of the gospel was serving to arouse the devil's wrathful response during these last few evil days in which he was living. The final *dies irae* would put an end to all earthly cities and states; no matter how carefully planned and beautifully constructed and securely defended, all of them would be replaced with "new heavens and a new earth" (2 Pet 3:13).

Of this new reality where "the righteous shall shine forth as the sun in the kingdom of their Father" (Matt 13:43), Luther observes, "How this will work we cannot know, except that it has been promised that there will be such a heaven and earth with no sin in it, only pure righteousness, and God's children will live there, as Saint Paul says in Romans 8. In that place there will be pure love, pure joy and pleasure, and nothing but God's kingdom." Anticipating possible concerns about the precise location of this kingdom, Luther continues: "At this point one might be concerned whether the blessed will be suspended in heaven or on earth. From the text here, it sounds as if we will live on earth, and so all of heaven and earth will be a new paradise in which God lives, for God does not live only in heaven but in all places."[151]

In a letter addressed to his six-year-old son Hans, Luther describes such a perfect place, filled with nothing but love and joy and pleasure, using the language not of kingdoms or cities, or even of a church, but of a simple, delightful garden filled with fruit and toys and friends:

> I know a pretty, beautiful, pleasant garden. There are lots
> of children in it, and they are wearing little golden cloaks.
> Under the trees they are picking up nice apples and pears,

cherries and yellow and red plums; they sing and jump and are happy. They also have nice little ponies with golden bridles and silver saddles. Then I asked the man who owns the garden, "Who are these children?" And he told me, "These are the children who love to pray and learn and to be good." Then I said, "Dear sir, I also have a son named little Hans Luther. Couldn't he come into the garden, too, so that he can eat such nice apples and pears, and ride on such fine ponies, and play with these children?" Then the man said, "If he loves to pray and learn and be good, he may come into my garden. Lippus and Jost [sons of Melanchthon and Justus Jonas] can come too. And when they all come together, they will also play fifes and drums and lutes and all kinds of other stringed instruments and dance and shoot little crossbows too." And there he showed me a fine mossy spot in the garden ready for them to dance in, where nothing was hanging except for golden fifes and drums and fine silver crossbows.[152]

Neither the ancient city of Rome nor the Holy Roman Empire, even with all of their complex governance structures and carefully devised regulations, could come close to approaching the simple perfection of this Edenic paradise as Luther conceives it. In this idyllic *Kindergarten*, we may catch a glimpse of Luther's dreamlike vision of a kingdom inherited not by the wise and powerful but only by those who become like little children. They are in a far better position to be admitted than adults (cf. Matt 18:3).

Even if he had no illusions about Rome's failings both as an ancient republic and as a medieval Christian "empire," Luther continued to respect the paradigmatic example of the former and the authoritative claims of the latter as he set out to address the time-honored question of how citizens of the heavenly kingdom should best live in the temporary kingdom of this world: wisely, safely, and dutifully as "good friends" and "trustworthy neighbors," to borrow

Luther's own language from his explanation of the fourth petition of the Lord's Prayer in his *Small Catechism*.[153] In Luther's mind, ancient Rome in this regard could still serve as a model, no matter how far removed in time it might be, and the Holy Roman Empire, no matter how creaky and ineffectual, deserved continued respect from its subjects, of whom he was one.

4

"If There Is a Hell, Rome Is Built on It"

THE CATHOLIC

IN THIS CHAPTER WE turn to Luther's relationship with the Roman church of his day, the church that identified itself as the Nicene Creed's "one, holy, catholic, and apostolic church." This unitary (one) and all-encompassing (catholic) sacred body has traditionally drawn its claim to unique ecclesial authority from its connection with the apostle Peter, upon whom Christ had vowed to build his church and to whom he entrusted the keys of the kingdom of heaven (Matt 16:18–19). Peter's crucified body is supposed to have been buried under what is now Saint Peter's Basilica. The Catholic Church's headquarters today is situated on 121 acres on the west bank of the Tiber River that constitute the sovereign state known as Vatican City (since 1929). Up until the time of the Avignon papacy in the fourteenth century, the pope had regularly resided in the Lateran Palace, near the basilica of Saint John Lateran. Today the pope's main residence is the papal palace (Palatium Apostolicum) adjoining Saint Peter's. Like many others before and since, Luther often used the word "Rome" metonymically to stand for this church.[1]

In studying Luther's rhetoric directed against the Roman church, it is important to acknowledge that strong, colorful, and abusive language was characteristic of the world of thought to which Luther belonged. All the same, even in an age that was more comfortable than our own with public invective, Luther's harsh words struck many of his contemporaries as excessive. We shall explore the possibility here that the very intensity of the mature Luther's hostile language not only indicates the depth of his antipathy toward papal Rome but also serves to underscore the strength of his original attachment to the church so closely associated with the figure of the pope, the man whom he once considered his "holy father."[2]

There are a number of possible ways to understand Luther as he castigates ecclesiastical Rome. It has been suggested that the increasingly vehement language he directed against the pope is partly a function of his growing older and sicker or even mentally unhinged as the years passed.[3] Luther would certainly not be the only human being whose physical infirmities and bodily pain dramatically soured his mood and colored his words. He suffered over the years from numerous ailments, including some or all of the following: constipation, anal fissures, hemorrhoids, headaches, dizziness (perhaps as a result of Meniere's disease), buzzing in the ears, ear infections, heart congestion, an open ulcer on his shin, excruciating kidney stones, gout, arthritis, and angina.[4] As Mark Edwards points out, the "intense pain" that Luther often experienced could very well have "aggravated his tendency to give way to anger." If he suffered from arteriosclerosis, "the question of possible senility or at least of reduced intellectual acuity in his later years" becomes a relevant one.[5]

On the other hand, as Edwards also observes, even late in life Luther "had not lost complete control" of himself, so the explanation that the increasing level of "vulgarity and violence" in his language must be due only to his illness and age "is not particularly illuminating historically." The fact that he was able "to turn it on and off as it suited his purposes" suggests that these factors, while influential, were not necessarily determinative. The late Luther seems to have remained aware of and in control of his verbal output.[6] Variable audience expectations as well as changing political and ecclesiastical circumstances surely also helped determine when and to what extent he would wax rhetorically aggressive. As he grew older and his eschatological sensibilities became increasingly acute,[7] Luther found himself writing more and more often for readers closer to home, who were already firmly committed to his cause and irreversibly opposed to Rome.

It could also be that Luther's visceral reaction to his spiritual father in Rome was shaped to some extent by psychological factors, including the not always easy relationship he had with his earthly father, as Erikson famously argued in *Young Man Luther*. Hans Luther had not approved of his son's decision to join the order of Augustinian hermits in Erfurt in 1505. Like so many other fathers (including John Calvin's),[8] the prosperous Hans had ambitious plans for his son's future in the world and wanted him to become a lawyer, not a churchman. The story of Hans's confrontation with his son at the time of his ordination to the priesthood is well known. Hans reminded Martin of the scriptural admonition to honor one's father and mother and wondered whether Luther's sudden decision to join the monastery was not divinely but diabolically inspired.[9] Perhaps Luther's later obsession with *il Papa* was somehow a transferal of his fixation on his real father, a demanding figure whose expectations for him the troubled Luther knew that he had failed to meet.

On the other hand, Luther seems to have had a fairly typical childhood as far as we can determine. Many sons have strong differences with their fathers, especially as they enter adulthood. Martin Brecht cautions against interpreting "Luther's struggle with God as a transferred father complex." Psychologists no less than historians need to recognize the limitations of their knowledge, he prudently suggests, especially "where sufficient data is lacking."[10] Psychoanalysis practiced from afar has its obvious limitations. This said, it is not hard to imagine that Luther may have suffered at least to an extent from what some psychologists today term "religious trauma syndrome," the intense emotional hurt that can come from leaving a church or religious group or, in Luther's case, being forced to leave it.[11]

Without discounting altogether these familiar explanations for understanding Luther's fierce invective against Rome, in the first part of what follows, I shall suggest a literary-critical consideration that has been less often taken into account. We should not forget that Luther was a literary artist who used language with playful dexterity and who rarely said or wrote anything that was merely prosaic or expected if he could express the same sentiment in a more vivid and striking way. Clearly, he did not mean literally all that he ever said and wrote. Luther could hardly have regarded Satan as "holy," and yet that is exactly how he once observed that he would address the devil in times of temptation, asking him sarcastically to pray for him (*Sancte Sathana, ora pro me*).[12] Nor surely did he consider Paul III to be anything at all like the pure Virgin Mary, who "never sinned and never will be able to sin," and yet that is how he describes this pope in 1545.[13] Modern readers might benefit, therefore, from trying to read Luther's writings not only as providing the underpinnings for systematic Lutheran theology or serving as primary source material for Reformation historiography but also as literary texts. We could then make helpful use of some of the theories about satire and persona familiar to literary critics. Much of what Luther had to say and to write about the Roman papacy has a satiric edge.

Like every other author (even professional theologians), Luther had a literary persona. Originally an Etruscan word for the mask worn by mimes, the word *persona* has evolved in more recent times. Carl Jung used it in a psychological sense to refer to the personality that individuals present to others as opposed to one's true self.[14] If we can speak of "brand Luther," as Andrew Pettegree has persuasively argued with regard to the careful and self-conscious attention Luther paid to "the look" of his published works, we may also be justified in speaking of "persona Luther" when it comes to analyzing his authorial presence in the texts that have come down to us under his name.[15] The literary persona that Luther projected may have been more calculated and less spontaneous than is often supposed.

Regardless of how we try to understand Luther's harsh language against Rome, what shall we say was its intended effect? Luther was above all else a theologian, and in the second part of this chapter, I offer a theological answer to the question of his relationship with the Roman church that relies on the dialectical relationship between law and gospel, one of Luther's most distinctive doctrines.[16] It is highly doubtful that Freudian speculation about fears of a "father figure" or even theories about the authorial "persona" developed by literary historians of satire would have made much sense to Luther. These surely would *not* have been the answers he himself would have provided had he been asked to explain why he once wished that his followers might be filled "with hatred of the pope."[17] Rather, he would doubtless have explained his animosity toward the papacy in terms of the dynamic of law and gospel. The angry criticisms and accusations he hurled at Rome were little different in his mind from the harsh preachment of prophets like Isaiah and Jeremiah against Jerusalem. The language of these Old Testament predecessors of Luther was so angry and vehement not because their God hated the inhabitants of his holy city built on Mount Zion but because he loved them.

The Home of the Antichrist

Without a doubt, Luther's invective against the city of Rome as the home of the papacy can sound extreme to modern ears. Consider, for instance, this torrential string of descriptive phrases characterizing Rome in one of the *Tischreden*:

> Rome is the realm of the antichrist, the prison of the sons of Israel, the theater of idols, the refuge for the wicked, the citadel for magicians and enchanters, the sewer of wickednesses, the plague of the world, the hammer of the earth, the land of bitter things, the pestilential mountain, the workshop of Satan, the opponent of the city of God (namely, Jerusalem—that is, the true church), worthy of being utterly destroyed, the land of idols that glories in omens, in which dragons and ostriches deservedly make their home, so that it may be left abandoned forever, and destroyed and overturned for generation after generation, and not be rebuilt nor tended by any human.[18]

And here are some of the opening lines of his late treatise *Against the Papacy in Rome, Founded by the Devil*, written after Luther had heard the news that the pope had finally agreed to hold a council to deal with reform issues:

> Meanwhile, we see and hear how the pope is such a masterful magician. For just like a magician, he puts gulden into the mouths of foolish people, but when they open their mouths, they are filled with horse manure. This is what this shameless fop, Paul III, also does. . . . For he wants to have a council over which he can exert his power and trample down everything that is decided upon in the council. The abominable devil thanks him for having such a council, and nobody else is admitted into the council except the abominable devil, along with his mother, his sister, and his whore children, the pope, the cardinals, and whatever other hellish dregs there are in Rome.[19]

Lest one imagine that Luther's harsh words directed against the "hellish dregs" of Rome and the devil's "whore children" came only from the later period of his life, we need look no further than his response to papal claims as articulated by Sylvester Prierias in 1520, less than a decade after his return from the modern "Sodom": "If we punish thieves with the forked gallows, brigands with the sword, and heretics with fire, why do we not use all of our arms to attack even more these masters of perdition, these cardinals, these popes, and this whole offscouring of Roman Sodom which corrupts the church of God endlessly (*sine fine*) and wash our hands in their blood, as though we were going to free ourselves and our own from a most dangerous conflagration threatening all of us?"[20] The Virgilian reference (*Aeneid* 1.279) to Rome's unlimited future (*sine fine*) helps underscore Luther's point here: the intolerable corruption of the current Roman regime is not at all new but rather began long ago under the empire ruled by Augustus's successors who persecuted the early Christians. Rome has always been an inveterate foe of the true church and no more deserves to continue to exist now than did Sodom, the city that God destroyed with fire and brimstone (Gen 19:24).

The variety of insulting epithets that Luther used to describe the avaricious, foolish, and diabolical Roman papacy over the years is impressive.[21] The following list is not exhaustive by any means: "Baalam," "ass," "whore," "screech owl," "louse," "monster," "king of the rats," "murderer of souls," "stench and abomination," "dragon," "idol," "Judas Iscariot," "murder cellar," "Nimrod," "tyrant," "sycophant," and "Hermaphrodite."[22] In a 1521 letter to Lucas Cranach, he calls the Romanists "apes and fools."[23] In another letter (of 1523), he refers to the "Roman lion and minotaur."[24] Luther's pope at the end of his life, the "werewolf" Paul III, is described as "a desperate scoundrel, the enemy of God and man, the destroyer of Christendom, and Satan's bodily dwelling."[25]

Perhaps the most theologically definitive term Luther used to describe the pope in Rome is "antichrist," the one who sits where Christ should be, presiding over the church as its head, claiming to be Christ's vicarious representative on earth but teaching and acting in a way that runs entirely counter to Jesus's own teachings and actions. As early as 1518, Luther had begun to identify "the one ruling in the Roman curia" as the antichrist.[26] In a letter of 1520, he speaks of the "tyranny of the Roman antichrist," and in another letter of the same year, he suggests that Satan is working through "the Roman antichrist."[27] More than once, Luther simply refers to the pope as the "Roman Satan."[28] The antichrist and Satan are two distinct entities, but they work in tandem, the former at the behest of the latter.

Luther was neither the first nor the last to refer to the bishop of Rome as the antichrist. As early as the late tenth century, Arnulf, bishop of Orléans, was accusing Pope John XV of being the antichrist. Some four hundred years before Luther's birth, Cardinal Benno had charged Pope Gregory VII with being the antichrist. In 1241, Pope Gregory IX was called "antichrist" at the Council of Regensburg. In the late fourteenth century, John Wycliffe published his treatise *On Christ and His Adversary, the Antichrist*. Wycliffe identified the latter as the pope. Very often it was the scriptural passage 2 Thessalonians 2:1–12, regarding "the son of perdition," who will sit in the temple of God as God, that was applied to the antichrist in question.[29]

Despite their strong differences on many other issues of style and substance, in the sixteenth century, Protestant leaders and their followers with few exceptions agreed wholeheartedly with Luther's identification of the pope with the antichrist. To be sure, there were some reform-minded individuals, like Erasmus, who did not appreciate Luther's *furor teutonicus*[30] and never actually parted company with the Roman church. Other reformers followed Melanchthon in expressing their critique of the papacy in more tempered prose than Luther's. Still, not only Melanchthon but Zwingli, Calvin, Thomas Cranmer, and John Knox, to say nothing of the leaders of the "enthusiasts" (*Schwärmer*), all connected the papacy with the antichrist.

In the centuries to come, the identification of the Roman pope as the antichrist continued to be central to Protestant identity. In North America as well as in Europe, Protestant leaders such as Roger Williams, John Wesley, Elijah Lovejoy, and many others were strongly opposed to all aspects of Roman Catholicism.[31] In 1884, C. F. W. Walther, president of the Missouri Synod of the Lutheran Church in America, declared that orthodox Lutherans in his country were entirely serious when they described the pope as the antichrist: "In line with the entire Church of the Reformation and in agreement with the Confessions of that Church, the orthodox American Lutheran Church of our time still and in full earnestness maintains the position that the pope is the antichrist." Even so, Walther also acknowledged that this might no longer be a majority opinion: "But that is, at best, regarded as an odd fancy of narrow-minded men who refuse to keep up with the times."[32]

Well into the twentieth century and even the twenty-first, confessional statements endorsed not only by Lutherans but also by other Protestant groups have continued to refer to the papacy as the antichrist. As late as 1988, Ian Paisley, an Irish politician and minister (Free Presbyterian Church of Ulster), publicly denounced Pope John Paul II as the antichrist, interrupting the pope as he was addressing a meeting of the European Parliament.[33]

On the part of many of those who are churched today, there is an unspoken expectation that verbal exchanges in ecclesiastical contexts should be unfailingly polite. The idea that a highly visible churchman such as Luther would use vulgar and abusive language in public is deeply disconcerting. In Europe and America, twenty-first-century readers may find it especially difficult to account for the extreme language of Luther and his contemporaries directed against the Roman church because recent decades have witnessed a genuine ecumenical rapprochement between Catholics and Lutherans.[34] Theologians from both church bodies have worked together productively to find ways to agree with each other on the historically divisive doctrine of justification (a joint agreement on the subject was reached in 1999).[35] Even those conservative Lutheran bodies that still identify the papacy as the antichrist are not inclined to make public pronouncements to that effect, and they certainly would never declare their convictions today as loudly, repeatedly, and colorfully as Luther once did.

Although Luther's excommunication has never been officially revoked by the Roman church, the attitude of its leaders toward Luther has mellowed somewhat in recent years. There is now even a piazza in Rome (on the Oppian Hill, overlooking the Colosseum), named Piazza Martin Luthero, with a sign that describes him simply (and politely) as "the German theologian of the Reformation" (*il teologo Tedesco della riforma*). Rome's city council approved the renaming of the piazza in 2010 to commemorate the five hundredth anniversary of Luther's trip, and the Vatican gave its consent to the idea in 2015.

At the same time, for many moderns there is another equally widely held assumption—namely, that the doctrinal differences that used to stir up ferocious controversy could not possibly have been worth so much angry attention, especially since they seem inconsequential for the well-being of humans in the twenty-first century.

But even though questions such as whether and how Christ's body is truly present in the Eucharist can sound arcane and irrelevant today, that does not necessarily mean that they were not of the most urgent importance for Luther and many others in his God-drenched century. One need only think of how seriously Shia and Sunni Muslims still take their disagreements about the proper lineage of the Islamic tradition after the prophet Mohammed's death. Distinctions that may seem relatively inconsequential to those who are not deeply involved in such controversies can be terribly important for those who are.[36]

All of these present-day expectations for proper ecclesiastical discourse must be put aside if we wish to understand correctly Luther's vituperations against papal Rome. Vituperation was in the air in the sixteenth century. Strongly worded scatological invective characterized the polemics not only of Luther but also of many of his contemporaries, including such a notable and respected Renaissance luminary as Thomas More. In his *Responsio ad Lutherum* (2,27), More demonstrates his own ability to spar verbally with the German master of scatological invective, whom he says has nothing "in his mouth, but sewage, sewers, privies, shit, and dung." He describes Luther as "the frantic little friar, the rest-room rascal, with his rantings and ravings, with his shit and his dung, shitting and being shat upon."[37] Such language was not confined only to the Grobianists of northern Europe but was employed by the literary geniuses of Italy as well.[38] Consider Dante's graphic description of how the apostle Peter describes what his papal successor has done to Rome: "He who usurps my place on earth, my place, the place that is empty in the presence of the Son of God, has made of my cemetery a sewer of blood and stench, with the result that the perverted one who fell from up here is now perfectly happy to be down there" (*Paradiso* 27.22–27).[39]

Over-the-top invective also characterized the discourse of sophisticated Italian humanists. Poggio Bracciolini uses an astonishing variety of abusive terms to describe his fellow humanist Lorenzo Valla, including the following: "a fanatical and crazy dreamer vomiting forth insanity, a most stupid ass, a beast grazing in the field of stupidity, . . . a mad dog, a raging reviler, a wrangling pettifogger, a misshapen hideous monster, a drunkard, a bastard, a prostitute, the worst kind of old sly-boots, a cook, a stable-boy, and a braggart."[40]

Luther threatened his adversaries and hurled names at them, but it could be said that he was only responding in kind. After all, the pope whom he had once addressed as his "most blessed father" had himself in the most public of ways called Luther a "boar from the woods" (*aper de silva*) loose in the vineyard that is Christ's church. Cochlaeus referred to Luther as a "child of the devil, possessed by the devil, full of falsehood and vainglory," motivated to reform the church only by his envy of John Tetzel and his lust "after wine and women." As far as Cochlaeus was concerned, Luther had no conscience and thought only of himself; he was "a liar and a hypocrite, cowardly and quarrelsome."[41] The anti-Lutheran invective continued long after Luther's death. The list of insulting epithets assigned to Luther in the acrostic *Elogium Martini Lutheri* by the French Jesuit Andreas Frusius (printed at Cologne in 1582) is an impressive *tour de force* of personal invective. There are eighty epithets whose first letters spell out Luther's full name in Latin (*Martinus Lutherus*) five times:

> *Magnicrepus* ("noisy"); *Ambitiosus* ("ambitious"); *Ridiculus* ("silly"); *Tabificus* ("infectious"); *Impius* ("irreverent"); *Nycticorax* ("nightjar"); *Ventosus* ("windy"); *Schismaticus* ("schismatic"); *Lascivus* ("lustful"); *Ventripotens* ("big bellied"); *Tartareus* ("Tartarean"); *Haeresiarcha* ("arch-heretic"); *Erro* [*Error*] ("mistake"); *Retrogradus* ("backwards"); *Vesanus* ("insane"); *Sacrilegus* ("blasphemous").
>
> *Mendax* ("liar"); *Atrox* ("cruel"); *Rhetor* ("talker"); *Tumidus* ("swollen"); *Inconstans* ("unfaithful"); *Nebulo* ("scoundrel"); *Vanus* ("vain"); *Stolidus* ("stupid"); *Leno* ("pimp"); *Vultur* ("vulture"); *Torris* ("firebrand"); *Horrendus* ("terrible"); *Execrandus* ("detestable"); *Reprobus* ("base"); *Varius* ("fickle"); *Satanas* ("Satan").
>
> *Morosus* ("peevish"); *Astutus* ("sly"); *Rabiosus* ("mad"); *Tenebrosus* ("gloomy"); *Impostor* ("swindler"); *Nugator*

("light-weight"); *Vilis* ("worthless"); *Seductor* ("seducer"); *Larvatus* ("bewitched"); *Vinosus* ("wine-bibber"); *Tempestas* ("storm"); *Hypocrita* ("hypocrite"); *Effrons* ("brazen"); *Resupinus* ("supine"); *Veterator* ("old fox"); *Sentina* ("bilge-water").

Morio ("fool"); *Apostata* ("apostate"); *Rabula* ("pettifogger"); *Transfuga* ("turncoat"); *Iniquus* ("unjust"); *Noxa* ("damage"); *Vulpecula* ("little fox"); *Simia* ("ape"); *Latro* ("brigand"); *Vappa* ("flat wine"); *Turbo* ("whirlwind"); *Hydra* ("serpent"); *Effronis* [*Effrenis*] ("unbridled"); *Rana* ("frog"); *Vipera* ("viper"); *Sophista* ("sophist").

Monstrum ("monster"); *Agaso* ("lackey"); *Raptor* ("plunderer"); *Turpis* ("shameful"); *Ineptus* ("improper"); *Nefandus* ("wicked"); *Vecors* ("senseless"); *Scurra* ("idler"); *Lanista* ("gladiator trainer"); *Voluptas* ("pleasure"); *Tyrannus* ("tyrant"); *Hermaphroditus* ("hermaphrodite"); *Eriunis* [*Erinys*] ("fury"); *Rebellis* ("rebel"); *Virus* ("poison"); *Scelestus* ("abominable").[42]

The Angry Satirist

A distinctive characteristic of Luther's harsh invective against papal Rome is its strongly satirical flavor. Satire is not confined to a specific literary form. It is true that it may be less often found in theological writings than in other genres, but its apparent scarcity may not mean that the element of satire is entirely absent, only that it is less often sought there in the first place.[43] No matter how serious the situations that Luther's various writings address, they fairly bristle with examples of satire. Some are quite brief, no more than a word or two, but others, like the parodic letter of 1537 from Beelzebub "to the holy papist church," go on for pages.[44] Occasionally, Luther's satire can be subtly Horatian, commenting on the foibles of other humans (and himself), but more often its tone is rough and angry, resembling the coarse and acerbic humor of Juvenal. As we have seen, Luther was familiar with both Latin poets. He ascribes a line from Juvenal's sixth satire (223) to "that foolish ass of a pope" who claims to be "lord over Scripture":

"Thus I wish it to be; thus I order it to be; let my will replace reason" (*Sic volo, sic iubeo, sit pro ratione voluntas*).[45] What if we were to construe some of the outrageous things that Luther said or wrote about papal Rome as though they were written by other mischievous, angry satirists who verbally attacked cities that they loved but sometimes also despaired of, like Juvenal's Rome or Samuel Johnson's London?[46]

Satire is an expression of humor, and we know that Luther had a lively sense of verbal humor.[47] He was an inveterate raconteur who enjoyed telling and retelling anecdotes about himself and others. He was fond of animal fables and peppered his discourse with maxims and proverbs. A gifted wordsmith, he was also an inveterate punster. For Luther, the philosopher Aristotle is "archfool" (*Ertzstultus*).[48] The pope is not "his holiness" but "his hellishness" (*Hellischeit* instead of *Heiligkeit*), and the Roman *curia* is *furia*.[49]

His Latin poem directed against "the shit-poet" Simon Lemnius, *Dysenteria Lutheri in merdipoetam Lemchen*, is a punning extravaganza. Luther plays with variations of the Latin word for "shit" (*merda*), using the figure of speech known as polyptoton, the repetition of words drawn from the same root (often with different endings in an inflected language like Latin). Various forms of *merda* occur twelve times within the space of ten lines:[50]

> *Quam bene conveniunt tibi res et carmina, Lemchen!*
> *Merda tibi res est, carmina merda tibi.*
> *Dignus erat Lemchen merdosus carmine merdae,*
> *Nam vatem merdae nil nisi merda decet.*
> *Infelix princeps, quem laudas carmine merdae!*
> *Merdosum merda quem facis ipse tua.*
> *Ventre urges merdam vellesque cacare libenter*
> *Ingentem, facis at, merdipoeta, nihil.*
> *At meritis si digna tuis te poena sequatur,*
> *Tu miserum corvis merda cadaver eris.*[51]

How well your verses and their subject matter suit you, little Lemnius! Your subject matter is shit and your verses are shit. Little shitty Lemnius was worthy of a poem of shit, for a poet of shit is worthy of nothing but shit. O, unhappy the prince, whom you praise with your poem of shit, whom you yourself make shitty with your shit. You try to press shit from your bowels and would really like to have a huge crap, but you produce nothing, O poet of shit. But if a penalty worthy of what you deserve follows you, you will be a miserable corpse, shit for the crows.

Luther uses scatological humor here to make a theological point. The word *merda* closely resembles the Latin word for "good works" (*merita*). The pun is more obvious if the poem is read aloud. Acoustically, *merda* and *merita* sound almost the same, but they are nonetheless different: one has an additional, albeit short, syllable; furthermore, the third consonant in *merita* is a voiceless stop, while in *merda* it is voiced. In terms of meaning as well, the words represent very different things, but they have some commonalities, too, that are especially significant from a Lutheran perspective. As far as achieving righteousness in God's eyes is concerned, good works have the same value as shit.[52]

As we have seen, Luther was a student of rhetoric, the art of persuasion; he knew how important it is to be able to move readers and listeners. Movement (*movere*) is arguably the most important of the three traditional *officia oratoris*. Even something as simple as a pun on *merda* and *merita* involves movement. Both the ear and the mind must make adjustments. Far from annoying or disturbing his readers and listeners, it was precisely rhetorical maneuvers such as these that doubtless delighted Luther's audiences and made them so eager to hear and read more of what he had to say and write. Delight (*delectare*) is another aim of rhetoric. Not all of Luther's readers were as sophisticated (or jaded) as Samuel Johnson, who denounced Shakespeare's use of puns (or "quibbles" as Johnson called them) because he considered them to be a low form of humor.[53] The purpose of rhetoric is also to teach (*docere*), its third traditional aim. Even though the poem against Lemnius is less obviously pedagogical than Luther's signature educational achievements, such as the *Small Catechism*, this nugatory bit of Latin verse makes a theological point that serves a higher didactic purpose. It is much more than merely entertaining. The poem ends not on a light note but with a serious warning for Lemnius: relying upon his own shitty merits means that he is on his way to death and destruction, the realm of the crows.

By all accounts, incongruity is one of the key elements of humor.[54] As a speaker and writer, Luther often capitalizes on the juxtaposition of incongruities as he makes his points. After his failure to celebrate Mass at Saint John Lateran (see the discussion in the first chapter), something that was apparently a terrible disappointment for him (and possibly for his mother too), he declares that he went out and ate some herring. The anticlimax of the story is arresting. We are moved abruptly from the high drama of expectations and disappointments connected with the celebration of the Holy Mass to the entirely ordinary. Eating is going to happen in either event: if Luther cannot eat the body of Christ, he will eat smoked fish instead. But the congruence only heightens the startling nature of the incongruity, as Luther redirects his audience's attention from the holy to the unholy, from celestial food to a common snack, from the incense-shrouded altar to the smelly marketplace.

There is a great deal of situational irony, that indispensable fuel for the satirist's fire, implicit in the idea of Rome as the seat of the antichrist. Sitting in the highest place of respect in the church, exactly where Christ should be, claiming to be his representative on earth, Luther's pope is proud instead of humble, wealthy instead of poor, and brutally powerful instead of meek and mild (cf. Matt 11:29).[55] His teachings are as bad as his behavior. The emphasis on good works instead of faith has transformed the gospel of salvation by God's grace alone into a religious system that breeds either perpetual doubt or smug self-righteousness. Instead of enjoying the divine gifts of repentance, peace, and joy, humans learn to become nervously reliant upon what they can do for God as opposed to what he has done for them. And what they do is never sufficient. So, paradoxically enough, the one place on earth that should be closest to heaven is actually hell on earth, as the popular proverb that serves as this chapter's title puts it: "If there is a hell, Rome must be built on it."[56]

Luther once cited this proverb to a visiting pastor from Thuringia who ate dinner with Luther and Spalatin and talked about his experiences in Rome. The pastor had made a total of four trips to Rome. Luther told him of his own impressions of the city: "In short, the wickedness in Rome is unbelievable. Nobody can be persuaded that there is so much evil unless they witness it for themselves with their own eyes, ears, and experience. This is the origin of the proverb: 'If there is a hell, Rome must be built on it.' For all sins are being committed there with a vengeance, not only the obvious manifestations of greed, but the hidden ones, contempt of God, perjury, Sodomitic sins, etc."[57] Luther makes the paradoxical contrast between the illusion of the holy city and its unholy reality dramatically clear in his open letter to Pope Leo of 1520 (in connection with Luther's treatise *On the Freedom of the Christian*): "In short, the [only] Christians are the ones who are *not* Roman" (*Breviter, Christiani sunt qui Romani non sunt*).[58] In Luther's time, the idea that it was actually detrimental to one's faith to be in Rome had become proverbial: "The closer to Rome, the worse the Christians are."[59] The Italian rhyme *Roma veduta, fede perduta* ("Once you have seen Rome, you lose your faith") is still well known.[60]

Satirists not only appreciate the irony of such situations but are also able to reflect and reproduce such irony in their own discourse. Verbal irony involves the use of words and the expression of sentiments that one does not really mean; in fact, the words expressed are usually quite the opposite of what the author means to say.[61] Since verbal irony is often signaled by emphasis or body language, it is not always easy to detect in written form. Even more so than other forms of humor, irony does not translate readily from one cultural context to another.

So how much of Luther's angry language against Rome was meant to be taken literally or seriously? How much of what he had to say was simply hyperbolic or tongue in cheek or posturing? And if so, how would we know? Is his anger real or feigned?[62] These questions become particularly relevant when one considers that Luther himself more than once deplores the use of violence to advance a cause in which the persuasive power of God's word alone must suffice to make real spiritual change happen. In 1522, he makes this abundantly clear: "By this destruction and demolition, however, I do not want it in any way to be understood that one should act with the fist and the sword. Because such punishment is unworthy, and nothing is accomplished by it either. But as Daniel teaches, the antichrist will be destroyed without force so that everyone will speak, teach, and maintain the word of God until of his own accord he is put to shame and is abandoned and scorned and goes to ruin. This is real Christian destruction."[63]

Earlier (1520), Luther had indeed entertained the idea that in order to rescue the church of God, the emperor and other leaders would be well justified in taking up arms against the papacy insofar as it was furiously continuing to corrupt the church: "But it seems to me that if the fury of the Romanists continues thus, there is no remedy left other than for the emperor, kings, and princes supported by armed force to attack these pests of the world and decide the matter no longer with words but with iron."[64] But in reaction to the overt bellicosity toward Rome of the militant Ulrich von Hutten, Franz von Sickingen, and others, Luther began more often and more clearly to reject the idea that the gospel itself could ever achieve its salvific effects through force. It was only through the word that the world had been conquered, and it was also only through the word that the church had been and would continue to be restored. Based on his reading of the eighth chapter of the prophet Daniel, especially verse 25, Luther was confident that the antichrist would be crushed "through the word" (*per verbum*), as he declares in a letter of 1521, "without the fist" (*sine manu*).[65]

That all of the expressions of anger on his part may not have been entirely spontaneous and involuntary is suggested by Luther himself. He can be quite deliberative about what kind of language he chooses to use or not to use. At the end of *To the Christian Nobility of the German Nation* (1520), he admits that he is "fully aware" that he has "sung high" and may have "attacked many things too sharply." But then he goes on to promise that he will sing "another little song about Rome" (*On the Babylonian Captivity of the Church*), which will be pitched even higher, suggesting that "dear Rome" knows very well what he means by this metaphor.[66] After rereading his angry treatise *Against Hanswurst*, Luther is amazed that he was as restrained as he was when he wrote it.[67] In the *Tischreden*, he speaks with a considerable degree of self-awareness about how he uses anger to motivate his discourse: "I have no better remedy than anger. If I want to write, pray, preach, I have to be angered; then my entire blood system is refreshed, my wit is sharpened, and all assaults give way before me."[68]

Luther is mindful of others' criticism of his angry polemics and more than once defends himself on this score. When two of his treatises were criticized as "sharp and urgent" (*scharf und geschwinde*), he explained to Elector John the Steadfast that the criticism was "truly true" (*warlich wahr*). He had not intended for his writings to be "boring and mild" (*stumpff und gelinde*), because the issues at stake were themselves "sharp and urgent." (Luther rhymes *gelinde* with *geschwinde*.) His only regret was that he had not written *more* sharply and vigorously.[69] In the preface he wrote for Melanchthon's commentary on Colossians in 1529, he contrasts his own rhetoric with that of his less polemical colleague: "I was born to do battle with the hordes and the devil and to take the field. This is why my books are so tempestuous and polemical. I have to dig out the roots and trunks, hack away the thorns and hedges, and fill up the pools. I am the rough forester (*waldrechter*) who has to blaze a trail and make it straight. But Master Philipp operates seriously and quietly, building and planting, sowing and watering with enjoyment, in accordance with the gifts that God has richly given him."[70]

One way in which literary critics have responded to the thorny question of what an author really intended to say with his words is to assume that the literary persona adopted by an author is not simply to be identified with the human being who issues these words. After all, how can we possibly determine with any degree of certainty whether someone like Luther, who lived and wrote five centuries ago, used a language that is not ours, and inhabited a world of thought so different from our own, really meant what he said? Even the intentions of contemporary authors who use one's own tongue and live in one's own native land can be difficult to determine. This is especially true if they are reclusive, decline to comment publicly on their motivations, give misleading explanations of their real intentions, feign authorial innocence, or use hyperbole and irony.[71] The authorial persona cannot simply be equated with the author. "I is someone else" (*Je est un autre*), the French poet Rimbaud once famously declared.[72] Luther is not unaware of such complexities. He speaks of "the two persons or double office" (*die zwo Personen odder zweierlei ampt*) for which all Christians must be responsible as they lead their lives in the two kingdoms.[73] The different roles we play in life will determine what we do and say in different situations.

Humor requires a certain degree of cool detachment, a momentary "anesthesia of the heart," as Henri Bergson puts it.[74] Since Luther often presents himself as an earnest and passionate speaker of the truth, famously criticizing Erasmus in *De servo arbitrio* for being too skeptical and not making assertions that come directly from the heart, it may be hard for us to appreciate just how self-aware he could be. Even when Luther indicates that his polemical language is inspired by God himself, he still seems quite conscious of what he is doing as he speaks and writes. With an almost cool objectivity, he is able to analyze his angry impulses and describe them to others, as he does in a 1519 letter to Staupitz: "I believe that you have received my *Acta*, that is to say, my wrath and indignation against Rome. God is snatching me, driving me, to say nothing of leading me. I am not in control of myself. I want to be quiet, but I am thrust into the midst of the commotion."[75] There are two Luthers, it would seem: the one who wants to be "quiet" (*volo esse quietus*) and the other who has been "thrust" by a force outside of himself into a tumultuous situation in which he did not himself seek to be involved in the first place. Who was this "quiet" Luther, we might well ask, and what in the world happened to him over the years? Was he any less real than the vociferous Luther we meet so often in print?

The persona of the satirist may have very little indeed to do with the "real" person behind the sardonic mask. The celebrity talk-show host or the stand-up comedian may well be an entirely different person when at home with family or out on the jogging path with friends. The public at large knows far less of these private individuals than of their celebrity personas. Maria Plaza describes the typical satirist's constructed persona thus: "The public personality, which the persona needs in order to be convincing in his fervent indignation, in his horror at the vice he sees around him, and in his unswerving moral judgement, is dominated by the bluntness and honesty mentioned above. These traits are often strengthened by rural origins, suggestive of pastoral innocence and a simple style in writing and living. In line with a country background, the public personality includes a simple, traditional moral code, a view of life in social not philosophical terms, and a tendency to assume heroic postures."[76]

Even within the persona itself there can be conflicting tensions. In his well-known study of Latin satire, William Anderson offers a definition of the internal conflicts faced by "the typical satirist." Some of them may apply fairly well to Luther: "The typical satirist experiences or exhibits internal conflicts on at least five levels: 1) he is a plain, blunt, simple, artless speaker who yet makes the most skillful use of rhetoric; 2) he proclaims the truth of what he says, while he wilfully distorts facts for emphasis; 3) although he loathes vice, he displays a marked love of sensationalism; 4) despite his moral concerns, the satirist can take sadistic delight in attacking his victims; 5) sober and rational as he may claim to be, he frequently adopts the most shockingly irrational attitudes."[77] I do not mean to suggest that Luther's language must always be read as the deliberate product of such a carefully constructed literary persona. Some of his statements surely represent the spontaneous expressions of a less self-conscious authorial self. Nonetheless, we are well advised not to take *all* of the contradictory, sarcastic, and overheated things that Luther has to say about so many different subjects, including Rome, as seriously and literally as has sometimes been done.

One reason perhaps that Luther's words *are* so often taken at face value is because Luther himself was so adamant about not having any persona at all. He made it abundantly clear on repeated occasions that he wanted to be understood only as a most earnest and sincere human being, speaking directly from his heart.[78] This is how he taught other human beings to express themselves too. He emphasizes the importance of sincerity in the first stanza of his German chorale version of the Lord's Prayer: "Make us pray not only with our mouths, / but ensure that our prayer comes from the depths of our hearts" (*von hertzen grund*).[79] There is a reason that the image of the monk standing before the emperor at Worms and bravely declaring that he cannot go against his conscience is so iconic. Even at the cost of losing his life, Luther would not say anything in such a setting that was not genuinely true and in accordance with his own deepest, most authentic thoughts. It is not surprising that modern theologians and historians, therefore, have understood all of Luther's language to be very seriously intended indeed. That is exactly what he hoped his audiences would do. We should not forget, however, that the abjuration of rhetorical sophistication is among the oldest and most sophisticated of rhetorical strategies. The declaration that one is speaking frankly and with utter candor without any sort of artifice is an example of what is sometimes called "rhetoric against rhetoric" (*rhetorica contra rhetoricam*).[80] Luther's mask is that he has no mask.

A great deal of art underlies Luther's apparent artlessness. His protestations to the contrary cannot really be taken seriously. In 1518, for instance, he declares of himself to Pope Leo X, "I am unlearned, ignorant by disposition, devoid of education."[81] This was thirteen years *after* he had earned his master of arts degree and six years *after* he was awarded his doctorate. Elsewhere he claims that he does not possess verbal eloquence like Melanchthon and Erasmus; his only talents, he suggests, lie in understanding well the substance that words are used to express: "Philipp has words and substance; Erasmus words without substance; Luther substance without words (*sine verbis*); Karlstadt neither substance nor words."[82] *Sine verbis* is a phrase that in no way can adequately describe the wordy Luther, a veritable *homo verbosatus*,[83] at his time "the most prolific living author since the dawn of printing,"[84] the man who single-handedly turned the European world on its head with his eloquent and persuasive words. His literary productions today occupy over a hundred stout volumes in the Weimar edition of his collected words.

As he regularly represents himself, Luther is a plain-speaking commoner, able to communicate clearly and straightforwardly the simple truth, no matter how hard that truth may be to declare or digest, defending the sincere interests of the German people against the powerful Roman papacy. Contrasting himself with sophisticated urban types, Luther claims to be from peasant heritage (he calls his father and grandfather *rechte Bauern*, or "genuine farmers")[85] and therefore well positioned to help the simple rural people of Germany resist the urban decadence of Rome. More than once he calls Rome "Sodom," the morally bankrupt biblical city that Abraham avoided in order to stay in the countryside with his flocks but that proved to be a fatal attraction for his nephew Lot. The latter's stay in Sodom did not end well (Gen 19:1–25).

Aspects of this persona of Luther's, of course, are based in actual fact and may well reflect genuine feelings on his part, but that does not mean that they are entirely true. In a certain way, whether they are true or not hardly matters, since these are the personal character-istics Luther chose to use as he constructed his public persona over the years. Certainly, this is the "Luther" with whom modern readers are often confronted in the texts that have come down to us under his name. But is this uncompromising, assertive straight talker, famous for his impatience with intellectual wafflers like Erasmus, the real Luther or the only Luther?[86] At the Leipzig Debate in 1519, Petrus Mosellanus found Luther to be "courteous, even cheerful," even if he did criticize "a bit too caustically and aggressively." Luther was wearing a silver ring and holding a flower that he smelled occasion-ally during the proceedings.[87] Mosellanus's Luther comes across as somewhat refined and urbane, certainly not a barbaric lumberjack. In fact, Luther was a child of relatively prosperous parents who could afford to send him to the best schools, a professor and university administrator with a doctorate, a European celebrity who corresponded with kings and emperors and popes, an urbanite, a musician and poet, and above all a talented wordsmith who paid careful attention to how his words would be presented to his reading public.

Perhaps in the end, Luther became something of a prisoner of his own formidable ability with language, a victim of his own rhetorical successes and dominating literary personality. Part of the reason this inveterate hyperbolist was so wildly popular was that he participated fully and even joyously in the heated invective so characteristic of his rhetorically aggressive age.[88] In time, he became a past master of the genre. Luther became so well known for his angry persona, so intimately associated with it, that others grew to expect such language from his pen and could hardly imagine that Luther himself might be something different from his familiar literary persona. As often happens in such instances, Luther had little choice but to become one with his vociferous persona. The "quiet" Luther effectively disappeared.

None of this, of course, is to suggest that the violence of the language of the time in which Luther lived did not reflect the threat of very real physical violence and was nothing more than verbal bullying. Just because we do not take all of Luther's "fierce words" and "hyperbolic outrage" entirely literally does not mean that they cannot still serve "as a sensitive barometer of religious concerns," as Constance Furey puts it in her study of invective in the language of Luther, Erasmus, and More: "Fierce words commonly appear in the midst of religious controversies, and one may choose to skim past this hyperbolic outrage in search of the real message. Insulting rhetoric, however, does provide a sensitive barometer of religious concerns in the sixteenth century and yields unexpectedly complex answers to a simple question. What does negative speech accomplish?"[89]

Luther himself argued "that he poked only with pigs' pokes" (not the sharpest of all possible goads) and that his language was not nearly as bad as that of others.[90] He never physically harmed any of his adversaries, and his harsh reprimand of the papists was no more than what he felt that their wickedness deserved and even required. His verbal scolding was "nothing in comparison to the unspeakable wickedness [of the papists], for what sort of scolding is it when I scold the devil as a murderer, rogue, traitor, blasphemer, and liar?"[91] No matter his stated intentions, however, Luther's words were hardly harmless in their effect, and they certainly ended up inciting and justifying countless acts of aggression and violence in his own lifetime and thereafter.

Theological disputes in the sixteenth century were quite literally matters of life and death. The opposition that Luther himself faced was murderous and real. He was quite sure, and with good reason, that he was himself unlikely to die peacefully in bed. His enemies were hoping to take him "alive and in chains to that homicidal Jerusalem, Rome."[92] In 1519, he wrote, "Rome burns for my destruction, but I am ice cold to their mockery of me. It is said that a Martin made of paper has been burned in public, cursed, and condemned in the Campo de' Fiori. I anticipate their anger."[93] From the *Catalogus haereticorum* of Bernhard of Luxembourg, we learn that Luther was indeed burned in effigy (along with his books) on the Piazza Navona, on June 12, 1521.[94] The statue of Giordano Bruno that stands today in the Campo de' Fiori, where he was burned at the stake in 1600, still reminds visitors to Rome that Luther's fear of a similar grisly fate for himself earlier in the sixteenth century was not at all exaggerated.[95]

Luther fully expected to be burned at the stake because this is what had happened to so many other outspoken critics of the church in the past. He was keenly aware of the fate of another would-be reformer of the church a hundred years or so earlier at the Council of Constance: Jan Hus, the Czech critic of the Roman church. His last name means "goose," and there was a story that just before he died, he turned to his executioners and predicted the coming of a "swan" whom they would not be able to eliminate so easily.[96] Luther spoke and wrote often of Hus and the grisly fate that so easily might have been his own. He was deeply moved by the death of two young

Augustinian followers of his who were burned at the stake in 1523 in Brussels. Luther wrote his first hymn to commemorate their martyrdoms.[97]

Law and Gospel

Regardless of how we adjust our assessment of Luther's "negative speech" against Rome in light of the norms of discourse in his times or in recognition of his satiric persona (or even taking into account his age and ill health or psychological considerations), we must still ask whether there was a positive purpose in the end that his angry words were intended to accomplish.

Even the angriest of satirists (perhaps *especially* the angriest of satirists), when pressed, regularly justify their savage critiques on the grounds that they are only trying in their own way to correct, repair, and improve the society that they are criticizing. Their mocking social commentary and cutting ridicule are to be seen as serving a constructive purpose higher than mere entertainment, an ultimate end that is not purely negative or destructive. "Satire may be mad and anarchic," G. K. Chesterton suggests, but "it presupposes a standard." The absence of satire, therefore, may be of more concern for a society than its presence. Chesterton continues sagely, "And the curious disappearance of satire from our literature is an instance of the fierce things fading for want of any principle to be fierce about."[98]

From a theological perspective, the harsh language Luther uses against papal Rome can be viewed as a severe preachment of the law. The failure of humans to meet God's expectation for holiness as it is revealed in the law results in God's judgment against them. The demands of God's law and the consequences for disobeying it must be so sternly and honestly proclaimed because it is of critical importance for human beings' salvation that they turn away from themselves and their own resources in order to throw themselves upon the mercy of God. Only when sinners have been brought to despair of their own righteousness can the promise of the gospel with its message of forgiveness and comfort be appreciated and appropriated. This is the theological explanation that may best account for the complexity of Luther's relationship with papal Rome, at one and the same time "holy" and the home of "the devil's bishop." If we use the theological dialectic of "law and gospel" to judge the motives of this man who considered himself to be a faithful son of Christ's church, Luther's criticisms of the papacy, no matter how harsh or vehement, can be seen as intended not to harm Rome ultimately but to help it.

To be sure, Luther hated Rome's current condition. "Hatred" is not too strong a word; Luther himself uses it to describe what he considers to be a reformer's ideal attitude toward the pope. When he was forced to leave the deliberations at Schmalkalden early because of illness in 1537, after making the sign of the cross, Luther bade farewell to his followers with the words "May the Lord fill you with his blessing and hatred of the pope."[99] The desire and ability to hate the pope is a divine gift. But however much Luther's rhetoric against papal Rome may have been motivated by hatred, it needs to be distinguished from "hate speech," if by that term we mean negative language meant only to demean or harm a group or class of people.[100] Luther's polemical program against Rome was something more in the way of stern "brotherly admonition," expressed in the colorful and angry language that he felt the drastic problems he was trying to address deserved. After all, if people without God's grace are doomed to hell instead of heaven, how could anyone who truly loves these people be anything less than forceful or even angry when talking about the factors that threaten their eternal bliss? As seen from this perspective, Luther's is not the language of misanthropy but the passionate rhetoric of one who intensely wishes to communicate the love of God to his brothers and sisters in Christ.

Certainly, this is how Luther himself defends his reforming zeal. In an early letter to his elector, he assures Frederick the Wise that he is entirely willing to retract any errors he has made in order not to "weaken the honor and power of the holy Roman church."[101] He assures Pope Leo X in 1519 that "the only thing" he is seeking to do is to keep "the Roman church, our mother, from being polluted by the foulness of alien avarice."[102] In his treatise of 1521 against Latomus, a theologian and professor at the University of Leuven, he testifies that even though to some readers his "shell" (*cortex*) might seem hard, nonetheless, his kernel is "soft and sweet." He wishes to harm no one but hopes "that everyone will confer with [him] as best as they possibly can." Of the beneficent purpose of his harsh language, he adds, "Furthermore, my severity harms no one, just as it deceives no one. Whoever avoids me will suffer nothing at my hands; whoever bears with me will profit. Solomon says in Proverbs 28[:23], 'Whoever rebukes someone will afterward be more appreciated than he who flatters with his tongue.'"[103]

This was also how Luther's defenders explained the motivation of his polemics. After his death in 1546, his mild-mannered colleague Melanchthon tried to account for the harshness of Luther's language in his funeral eulogy: "But some people, not evil, have complained that Luther was more severe than he had to be. I will not argue against that view but respond with what Erasmus often said: 'God gave this latter age a harsh doctor in view of the gravity of our maladies.'" Luther was an ecclesiastical surgeon, according to Melanchthon, operating not with scalpels but with words. Like surgery, this kind of invective is painful, but it is sometimes more efficacious for the purposes of healing than a less drastic medicinal treatment. Melanchthon acknowledges that "it is common for moderate and temperate minds to disapprove of more ardent impulses whether good or evil."[104] No doubt he included himself in the company of "moderate and temperate minds" and Luther among those with "more ardent impulses," but both of them were laboring in the service of the good. The ultimate purpose of the scalpel is not to harm but to heal.

There were others besides Luther himself who used the metaphor of the forester or lumberjack to describe his polemical purpose. Chancellor Gregor Brück, the so-called lawyer of the Reformation, described Luther "as hewing away vigorously with his wooden ax, which he does, by God's grace, with greater spirit than other men."[105]

When it comes to the language of ecclesiastical reform, Luther is a logger who must use a great deal of brute force to bring down recalcitrant trees. Other reformers may perform more delicate pruning operations, but sometimes nothing will do except a drastic clearing out of the forest. Great trees will come crashing down to the forest floor in the process, but ultimately the woods will be easier to tend and healthier if they are thus thinned.

Insofar as Luther's entire mentality may be judged to be more premodern than modern, we would do well to consider Mikhail Bakhtin's distinction between what he calls "the pure satire of modern times," with its laughter that places the satirist "above the object of his mockery," and that of the medieval satirist who knows that he still does belong in some important way to the world at which he is laughing.[106] In many ways, Luther belonged to the Rome that he was mocking, scolding, and reviling, just as it belonged to him. For Protestants in the generations following Luther, most of whom had never even visited Rome, the city and the papacy had become no more than distant symbols of religious evil incarnate, the quintessential "other." By contrast, Luther was intimately acquainted with Rome, the city and the ecclesiastical institution headquartered there against which he so frequently railed. Even more important, he had considered himself to be an actual part of it for much, if not all, of his life. This fact alone could account for the special urgency to Luther's language, the extra degree of bitter resentment that characterizes his polemics, especially when he is compared with other later critics of the church who never had such close ties with Rome as he once had.

Luther's relationship with the Roman church was never just a purely formal arrangement, devoid of real emotional significance. Luther did not simply "join" the Roman church as one might another institution. He was baptized into this church when he was just a day old. He grew up to become a monk, a priest, an ecclesiastical administrator, and a professor in the service of this church, all before his excommunication. As Luther puts it in a sermon preached in 1537, he was "a member of this same body, the Roman church twenty years ago."[107] To be a "member" of "the body of Christ" is traditional terminology, to be sure, but just because it is familiar does not mean it is merely formulaic. The word "member" suggests that the individual is inseparably connected with other members individually and with the body collectively.[108] It is hard to imagine wording that could indicate a closer personal intimacy. For a former church member to become detached from the church body is potentially as painful and detrimental a process as losing a physical limb.

Traditionally, Christians have used the language of love to describe their attachment to God or Jesus or Mary or the church. Luther is still able to describe Rome as "dear Rome" (*liebes Rom*) as late as 1520.[109] And he continues to refer to the holy and apostolic church itself, even if no longer equated with the Roman church, in terms of personal endearment, as, for instance, in his seldom sung hymn of 1535, "A Song of the Holy Christian Church." The first stanza especially is filled with highly emotional terminology: "I hold her dear, the worthy maiden, and can never forget her." Not only has she "possessed my heart," Luther goes on to sing, but "I am entranced of her." Regardless of how many mishaps might befall him, "she will make it up for me with her love and trust in me . . . and fulfill all my desires."[110]

In the last stanza of the chorale, Luther refers to the church no longer as a "maid" but as "mother" (*die Mutter*). Like Augustine and many others before him, Luther had once thought of "the Roman church" as "our mother" (*mater nostra*).[111] The import of the powerful filial metaphor in *mater ecclesia* no doubt had faded considerably over the centuries due to its common use, but it is nonetheless striking. After all, there are few human attachments more powerful and enduring than that of mother and child. When Luther appeals to jurists involved in an excommunication case in 1539 not to "act against the interests of our church," he uses the most simple and powerful familial argument one could imagine: "She is mother."[112] This is the cogent language of love. The intensity of Luther's feelings did not fade even after he came to realize that the city he had for so long associated with his ecclesiastical mother was really a prostitute (*meretrix*).[113]

Years earlier, when he entered the monastery in Erfurt in 1505, Luther was following quite literally Jesus's strongly worded advice about the need for his disciples to love him more than their fathers and mothers (Matt 10:37). In the letter in which he dedicates his *Judgment of Martin Luther on Monastic Vows* (1521) to his father, Luther refers to this New Testament precept.[114] Once he became a monk, Luther's real "family" was no longer his immediate biological family only but the church as well. His ecclesiastical superiors were to be addressed as his "fathers." His fellow Augustinians were, as the word "friar" connotes, his spiritual brothers. (Technically speaking, "friar" is a more accurate designation for Luther's ascetic status than "monk," although he did more than once use the latter term to describe himself.[115]) For years Luther worked hard to be an obedient Catholic, subordinating himself completely to the pope. Looking back at his career in the preface to his collected works in Latin in 1545, Luther says that he was such a "crazy papist" early on, so fanatically "intoxicated" (*ebrius*), that he would have murdered anyone who questioned obeying the pope. Unlike others who merely played around with the idea of being religious and went about fulfilling their spiritual obligations in a fairly casual fashion, Luther claims that he took it all with the utmost seriousness.[116]

In this connection, therefore, the language Luther uses to describe himself vis-à-vis his ecclesiastical superiors may be not only rhetorically conventional but actually significant. He addresses Archbishop Albrecht of Mainz in 1517 as his "father and most illustrious prince," "the pinnacle of your exaltation," and "your highness" while describing himself as "the dregs of humanity" and "mere dust." He signs off as "your unworthy son."[117] Whether this language is meant sincerely or not, it clearly signals an acknowledgment on Luther's part of what was supposed to be a close, familial relationship between the two of them. The language in which Luther refers to himself in his correspondence with Leo X in 1519 is also remarkably humble and filial: "Most blessed father, necessity again compels me, the dregs of humanity and the dust of the earth, to speak to your blessedness and to your great majesty. For which reason may your blessedness deign meanwhile to lend most mercifully those fatherly and truly Christlike ears to this little lamb of yours and listen attentively to this bleating of mine."[118] Even in such a respectful letter as this, there is an element of verbal humor as Luther plays with the imagery of religious shepherding. He takes the faded metaphor literally. Luther is one of the "little sheep" in the flock belonging to the pope, who is the pastor of the entire church. His own words in the letter represent nothing more than his humble "bleating."

The degree of his expressed submissiveness to the pope a year earlier is even more striking. The pope may feel free to do anything he wishes with him, Luther declares, including killing him: "For this reason, most blessed father, I offer myself prostrate at the feet of your blessedness with everything that I am and have. Bring me to life, kill me, call me, recall me, approve me, reprove me, as you please. I acknowledge your voice as the voice of Christ present and speaking in you. If I deserve death, I will not refuse to die. For the earth and its fullness is the Lord's, who is blessed through the ages, Amen, and may he preserve you forever."[119] In 1519, in a letter to Frederick the Wise, Luther humbly declares himself ready to honor the Roman church and to regard it as superior to everything else on earth and in heaven except for God himself and his word.[120] As late as 1520, Luther continues to use deferential language to the pope in the prefatory letter to *On the Freedom of the Christian*.[121] He need not have done so. It was quite possible to ignore customary epistolary etiquette when addressing the pope, as we can see in a letter from Philip the Fair (king of France from 1285 to 1314) to Boniface VIII: "To Boniface, who calls himself pope, little or no greeting. Let your stupendous fatuity know that in temporal matters we are subject to no man."[122]

To be sure, these letters of Luther to the pope were written fairly early on in the career of a man who was a friar and not a king. It is highly unlikely that Luther would ever have written a letter to a later pope with the same degree of deference. Indeed, in the late 1530s, he explicitly acknowledges the dramatic change over time in his attitude toward the pope: "If I now had to defend everything that I said or did years ago, especially at the beginning, I would have to worship the pope."[123] By 1537 at the meeting of the Schmalkaldic League, confessional positions had hardened to such an extent that Luther found no way at all in which it would now be possible to consider the pope as "the church's head even by human ordinance."[124]

But these firm antipapal convictions did not develop suddenly. Luther could still declare as late as 1528, seven years after his excommunication, "If the pope and all of them would only grant that they will not force us to teach anything or live contrary to God's word, we would gladly and willingly accept and follow everything that they require of us or they command."[125] Even in the 1530s, Luther was still expressing his personal willingness to submit to the authority of the pope, to kneel before him to kiss his feet, if the church could be corrected along the lines he was demanding. In his commentary on Galatians, he writes, "Pope, I am willing to kiss your feet and to recognize you as the highest pontiff if you will adore my Christ and allow us to have the forgiveness of sins and eternal life through his death and resurrection and not through the observation of your traditions. If you yield on this point, I will not take away your crown and your power."[126]

For Luther, the central problems facing the church of his day did not revolve around the issue of worldly power. His appeals for ecclesiastical reform did not arise primarily from an inherent dislike of hierarchy on his part. He had no principled "Protestant" reservations that would prevent him from contemplating kissing the pope's feet. Indeed, proper church governance, with a structured hierarchical authority, was absolutely necessary to his mind, if proper order was to be preserved in the new churches. What needed so urgently to be corrected was not the church's governance system per se but rather fundamental theological deficiencies, especially those having to do with repentance and the forgiveness of sins and the relationship between works and faith. It was the failure to appreciate the doctrine of justification by faith, not its administrative structures, that the mature Luther believed lay at the heart of the institution's current malaise.

As far as worship was concerned, Luther was more interested in an internal reformation in people's minds and hearts than in any specific reconstitution of the traditional liturgy. The forms of worship as they took place in some of the "Lutheran" churches that began to be established later in Luther's life would not have struck most observers as so very different from those of "the old believers." This is not surprising, especially given Luther's understanding of Christ's real presence in the Eucharist. In the end, the contours of the worship service followed in Wittenberg had changed so very little from that of the traditional Roman Mass and the liturgical year that it was hard "for a visitor from the Romance lands" in 1541 to "notice that he was not in a Catholic church."[127]

The reason that Luther was so angry and disappointed with Rome was precisely because he had once thought of it as *his* "holy" place.[128] What could possibly ever replace it in his mind? He loved the Roman church. In 1518, he contrasts his own loving fidelity to an impure church with the schismatic heretics who simply run away from it and seek purity apart from it: "Alas, we recognize our dilemma and we grieve, but we do not flee like the heretics and pass by the half-dead man as though we feared being contaminated by someone else's sins. . . . But the more miserably the church struggles, the more faithfully we assist it and run to help it by crying, praying, warning, and pleading. For love commands one to bear the burdens of another."[129] We should not discount the seriousness with which the young Luther took the obligations of love that bound him to the Roman church. To illustrate his own attitude toward his struggling church, he refers to the parable of the good Samaritan (Luke 10:30), one man who assists another for no other reason than love. Luther is helping Rome because love commands us to do so.

Far from being a "renegade," as a recent biographer describes him, someone who willfully rejects his obligations and allegiances, Luther did not forsake his monastic vocation or leave the Roman church and the Holy Roman Empire of his own volition.[130] In a letter to Spalatin written in 1519, he declares that he never "wished to be cut off from the Roman Apostolic see. In the end, I am content that it should be called (or even be) the lord of all. What is that to me?"[131] In 1532, he is still insistent that it was not he but duly appointed officials who had cut their mutual ties: "I was excommunicated three times, first by Dr. Staupitz, . . . secondly by the pope himself, and thirdly by Caesar himself. Therefore, I cannot be accused of putting aside my habit."[132] The use of the passive voice (*excommunicatus*; *absolutus*) is striking in this context. Veit Dietrich, Luther's amanuensis, relates that he saw a similar statement written in Luther's own hand: "In 1518, Doctor Staupitz released me from obedience to the order and left me to God. In 1519, Pope Leo excommunicated me from his church, and thus I was released from a second order. In 1521, Caesar Charles banned me from imperial territories, and thus I was released for a third time. As the Psalm says, 'But the Lord has taken me up.'"[133]

It was not Luther but those superior to him and with the authority to do so who had released him from his vows and removed him from the institutions to which he formerly belonged. Luther emphasizes the titles of those involved: "Doctor," "Pope," and "Caesar." He is the object of their executive actions. In this connection, Luther derives comfort from Psalm 27:10: "When my father and my mother forsake me, then the Lord will take me up." What could be more emotionally devastating for any child than to be abandoned by both parents? The sense of loss may well have been extremely distressing for this erstwhile "true believer."[134] At first, as Luther recalls his religious development, he had "believed everything" he was told by his church,[135] but as the years went by, he became increasingly removed if not alienated from what had once been his most intimate religious affiliations. He had expected a paternal blessing from Rome for all of his efforts to aid in its reformation but received "lightning and thunder" instead.[136] While Luther may not have immediately felt the deprivation or ever fully acknowledged it, we may not simply assume that it would not have had a traumatizing effect over time on a sensitive soul like his.

Luther's God himself is a lover and a hater. He, too, has more than one persona, as it were, and the shining face that he lifts upward to bestow his graciousness and peace upon humanity (cf. Num 6:24–26) is not always clearly visible. He hates the wicked (see, e.g., Ps 5:5 and Hos 9:15) and punishes sinners often and severely (see, e.g., Exod 22:20 and Isa 51:17). He wreaks divine havoc on heathen cities such as Sodom or Babylon, and he does not spare even his own beloved Jerusalem when his wrath is deserved. According to Luther, neither Rome nor Germany will be immune from his angry judgment: "The text [Matt 3:12] says, 'He will burn it with an unquenchable fire.' This is what he did with Rome too. . . . And thus he will deal also with Germany. He will take up the pious and after that make an end of the land of Germany, for it has well deserved the punishment in the past and still has not ceased to do so."[137]

But in the final analysis, according to Luther, such destructive activity (or its threat) is not God's only work or even his real work but his "alien" work: "He who sees God as angry does not see him aright but looks upon him as through a curtain or blanket, yes, as if a dark cloud had been drawn over his face."[138] God hides *sub contrario*—that is to say, "under the sign of his opposite."[139] One of the characters in Graham Greene's novel *The Honorary Consul* makes a similar point about how God is to be viewed, using similar language: "The God I believe in must be responsible for all the evil as well as for all the saints. He has to be a God made in our image with a night side as well as a day side."[140] Only when one views God as his crucified son does one see his "day side," the true "face of the Father" (*facies patris*).[141] God is not only justice but mercy.

Christ himself could be seen from two very different perspectives. In a Christmas sermon of 1540, Luther says that he had not really known "the little boy Christ" (*puellum Christum*) while he was in the monastery.[142] He had seen him only as the divine judge who would return in glory at the right hand of the Father to judge the living and the dead, not as the vulnerable Christ child, "playing in the lap and at the breast of his most gracious mother."[143] Christ is not only "true God" but also "true man," who became incarnate not in order to condemn lost sinners but to redeem them "from death and from the power of the devil" so that they might become Christ's "own," living with him in his kingdom and serving him "in everlasting righteousness, innocence and blessedness." This, Luther concludes in his explanation of the second article in his *Small Catechism*, "is most certainly true."[144] Here is the simple and clear declaration of the gospel articulated by the man who was described as the sweet-singing "nightingale of Wittenberg" in a 1523 poem by Hans Sachs. Both during his own life and for centuries thereafter, Luther was known by his devoted followers not only as the author of harsh pronouncements and scatological invective aimed at Rome but also as the winsome proclaimer of the gospel of the forgiveness of sins, a fifth evangelist.

God's hatred of sin, his punishment of those who violate his holy commandments, and his fierce anger against those who rebel against him have a positive purpose. So, too, does his holy law. In addition to providing guidelines for Christian living and curbing public crime, the law serves to accuse and condemn and punish sinners in order to drive them to despair of their own righteousness. It always does this. "The law always accuses" (*Lex semper accusat*).[145] Only then does the gospel "enter in" with its welcome declaration of a loving God's forgiveness, blessedness here on earth, and eternal life hereafter, as expressed in one of the stanzas of the most doctrinal of the early Lutheran chorales, "Salvation unto Us Has Come" (written by Paul Speratus and included in the first Lutheran hymnal, the *Achtliederbuch* of 1524): "The Law reveals the guilt of sin / And makes men conscience-stricken; / The Gospel then doth enter in / The sinful soul to quicken. / Come to the cross, trust Christ, and live; / The Law no peace can ever give, / No comfort and no blessing."[146] The negative in such a context never stands alone. It is a means, not an end. Divine hatred operates only in the service of divine love. This is how Luther puts it in his commentary on Isaiah 28:21:

> This allegorical operation of God is depicted beauti-
> fully in Isaiah 28: "That he may do his work—his work

is strange—and that he may work his work—his work is alien." It is as if he were saying that even though he is the God of life and salvation, and these are his proper works, nonetheless in order to make them effective, he kills and destroys, which are alien works for him, in order to get through to his proper work. For he kills our will so that his own may be established in us. He mortifies our flesh and its desires so that the spirit and its desires may come to life.[147]

As seen in this light, Luther's hatred of the Roman papacy, even as expressed in the most vehement of terms, is akin, *mutatis mutandis*, to God's "alien" work. The ultimate aim of all of these apparently destructive threats is to bring about not enmity to God but true repentance, that key theological principle of Luther's Reformation, the subject of the first of his Ninety-Five Theses, and the "principle" reason that he went to Rome in the first place.

Luther uses the same kind of dialectic terminology when he describes the failure of the Roman church to understand the purpose of his own reform efforts. They complain that Luther is an "alien" who has set himself up in opposition to the Roman church when, as he sees it, he "is cherishing in the purest way possible not only Rome but the whole church of Christ."[148] Luther is doing God's "alien" work in judging Rome. He is the preacher of the law, and if Rome listens to him, it will be saved by the gospel. Theologically speaking, therefore, Luther aims to do much more than serve as an Erasmian satirist, the wry critic of society and its foibles.[149] Luther is not only a satirist but a passionate and unwavering biblical prophet who is speaking on behalf of God and at his behest as he issues his condemnatory proclamations and promises of comfort and redemption in the most absolute of terms.

For many of his followers, including Melanchthon, Luther was indeed a prophet, a latter-day Elijah.[150] He continued to be regarded as a prophet by his followers long after his death.[151] Luther refers to himself, only half-teasingly, as "the prophet of the Germans" in

Warning to His Dear Germans (1531).[152] Being a prophet means that he has no choice but to speak for his divine master and to say only what he is commanded to say. At the end of *To the Christian Nobility of the German Nation* (1520), Luther tells his readers that he is "compelled" by God to continue speaking out against his enemies. He would rather face the wrath of the world, even risk his life, than incur the wrath of God by not speaking out. Whether he wishes to or not, he has no choice but to serve as God's prophet against Rome: "But as I see it, God has compelled me through them [my adversaries] to open my mouth ever wider."[153]

Luther was deeply immersed in the thought and language of the Old Testament prophets, whose works he translated in the years preceding the publication of the complete Bible in German (1534) and whose works he also taught in his capacity as professor at the University of Wittenberg. These prophets were surely his models in this regard. In one of the *Tischreden* of 1539, Luther explicitly identifies his own mournful witness against the "once holiest" of cities, Rome, with that of the prophet Isaiah, who warned Jerusalem, his beloved city, of its imminent demise: "The same thing is happening to us as to the prophets who lamented in a similar way [cf. Isa 1:21]: 'The faithful city has become a harlot.'"[154] Jerusalem was taken by the Babylonians in 587 or 586 BCE and utterly destroyed.

More than once Luther refers to Rome as Babylon, the great hostile empire that figures so often in the warnings and denunciations of the prophets of the Old Testament.[155] With its great walls and efficient army and its murderous intent against God's chosen people, even centuries later Babylon was understood by early Christians to be a type of Rome. Many biblical scholars have taken the cryptic names assigned to the great whore in Revelation 17:5 ("Babylon the Great, the Mother of Harlots and Abominations of the Earth") as meant to refer to Rome. In his 1523 exegesis of the First Epistle of Peter, Luther explains that the greeting from "the church that is at Babylon" (1 Pet 5:13) could be understood as a reference to the city of Rome.[156] Whether Babylon or Rome, such a powerful, godless city represented a serious threat to the pure religion of the beleaguered first-century Christians contemporary with Peter as well as to the pious Germans of Luther's day and deserved to be denounced with prophetic zeal.

If Luther's language could be seen as harsh and offensive, so also could that of the divinely inspired prophets: "If every form of rebuke (*increpatio*) is a slander (*convitium*), then nobody is more guilty (*criminantior*) of slander than the prophets."[157] God's word, as delivered by the prophet Jeremiah, is as intense "as fire" and as powerful as the "hammer that breaketh the rock in pieces" (Jer 23:29). Of Psalm 2:9 ("Thou shalt break them with a rod of iron"), Luther observes that this sort of expression "does not belong to Cicero or Virgil" but is rather the language of "lightning and thunder."[158]

Luther's rhetorical model in this regard would have been not only the Old Testament prophets but also the Jesus of the canonical Gospels. Luther's stern prophetic language of judgment, his own verbal thunder and lightning against Rome, has plenty of precedent in the New Testament as well as the Old. Jesus was capable of pronouncing thundering "woes" against his religious adversaries even as he was graciously delineating the "blessings" that would accrue to his followers (Luke 6:17–49). At the end of the world, according to one of his parables (Matt 13:50), the wicked will be cast into a "furnace of fire," where there will be "wailing and gnashing of teeth." But Jesus also wept over the city that was known for killing prophets like himself even as he expressed his deep desire to gather Jerusalem's children to himself as tenderly as a hen covers her chicks with her wings (Luke 19:41 and Matt 23:37).

Luther's Last Words

As we have seen, Luther's profound disillusionment and disappointment with Rome did not begin all at once.[159] Early on, he really did believe that things might change for the better in the Roman church, thanks to his own reforming efforts and those of others. After the death of Julius II in 1513, the ascendancy of the humanist Leo X, a

Medici, to the papal throne had inspired hope among many that much-needed changes in Rome would now actually begin to happen. Venus and Mars, the pagan deities who might be thought to have inspired the licentious Borgia pope Alexander VI and the warrior pope Julius II, respectively, had now been replaced by Minerva, the goddess of wisdom.[160] There was good reason during these early years for Luther to hope that Leo might respond favorably to him. After all, there had been successful reform movements in the church before, such as the rise of the Franciscan order in the thirteenth century. There is no reason to doubt Luther when he says in 1545 that the reason he wrote so critically about the abuse of indulgences in the first place was to honor Leo X, not simply to annoy or provoke him.[161]

By the end of his life, however, Luther had grown far less optimistic about the possibility of the conversion of Rome. His language directed against the Roman papacy became almost entirely condemnatory, even abusive, and his humor turned more sardonic and bitter. In 1531, a far from hopeful Luther declares his commitment to continue inveighing against the obdurate papists "all the way to [his] grave":

> For longer than ten years, I have often humbled myself and have used the very best language, but the result is that the longer I have done so, the worse they have become. . . . But now, since they are hardened and have decided to do nothing but evil and no good at all, there is no hope for them, and from now on I will curse and scold these scoundrels all the way to my grave, and no good word shall be heard from me. I will thus ring them all the way to the grave with my thunder and lightning.[162]

Whether he is railing against Rome, or German peasants, or Jews, or Turks, if there is one consistent motivation for Luther's harshest invective, it is his conviction that hearts have been unalterably "hardened" and that the gospel is being deliberately ignored or actively subverted.[163] The gradual dashing of his hopes for the conversion of the Jews to the gospel helps explain why he can speak of them with a certain degree of generosity and optimism earlier in life, reminding his readers that Jesus himself was Jewish in his 1523 treatise *That Jesus Christ Was Born a Jew* only to turn around twenty years later and pen such vitriol against them as he does in *On the Jews and Their Lies.*

Nothing else that he wrote earlier in life against Rome can match the angry intensity of "the most bitter of Luther's polemic writings,"[164] *Against the Papacy in Rome, Founded by the Devil*, published in 1545, the year the Council of Trent was scheduled to convene and less than a year before he died. Did the aging Luther forget that this and all of his other polemical writing against Rome represented God's "alien" work? Did he lose the last glimmer of hope that his efforts to change the church's teaching might have some positive effect on Rome, all appearances to the contrary? Would the late Luther have recognized himself in the figure of the disgruntled prophet Jonah, whom he had described years earlier (1526) as "a strange and unusual saint, who is angry when God is merciful to sinners"?[165] Jonah lost sight of the goal of his preachment of the law to Nineveh—namely, that the fear of God's judgment upon their city would drive its inhabitants to repentance and salvation. Instead of rejoicing when the citizens of Nineveh actually did repent and were not destroyed, Jonah grows angry and pouts. He complains that God is always so "gracious" and "merciful" and resents the fact that he is "slow to anger, and of great kindness" (Jonah 4:2). God has to remind Jonah with a vivid object lesson (the gourd that shades him from the sun's rays is withered) that the ultimate purpose of the preaching of divine judgment is not a negative but a positive one. The whole point of the prophetic exercise was for God to "spare Nineveh, that great city, wherein are more than sixscore thousand persons that cannot discern between their right hand and their left hand; and also much cattle" (Jonah 4:11). Of course, Nineveh *had* repented, and Rome, from Luther's frustrated perspective, had *not.*

One of Luther's most insistent critics, Duke George, questioned Luther's stated positive intentions for his polemics and suggested that if he were "a real preacher of the gospel," he would not spend so much time in "reviling, slandering, cursing, and scolding" (*schenden, lestern, fluchen, schelden*). Rather, the duke continues, "he would chastise the transgressions and misdeeds of those who oppose him in all patience and gentleness, seeking not their destruction but rather their improvement."[166] Especially in his later years, as Erikson observes, "Luther displayed an extraordinary ability to hate quickly and persistently, justifiably and unjustifiably, with pungent dignity and with utter vulgarity."[167] There is not nearly as much evidence of "love" as "hate" in Luther's later writings for those who set themselves in opposition to his prophetic proclamations. This is certainly the case if, like Duke George, we associate love exclusively with gentler emotions such as "patience and gentleness."

Of course, what mattered ultimately from the perspective of the theology of the mature Luther was not the extent or quality of his own love (or lack thereof) toward God and others but the reality of God's love for the entire world. This is the "proper" work of the God who is simply defined in the First Epistle of John (4:8–10) as "love." It is this divine love that is bestowed upon Luther and other believers purely as a result of God's own goodness and mercy and not because of "merits or any worthiness" on the part of humans, as Luther puts it in his explanation of the first article of the Apostles' Creed in his *Small Catechism*.[168] This is the gift of divine *caritas* that Luther had been trying to communicate as a preacher of the word and prophet of the gospel to his church and others beyond it for years.[169]

Even if later on Luther himself grew far less hopeful and increasingly impatient when it became clear to him that his message was being rejected, he still continued to appreciate God's patience. In 1536, he told a story about a Jewish convert to Christianity who visited Rome before his baptism. Far from being revolted by the horrible things he saw in the city, he returned fully committed to worshipping the Christian God because, as he said, if God was patient enough to put up with the folly of Rome, he would easily be able to bear all the wickedness of the world.[170]

At least at the very end of his life, if not before, Luther may have realized that his own work as an interpreter and communicator of God's word had been anything but perfect or complete. Just a few days before his death in Eisleben on February 18, 1546, he wrote,

> No one is able to understand Virgil in his *Bucolics* and *Georgics* who has not first been a shepherd or a farmer for five years. No one understands Cicero in his epistles in the second place who has not been involved in the affairs of some important republic for twenty years. Let no one who has not governed the churches with the prophets for a hundred years think that he has tasted enough of the Holy Scriptures. This is why the miracle of John the Baptist first of all, but secondly of Christ, and thirdly of the apostles, is so great. "Do not challenge this divine *Aeneid*, but rather worship prostrate at its feet." We are beggars. This is true.[171]

If these are indeed Luther's final written words (in Latin except for three words), it is tempting to ascribe them special significance and to give them special weight. Last words often become momentous, whether they were originally intended to be or not. Let us start by noting what Luther does not say. He makes no mention of his wife and children, whom he loved so deeply. Nor does he refer to any of his close friends and colleagues, like Melanchthon or Bugenhagen. He says not a word about the monumental ecclesiastical struggles or the provincial politics that had consumed so much of his time throughout his life. Nor does he say anything as simple and affirmative as the clear *Ja* he is supposed to have uttered (his final spoken word) when asked by Justus Jonas at his bedside whether he continued to uphold the theological truths for which he had fought so hard during the course of his life.[172]

No, at the end of his life, at least to judge from these written observations, Luther was concentrating his attention on the ancient Romans, the "most powerful and wisest" of all peoples,[173] and the city whose ruined remains he had visited so many years before. As he prepared to die, Luther was thinking of Virgil, the Roman poet from whom he had learned how to write his famous chorales, and Cicero, the Roman philosopher and rhetor whom he loved and wished could be in heaven with him. Luther even quotes a passage from the Latin poet Statius (*Thebaid* 12.816–17), who modestly advised his own poem not to challenge the *Aeneid*,[174] as he tries to find words adequate to express his own deep admiration of the Scriptures and his sense of personal failure to have done full justice to them despite all of his diligent study.[175]

There is no criticism here of ancient Roman paganism, no biting references to the Roman pope or the curia, just an admission of his own humble beggarliness in his vocation as a *Doctor in Biblia*. Professor Luther had tried in his own limited way—not for a hundred years but for some decades—to understand the Bible. What is on Luther's mind at the end of his life is Scripture, the only authority that could ever replace Rome, whose powerful claim to ultimate authority may be discerned in the phrase often attributed to Augustine: "Rome has spoken; the case is finished."[176] At the end of these observations, Luther lays himself metaphorically prostrate (*pronus*) before this "divine *Aeneid*," just as once long before he had literally thrown himself to the ground (*in terram prostratus*) at the sight of the city of Rome.

Scripture, and Scripture alone, had become the matrix for all of Luther's beliefs, the fundament for his hopes for this world and the next, the sole basis for his life's work and its validity. Previously the Roman church may have been his mother and the pope his father, but now Paul's letter to the Galatians was his intimate "betrothed," his Katie von Bora.[177] If no other city could replace Rome in Luther's mind, Paul's letter to the Romans could. In one of his *Tischreden*, he uses a spatial metaphor to describe the Bible itself as though it were a physical place, declaring, "The Scripture is a very large forest, but there is not a single tree which I have not shaken with my hand."[178] Rather than taking pilgrimages to Rome, according to this new Lutheran sensibility, everyone would be better served spiritually by strolling through the pages of the Bible. Whether they were expert theologians who taught the ancient languages or university students who studied the Bible in the original or schoolgirls who had learned to read the Bible in translation, "Lutherans" had a new, inexhaustible, holy place that they could visit with all due reverence and from which they could draw endless sustenance for their faith life—not a city but a book, the book of books: "We do not allow ourselves to be concerned about how big and holy Jerusalem is or how lofty and powerful Rome is. We seek neither Jerusalem nor Rome but Christ the king in his Scriptures."[179]

If Luther's last written statement speaks to his own sense of inadequacy at the end of his career as a preacher and professor of the Bible, his very last six words, "We are beggars. This is true" (*Wir sein Pettler. Hoc est verum*), may hark back to the time he spent in Erfurt as a mendicant monk in earlier years. The Augustinians were known for their practice of rigorous collective poverty. Indeed, the question of how seriously Luther's order was supposed to pursue ascetic principles, as we have seen, was quite possibly behind the observant Augustinian's trip to Rome in the first place. Luther's later excoriation of monks and monasticism should not make us forget that he was once deeply impressed by strict ascetic practice. As a young schoolboy in Magdeburg, Luther had been struck by the sight of the emaciated prince of Anhalt, wearing a skullcap, bent over with a heavy pack on his back, begging for bread. Luther observes many years later that those who saw him "could not help being ashamed of their own worldly condition."[180]

In this context, the expression "we are beggars" sounds like something more than an expression of false modesty. Throughout his life, Luther had indeed used a lot of self-deprecation, not always in full earnestness, but in these, the final moments of his life, he was doubtless feeling more serious about everything as he came to final grips with his own mortal limitations. When he penned these last lines, he may have been feeling not so very different from those "mouse droppings" or that "maggot-sack" to which he had likened himself earlier in life.[181] Why otherwise would he add the final sentence "This is true" (*Hoc est verum*)? It is as though he is echoing the familiar phraseology that serves as the emphatic summary of each of the three articles of the Apostles' Creed in the *Small Catechism*: "This is most certainly true" (*Hoc certissime verum est*).

Counterintuitive as it might seem to modern sensibilities, Luther's last words describing himself and others as "beggars" would not have had entirely pejorative connotations for many of his followers who read this note. In the Gospel of Mark (10:17–31), Jesus recommends that the rich young ruler give up everything he has in order to follow him if he wishes to "inherit eternal life." Jesus describes himself as homeless. He has less in the way of housing security than foxes and birds, who at least have dens and nests in which to live (Matt 8:20). But this apparent lack is actually a blessing. In Jesus's "Beatitudes" in the sixth chapter of Luke, it is the hungry who will be filled. As the Magnificat so memorably explicated by Luther in 1521 puts it, "He hath filled the hungry with good things; and the rich he hath sent empty away" (Luke 1:53).[182] The beggar's sack can only be filled if it is first empty. In his final words, Luther may be suggesting that it is only when humans recognize their own inability to master the sacred Scriptures that they may begin to be mastered by them and thus appropriate them aright.

The use of the first-person plural in the statement "*we* are beggars" may be as significant in this context as it was in Luther's earlier Latin poem about "our" Rome. There is something catholic about the sweeping inclusiveness of the pronoun here. It takes in potentially all of humanity. Luther could have employed the singular if he had meant the reference to apply only to himself. Surely, he would have used the second person pronoun if he had intended to criticize others. It is possible that at the very end of his life, Luther meant to include not only himself and his adherents in the first-person plural "we" but also those whom he had so often identified as "you" in earlier days: the ancient pagan Romans, the marauding peasants, the Jews, the Anabaptists, the Turks, and of course, *his* Roman papists.

Luther's last six words suggest that all of humanity as a collective whole must be judged as woefully deficient (along with himself) in the presence of God and his profoundly significant word.

At the same time, however, when sinful humans confess that they are nothing more than beggars and can do nothing themselves to earn their own salvation, they are then (and only then) in a position to be given the righteousness of God. Hence the familiar phrase "at one and the same time sinner and saint" (*simul peccator et iustus*).[183] As Luther puts it in his lectures on Genesis, "For this is the rule: cross and affliction always precede comfort. For God comforts only those who are sad, just as he brings to life only those who are dead and justifies only those who are sinners."[184] As beggars, then, "we" are ourselves at one and the same time as "lacerated" and yet also as "holy" as the city that lay in the distance before the young Augustinian mendicant when he stretched himself prostrate on the ground and saluted the Rome that he would love and hate for the rest of his life.

Abbreviations

Brecht — Brecht, Martin. *Martin Luther.* Vol. 1, *His Road to Reformation, 1483–1521*; vol. 2, *Shaping and Defining the Reformation, 1521–1532*; and vol. 3, *The Preservation of the Church, 1532–1546.* Translated by James L. Schaaf. Minneapolis: Fortress, 1985–99.

CR — *Corpus Reformatorum. Philippi Melanthonis Opera Quae Supersunt Omnia.* Edited by Karl Gottlieb Bretschneider and Heinrich Ernst Bindsell. Volumes 1–28. Halle: Schwetschke, 1834–60.

Enchiridion — *Enchiridion. Catechismus minor D. Martini Lutheri pro parochis et concionatoribus. Die Bekenntnisschriften der evangelisch-lutherischen Kirchen.* 10th ed. Göttingen: Vandenhoeck & Ruprecht, 1986.

LW — *Luther's Works: American Edition.* Edited by Jaroslav Pelikan and Helmut Lehmann. 55 volumes. St. Louis: Concordia, 1955–86.

MGH — *Monumenta Germaniae historica.* Edited by G. H. Pertz et al. Hanover, 1826–.

MLiR — Matheus, Michael, Arnold Nesselrath, and Martin Wallraff, eds. *Martin Luther in Rom. Die Ewige Stadt als kosmopolitisches Zentrum und ihre Wahrnehmung.* Berlin: De Gruyter, 2017.

Oberman — Oberman, Heiko. *Luther: Man between God and the Devil.* Translated by Eileen Walliser-Schwarzbart. New Haven, CT: Yale University Press, 1989.

PL — *Patrologia Latina.* Edited by Jacques-Paul Migne. Paris, 1841–55.

WA   *D. Martin Luthers Werke. Kritische Gesamtausgabe.*
        Weimar: Böhlau, 1883–2009.

WAB   *D. Martin Luthers Werke. Kritische Gesamtausgabe,*
        Briefwechsel. Weimar: Böhlau, 1930–78.

WADB   *D. Martin Luthers Werke. Kritische Gesamtausgabe, Die*
        deutsche Bibel. Weimar: Böhlau, 1906–91.

WAT   *D. Martin Luthers Werke. Kritische Gesamtausgabe,*
        Tischreden. Vol. 1, *Tischreden aus der ersten Hälfte*
        der dreissiger Jahre; vol. 2, *Tischreden aus den dreissiger*
        Jahren; vol. 3, *Tischreden aus den dreissiger Jahren*; vol. 4,
        Tischreden aus den Jahren 1538–1540; vol. 5, *Tischreden*
        aus den Jahren 1540–1544; and vol. 6, *Tischreden aus*
        verschiedenen Jahren. Weimar: Böhlau, 1912–21.

Notes

Prolegomena

1. Nathaniel Hawthorne, *The Scarlet Letter: A Romance* (Boston: James R. Osgood, 1871), 303.

2. Lucien Febvre, *Martin Luther: Un Destin* (Paris: Presses Universitaires de France, 1928), 22. Here and elsewhere, translations are my own, unless indicated otherwise. Andrew Wilson includes this passage at the beginning of his engaging account of his own recent pilgrimage to Rome, *Here I Walk: A Thousand Miles on Foot to Rome with Martin Luther* (Grand Rapids: Brazos, 2016), 2–3.

3. Jim Holt, *Why Does the World Exist? An Existential Detective Story* (New York: Liveright, 2012), 78.

4. Hans Hillerbrand, "Martin Luther and the Bull *Exsurge Domine*," *Theological Studies* 30 (1969): 108–12.

5. WA 40.3,94. This and subsequent notes provide references to the Latin and German texts in the *Weimarer Ausgabe* that serve as the basis for my translations of Luther throughout the book.

6. WAT 5,317–18,#5677. See a full discussion at the end of chapter 4.

7. In an interview with Alvin Sanoff, "One Must Not Forget," *US News and World Report*, October 27, 1986, 68.

8. WAT 4,501,#4784.

9. Stephen Paulson, *Luther's Outlaw God*, vol. 2 (Minneapolis: Fortress, 2019), 289. On the importance of paradox in early Christian thought, see Philip Hardie, *Classicism and Christianity in Late Antique Latin Poetry* (Oakland: University of California Press, 2019), 163–87.

10. See Erik Erikson, *Young Man Luther: A Study in Psychoanalysis and History* (New York: Norton, 1962). Harry Haile expresses the dilemma facing biographers of Luther in the first pages of *Luther: An Experiment in*

Biography (New York: Doubleday, 1980). He confines himself to presenting "no more than the character of the man in his later years" (2). Other biographers have focused on the young Luther. Such compartmentalization is understandable. In this study, of necessity, we must reckon with both Luthers, the young man who visited Rome and the older man who talked and wrote about his experiences there later in life.

11. LW 22,xi.

12. WA 40.2,593.

13. Oberman is open to possible insights into Luther's identity that can be offered by psychology: "Evidence that would enable us to answer all such questions is extremely scarce; but for that very reason, no helping hands may be disregarded—and all suspicions against psychohistory must be put aside" (82).

14. See Shane Butler, ed., *Deep Classics: Rethinking Classical Reception* (London: Bloomsbury Academic, 2016), 1–19.

15. Patrick Baker, Johannes Helmrath, and Craig Kallendorf, eds., *Beyond Reception: Renaissance Humanism and the Transformation of Classical Antiquity* (Berlin: De Gruyter, 2019), 4. There is now (since 2009) an international journal devoted to the subject, *Classical Receptions Journal*.

16. For a comparative analysis of the ways in which Luther and his contemporary Rabelais used scatology, see David Bagchi, "The German Rabelais? Foul Words and the Word in Luther," *Reformation and Renaissance Review* 7 (2005): 143–62.

17. See, for example, the essays collected in Ray Laurence and David Newsome, eds., *Rome, Ostia, Pompeii: Movement and Space* (Oxford: Oxford University Press, 2011).

18. On the function and importance of religious spaces, see the introductory observations in John Corrigan, ed., *Religion, Space, and the Atlantic World* (Columbia: University of South Carolina Press, 2017), 1–21; and Elizabeth Lewis Pardoe, "Confessional Spaces and Religious Places: Lutherans in America, 1698–1748," in the same volume, 246–66.

19. On this persistent topos, see Ernst Robert Curtius, *European Literature and the Latin Middle Ages*, trans. Willard R. Trask (Princeton, NJ: Princeton University Press, 1953), 157–58.

20. WAT 2,284,#1971.

21. See the first five books of Livy's *Ab urbe condita* for the history of the city from its foundation to its capture by the Gauls.

22. WA 19,589.

23. As quoted in James Salvo, *Reading Autoethnography: Reflections on Justice and Love* (New York: Routledge, 2020), 39.

24. As quoted in Charles Swann, *Nathaniel Hawthorne: Tradition and Revolution* (Cambridge: Cambridge University Press, 1991), 199.

25. Rose Macaulay, *Pleasure of Ruins* (London: Thames & Hudson, 1953), 171.

26. Nathaniel Hawthorne, *The Marble Faun: or, the Romance of Monte Beni* (Boston: Houghton Mifflin, 1891), 442.

27. See Andrew Gallia, "'Some of My Best Friends . . .': Reading Prejudice in Juvenal's Third Satire," *Classical Journal* 111 (2015/2016): 319–46.

28. See also Barbie Latza Nadeau, "Rome's Sad Decline Sums up Italy's Problems," CNN, March 4, 2018, https://tinyurl.com/romes-sad-decline.

29. On the use and abuse of Tacitus's *Germania* through the ages, see Christopher Krebs, *A Most Dangerous Book: Tacitus's* Germania *from the Roman Empire to the Third Reich* (New York: Norton, 2011).

30. "The Autobiographical Animal" was the title of Jacques Derrida's address in 1997 at the *Colloques de Cerisy* in Normandy.

31. Adam Kirsch, "The Empire Strikes Back: Rome and Us," *New Yorker*, January 9, 2012, 68.

32. Anthony Burgess's candid but affectionate 1978 video about Rome includes comments on the city's pungent odors; see Anthony Burgess, *Anthony Burgess's Rome* (New York: Learning Corp. of America, 1978), https://tinyurl.com/anthonyburgessrome.

33. As quoted in Heinrich Böhmer, *Luthers Romfahrt* (Leipzig: Deichert, 1914), 1.

34. Hawthorne, *Marble Faun*, 372–73.

35. As quoted in Susan Cahill, *The Smiles of Rome: A Literary Companion for Readers and Travelers* (New York: Ballantine, 2005), xx.

Chapter One

1. WAT 3,349,#3479a.

2. For the importance of "emplotment" in the writing of history, see Hayden White, *Metahistory: The Historical Imagination in Nineteenth-Century Europe* (Baltimore: Johns Hopkins University Press, 1973). The novelist E. M. Forster distinguished between "story" and "plot," suggesting that causality is essential to plot, whereas a story is simply a narrative that concentrates on temporal sequence: "'The king died and then the queen died' is a story. But 'the king died and then the queen died of grief' is a plot. The time-sequence is preserved, but the sense of causality overshadows it" (as quoted by Alan Palmer, *Fictional Minds* [Lincoln: University of Nebraska Press, 2004], 180). In this chapter, as the reader will discover, both sequence and causality will be important and not easily untangled considerations.

3. For a recent historical novel devoted to the subject, see Michael Thompson, *To Rome and Back with Martin Luther: The Pilgrimage That Would Ultimately Lead to the Protestant Reformation* (Kingwood, TX: Charis, 2010). The subtitle indicates how consequential the author believes Luther's trip to Rome to have been. Still worth reading is Levin Schücking, *Luther in Rome; or, Corradina, the Last of the Hohenstaufen: A Religio-historical Romance*, trans. Eudora Lindsay South (Boston: Thayer, 1890).

4. Studies in recent years include Peter Maier, "Aussagen Luthers über die Stadt Rom seiner Zeit," in *Lutheriana: Zum 5. Geburtstag Martin Luthers von den Mitarbeitern der Weimarer Ausgabe*, ed. Gerhard Hammer and Karl-Heinz zur Mühlen (Cologne: Böhlau Verlag, 1984), 281–90; Stefan-Bernhard Eirich, "'Ich wolt nich gros geldt nemen das ich zu Roma nicht gewesen war': Martin Luther und seine römischen Erinnerungen," *Korrespondenzblatt: Collegium Germanicum et Hungaricum* 101 (1992): 77–97; Italo Michele Battafarano, "Luthers Romreise in den erinnernden 'Tischreden,'" in *Deutsche Handwerker, Künstler und Gelehrte im Rom der Renaissance*, ed. Stephan Füssel and Klaus Vogel (Wiesbaden: Harrassowitz, 2001), 214–37; Eva-Maria Jung-Inglessis, *Auf den Spuren Luthers in Rom* (St. Ottilien: EOS Verlag, 2006); Corinna Landi, *Con Luthero nella*

     Roma del 1510 (Rome: Com Nuovi Tempi, 2013); Hans-Albert Genthe, ed., *Auf Luthers Spuren unterwegs: Eine Reise durch Deutschland, die Schweiz und Italien* (Göttingen: Vandenhoeck & Ruprecht, 2010); and Jürgen Krüger and Martin Wallraff, *Luthers Rom: Die ewige Stadt in der Renaissance*, 2nd ed. (Darmstadt, Germany: Philipp von Zabern, 2015).

5. Böhmer, *Luthers Romfahrt*, 76–77. Böhmer himself is hardly beyond reproach in this regard, as he himself draws a number of definitive conclusions from assumptions that are not always entirely certain.

6. Scholars have often assumed, for example, that Luther must have visited Bologna on his way home from Rome. As Böhmer points out, "The assertion that he 'also surely saw Bologna' is in any case not entirely uncertain only if he stopped by San Benedetto Po. But for now that is only a good hypothesis" (*Luthers Romfahrt*, 79). No matter how good a hypothesis may be, it is still just that, a hypothesis.

7. The title of this subchapter also served as the title for John Morris's English adaptation of a German novel by Karl Gottlieb Bretschneider, *To Rome and Back Again, or The Two Proselytes* (Baltimore: T. Newton Kurtz, 1856).

8. Hans Schneider, *Martin Luthers Reise nach Rom—neu datiert und neu gedeutet* (Berlin: De Gruyter, 2011), 114–15.

9. On separate occasions Luther indicates 1509, 1510, and 1511 as possible dates for the trip to Rome, but most often his departure is in 1510 with a return in 1511 (Schneider, 26).

10. WA 54,219. See also WAT 5,75,#5344. One possible source of confusion regarding this and other dates in Luther's life is the medieval practice of beginning the new year on March 25, the day Gabriel was thought to have announced the birth of Christ to Mary (Richard Marius, *Martin Luther: The Christian between God and Death* [Cambridge, MA: Harvard University Press, 1999], 80).

11. Melanchthon's chronology "fits better with the known dates of Luther's lectures in Erfurt and Wittenberg" (Christopher Boyd Brown, ed., *Luther's Works Companion Volume: Sixteenth-Century Biographies of Martin Luther*, trans. Matthew Carver and Kevin Walker [St. Louis: Concordia, 2018], lvii, n. 196).

12. Schneider, *Martin Luthers Reise nach Rom*, 11, n. 21.

13. Melanchthon cites "the controversies of the monks" as the reason for Luther's trip to Rome (CR 6,160).

14. According to Luther's early but hostile biographer, Johannes Cochlaeus, Luther was chosen by the "dissenting monasteries" to represent their cause in Rome (Böhmer, *Luthers Romfahrt*, 9).

15. Böhmer, 58, n. 2. Nicholas Besler was "virtually imprisoned" by the leaders of the order in Rome in 1505 because he had bypassed them in order to deal directly with the Roman curia (Brecht 1,98).

16. Brecht 1,101; Gustav Kawerau, "Aus den Actis generalatus Aegidii Viterbiensis," *Zeitschrift für Kirchengeschichte* 32 (1911): 604; Schneider, *Martin Luthers Reise nach Rom*, 66.

17. Cochlaeus says that Luther "succumbed to his Staupitz." "Submitted" might be a more accurate verb (Oberman, 144).

18. Oberman, 143.

19. Oberman, 146.

20. For Luther's overly busy schedule in the monastery, which meant that he sometimes had to pray the entire day long on Sunday to make up for the prayers that he had not had time to say during the week, see WAT 4,654,#5094.

21. Oberman, 144.

22. On Staupitz and his importance, see Franz Posset, *The Front-Runner of the Catholic Reformation: The Life and Works of Johann von Staupitz* (Aldershot, UK: Ashgate, 2003).

23. For the possibility that it was a pastoral concern that prompted Staupitz to send Luther to Rome, see Schneider, "Luthers Romreise," in *MLiR*, 11. Staupitz knew of Luther's intense spiritual struggles and at one point urged him to pursue doctoral studies so that he would have "something to do" (WAT 1,442,#885).

24. Schneider, *Martin Luthers Reise nach Rom*, 7, n. 8.

25. Cochlaeus mentions Kress in his discussion of why Luther made the trip to Rome (Böhmer, *Luthers Romfahrt*, 8). According to Schneider (*Martin Luthers Reise nach Rom*, 112, n. 499), Kress was not himself an Augustinian monk. On Johannes Klein as a possible third travel companion, see Schneider, 113–14.

26. Andrew Pettegree, *Brand Luther* (New York: Penguin, 2015), 34. According to Hieronymus Dungersheim, *Dadelung des obgesatzten bekentnus oder untuchtigen Lutherischen Testaments* (Leipzig, 1530), Luther had traveled with Nathin once before, to Halle (Böhmer, *Luthers Romfahrt*, 57, n. 2).

27. See WAB 1,53, n. 10.

28. See Dietrich Denecke, "Wege und Städte zwischen Wittenberg und Rom um 1510: Eine historisch-geographische Studie zur Romreise Martin Luthers," in *Genetische Ansätze in der Kulturlandschaftsforschung: Festschrift für Helmut Jäger*, ed. Wolfgang Pinkwart (Würzburg, Germany: Steiner, 1983), 77–106. The 1500 *Romweg* of Erhard Etzlaub (oriented "south up") is helpful for trying to plot possible pilgrim itineraries at the time; see Herbert Vossberg, *Im Heiligen Rom: Luthers Reiseeindrücke 1510–11* (Berlin: Evangelische Verlagsanstalt, 1966), 14.

29. WAT 5,638,#6392; WA 1,133.

30. WAT 3,611,#3781.

31. Brecht 1,100: "Luther must have gone through Memmingen. He noticed the dialect of Swabia and the Allgäu. The hospitality of the Swabians and the Bavarians (on the return) stuck in his memory."

32. Mary Shelley describes the "singular and sublime" Splügen Pass in some detail in her *Rambles in Germany and Italy in 1840, 1842, and 1843* (London: Edward Moxon, 1844), 1,56–61. The pass (without the umlaut) is also mentioned by Arthur Conan Doyle in his story "The Adventure of the Illustrious Client," in *The Complete Sherlock Holmes* (New York: Barnes & Noble, 1992), 985.

33. WAT 4,285,#4385.

34. WAT 4,646,#5081.

35. Heinrich Böhmer, *Road to Reformation: Martin Luther to the Year 1521*, trans. John W. Doberstein and Theodore G. Tappert (Philadelphia: Muhlenberg Press, 1946), 73.

36. See Wilson, *Here I Walk*, 115–17.

37. Böhmer, *Luthers Romfahrt*, 80, n. 6. The Augustinian convent connected with Santa Maria delle Grazie in Gravedona was consecrated in 1496. It is now a municipal library.

38. WAT 5,621,#6360.

39. Marco Poli and Simona Costato, "Martin Lutero in un Affresco alla Misericordia? Ipotesi per una ricerca storico-artistica," *Strenna Storica Bolognese / Comitato per Bologna Storica e Artistica* 47 (1997): 425–38. The bottom half of the fresco of Augustine giving his rule to four friars was only uncovered in the 1930s. Schneider considers the idea that one of them is a portrait of the young Luther "quite unlikely" ("Luthers Romreise," in *MLiR*, 14, n. 54).

40. WAT 4,654,#5094.

41. For many pilgrims coming to Rome from the north, Bologna served as "the entrance point for paths over the Apennines" (Vossberg, *Im Heiligen Rom*, 27). For Luther's experiences in Florence and Siena, see WAT 4,17–18,#3930 and WA 51,207, to be discussed in chapter 3.

42. WAT 5,467,#6059. Liborius Magdeburg, who was often a guest at Luther's table in 1537 and 1538, participated in this *Table Talk*.

43. I follow the Latin text as it is found in Eugene Strittmatter, "Classical Elements in the Roman Liturgy," *Classical Journal* 18 (1923): 197–98. See Jan van Herwaarden, *Between Saint James and Erasmus: Studies in Late-Medieval Religious Life: Devotion and Pilgrimage in the Netherlands* (Leiden: Brill, 2003), ch. 6, on medieval pilgrims traveling to Rome from the north and their reactions to the city.

44. See Michael Roberts, "Rome Personified, Rome Epitomized: Representations of Rome in the Poetry of the Early Fifth Century," *American Journal of Philology* 122 (2001): 533–65.

45. According to WAT 5,467,#6059, n. 7, the reading here should "perhaps" be the Latin *Ita* instead of the German *Ja*.

46. WAT 3,347,#3478.

47. For a lively example, see Oberman, 157.

48. See Birgit Stolt, *Die Sprachmischung in Luthers Tischreden: Studien zum Problem der Zweisprachigkeit* (Uppsala: Almqvist & Wiksell, 1964), on Luther's "code-switching" at table.

49. Adolf Hausrath, *Martin Luthers Romfahrt nach einem gleichzeitigen Pilgerbuche erläutert* (Berlin: Grotesche Verlagsbuchhandlung, 1894), 28.

50. The new gate (its inner facade was designed by Bernini) was ready in 1655 to greet the ex-Lutheran queen Christina of Sweden when she entered the city.

51. Armando Ravaglioli, *Heart of Rome* (Rome: Edizione di Roma Centro Storico, 1984), 5–7.

52. For historical background, see Katherine Walsh, "The Observance: Sources for a History of the Observant Reform Movement in the Order of Augustinian Friars in the Fourteenth and Fifteenth Centuries," *Rivista di storia della chiesa in Italia* 31 (1977): 40–67.

53. See Vossberg, *Im Heiligen Rom*, 40; and Brown, *Sixteenth-Century Biographies*, 128.

54. Proposed already by Hubert Jedin, "Die römischen Augustinerquellen zu Luthers Frühzeit," *Archiv für Reformationsgeschichte* 25 (1928): 256–70. See Schneider's discussion in "Luthers Romreise," in *MLiR*, 21–22. The rebuilt convent and the Biblioteca Angelica (open to the public since 1604) were owned by the Augustinians until the early 1870s, when they were confiscated by the Italian government.

55. John W. O'Malley, *Giles of Viterbo on Church and Reform: A Study in Renaissance Thought* (Leiden: Brill, 1968), 49.

56. In connection with his comments on Egidio, Luther tells a gruesome story about the death of two other Augustinians in Rome who were critical of the papacy. They were found dead on the street one morning with their tongues cut out and stuck up their rectums (WAT 2,347–48,#2174). For a briefer (and less gruesome) version, see WAT 3,345,#3478.

57. Schneider, *Martin Luthers Reise nach Rom*, 116.

58. Schneider, 136. The convent of S. Susanna was demolished in the 1920s to make way for the road connecting Piazza Barberini with the train station (Termini). Another monastery, next to Santa Prisca, on the Aventine, was given to the Augustinians only in the seventeenth century.

59. WAT 3,431–32,#3582A–B. See also Georg Mylius's preface to Romans (1590) for this perspective on Luther's motivation (Julius Köstlin, *The Theology of Luther in Its Historical Development and Inner Harmony*, trans. Charles E. Hay [Philadelphia: Lutheran Publication Society, 1897], 1,86).

60. WA 31.1,226. The WA editor suggests that *schier leid* is probably to be translated as "almost sorry" (n. 3). Böhmer and others take it to mean something more like "downright sorry" (*Road to Reformation*, 64). Either translation is possible (see the entry for *schier* in the Grimm brothers' *Deutsches Wörterbuch*).

61. WAT 2,613,#2717, n. 9. For *Satanae* instead of *Staupitii*, see Volker Leppin, "Salve, Sancta Roma," in *MLiR*, 43.

62. Oberman, 144. See also Brecht 1,155–61.

63. Leppin, "Salve, Sancta Roma," in *MLiR*, 46.

64. See Debra Birch, *Pilgrimage to Rome in the Middle Ages: Continuity and Change* (Woodbridge, UK: Boydell & Brewer, 1998).

65. WA 50,577.

66. See Adrian Boas, *Jerusalem in the Time of the Crusades: Society, Landscape and Art in the Holy City under Frankish Rule* (London: Routledge, 2001).

67. A fresco still in Saint John Lateran may have been intended to illustrate Boniface's declaration of the first such Jubilee (Riccardo Cattani, *St John Lateran* [Rome: Macart, n.d.], 12).

68. Herbert Kessler and Johanna Zacharias, *Rome 1300: On the Path of the Pilgrim* (New Haven, CT: Yale University Press, 2000), 2.

69. An unusually large number of Germans made the pilgrimage to Rome in 1500 (LW 44,171).

70. WAT 2,484,#2488a–b. See also Luther's discussion of two papal bulls of Clement VII for the Jubilee Year of 1525 in WA 18,255–69.

71. On the origins of the cult of relics in the fourth century and the theological controversies surrounding their veneration, see Robert Wiśniewski, *The Beginnings of the Cult of Relics* (Oxford: Oxford University Press, 2019), especially ch. 10.

72. WA 34.1,91. Luther mentions S. Sebastiano and S. Paolo fuori le Mura in WA 54,223.

73. WA 47,425. For the history of this church, see Michael Matheus, ed., *S. Maria dell'Anima. Zur Geschichte einer "deutschen" Stiftung in Rom* (Berlin: De Gruyter, 2010). The "German pastor" to whom Luther refers may have been a sacristan named Heinrich Bode (Vossberg, *Im Heiligen Rom*, 108) or Gottfried Velderhoff von Beeck (*MLiR*, 380). There was also a cemetery south of the Vatican (Cimitero Teutonico) for the use of Germans in Rome.

74. Ernest Schwiebert, *Luther and His Times: The Reformation from a New Perspective* (St. Louis: Concordia, 1950), 191.

75. WAT 3,349,#3479a.

76. WA 54,223.

77. For a recent consideration of the history of this church in the Middle Ages, see Claudia Bolgia, *Reclaiming the Roman Capitol: Santa Maria in Aracoeli from the Altar of Augustus to the Franciscans, c. 500–1450* (New York: Routledge, 2017).

78. See Aldo Nestori, "La basilica di S. Pancrazio in Roma," *Rivista di Archeologia Cristiana* 36 (1960): 213–48.

79. See Umberto Fasola, "La 'regio IV' del cimitero di S. Agnese sotto l'atrio della basilica costantiniana," *Rivista di Archeologia Cristiana* 50 (1974): 175–205.

80. Schneider, "Luthers Romreise" (*MLiR*, 22). On the reliability of this guidebook, see Dale Kinney, "Fact and Fiction in the Mirabilia Urbis Romae," in *Roma Felix*, ed. Éamonn Ó Carragáin and Carol Neuman De Vegvar (Aldershot, UK: Ashgate, 2007), 235–52. There is a well-used copy with annotations in the Vatican Library (Cod. Vat. Lat. 3973).

81. Cattani, *St John Lateran*, 28. The current building that houses the Holy Steps was designed by Domenico Fontana and completed in 1589.

82. WA 51,89. Given the context, I have translated the imperfect Latin verb that Luther uses here, *cogitabam*, not as a simple past tense ("I thought") but as an iterative ("I kept thinking").

83. According to Schwiebert (*Luther and His Times*, 187), there were "similar quotations already associated with the story of the *Scala Sancta* in the sixteenth century." A plate in a museum in Delft depicting the Holy Steps has the words *Wie weet, of het wel waar is* inscribed upon it.

84. WA 1,390.

85. WA 31.1,226.

86. Cattani, *St John Lateran*, 1. For Luther's description of an inscription on the facade of Saint John Lateran, see WA 2,159.

87. WA 31.1,226.

88. WA 34.1,91.

89. In 1453, the Croats in Rome were given the old church of S. Marina, which they rebuilt and dedicated to Saint Jerome along with a hospice and infirmary on the Via di Ripetta, not far from S. Agostino.

90. Ferdinand Gregorovius, *The History of the City of Rome in the Middle Ages*, trans. Annie Hamilton, 2nd ed. (London: G. Bell & Sons, 1900), 8.2,582.

91. Luther refers to the display of the veil in WA 54,255. Vossberg (*Im Heiligen Rom*, 90) suggests that Luther's vivid description of the veil "gives the impression that he himself saw it."

92. WA 47,394.

93. WA 47,817.

94. WA 51,136.

95. The cathedral in the city of Amiens was built for a different head of John the Baptist brought to France from the Holy Land by a crusader in the early 1200s.

96. WAT 2,21,#1272.

97. There is an early mosaic depiction of Jesus handing a very heavy key to Peter still to be seen in the mausoleum of Santa Costanza. On the supposed filings from the chains with which Peter was bound while in Rome preserved in a key, see George Demacopoulos, *The Invention of Peter: Apostolic Discourse and Papal Authority in Late Antiquity* (Philadelphia: University of Pennsylvania Press, 2013), 151.

98. In the Cincinnati Art Museum, there is a painting, dated to 1525, by Lucas Cranach the Elder of Helena holding the cross in her right hand.

99. J. W. and A. M. Cruickshank, *Christian Rome*, 2nd ed. (London: Grant Richards, 1911), 236.

100. WAT 4,253,#4355. For more on this site and the traditions associated with it, see David L. Eastman, *Paul the Martyr: The Cult of the Apostle in the Latin West* (Atlanta: Society of Biblical Literature, 2011), 62–69.

101. WAT 4,291,#4391. A catalog of relics to be sold in 1753 at auction at Saint Peter's lists "a piece of the rope Judas hanged himself with" as coming "from Amras, near Inspruck" (Josephus Tela, ed., *A Catalogue of the Most Eminently Venerable Relics of the Roman Catholic Church* [London: Souter, 1818], 15).

102. Böhmer, *Road to Reformation*, 66.

103. As quoted in Darran Anderson, *Imaginary Cities: A Tour of Dream Cities, Nightmare Cities, and Everywhere in Between* (Chicago: University of Chicago Press, 2017), 184.

104. WA 31.1,226. In the *Tischreden*, Luther remembers the presence of "two Franciscans" in the catacombs (WAT 5,676,#6463), a detail that suggests

that he actually visited the catacombs himself and was not simply relying on the reports of others.

105. Ivana Della Portella, Giuseppina Pisani Sartorio, and Francesca Ventre, *The Appian Way: From Its Foundation to the Middle Ages* (Los Angeles: J. Paul Getty Museum, 2004), 59.

106. WAT 3,349,#3479a.

107. WAT 5,667,#6447; WAT 5,675,#6463.

108. WAT 2,609,#2709b.

109. Its precise location was only rediscovered in the nineteenth century by the archeologist Giovanni Battista de Rossi, author of *La Roma sotterranea cristiana*.

110. MGH, *Chronica minora* 1,71–72.

111. WA 1,655. See Schneider, "Luthers Romreise," in *MLiR*, 24–25, n. 120.

112. WA 1,655.

113. WAT 5,467,#6059. See Michael Camille, "Dr Witkowski's Anus: French Doctors, German Homosexuals and the Obscene in Medieval Church Art," in *Medieval Obscenities*, ed. Nicola McDonald (York, UK: York Medieval Press, 2006), 26–27. Luther also refers to Marcolf in WAT 2,374,#2242. For a full discussion of whether Luther saw the pope, see Schneider, *Martin Luthers Reise nach Rom*, 129–34. For a recent biography of Julius, see Christine Shaw, *Julius II: The Warrior Pope* (Oxford: Blackwell, 1996).

114. WAT 5,667,#6447.

115. An abbreviated Latin inscription on the relief statue, *Pa. Pater Patrum P. P. P.*, was read as "a pope, father of fathers, bore a little pope while she was a popess" (*Papa, pater patrum, peperit papissa papellum*). More likely it is to be expanded as "Papirius, father of fathers, put in place [this monument] with his own money" (*Papirius, pater patrum, propria pecunia posuit*). See Vossberg, *Im Heiligen Rom*, 76.

116. On the possible historical basis for the legend of Pope Joan, see E. R. Chamberlin, *The Bad Popes* (New York: Barnes & Noble, 1969), 25. For the eventual disposal of the statue, see Bruce Ware Allen, *Tiber: Eternal River of Rome* (Lebanon, NH: University Press of New England, 2018), 119.

117. WA 1,235.

118. WA 42,466.

119. WAB 1,111. For a full consideration, see Hans Hubert, "Luther und die Peterskirche," in *MLiR*, 435–70.

120. See Alan Thacker, "The Cult of Peter and the Development of Martyr Cult in Rome: The Origins of the Presentation of Peter and Paul as Martyrs," in *The Early Reception and Appropriation of the Apostle Peter (60–800 CE)*, ed. Roald Dijkstra (Leiden: Brill, 2020), 251.

121. Luther's silence in this regard is striking, since he clearly had a deep appreciation of beauty. See, in general, Mark Mattes, *Martin Luther's Theology of Beauty: A Reappraisal* (Grand Rapids: Baker Academic, 2017).

122. Böhmer, *Luthers Romfahrt*, 137.

123. WA 6,427.

124. WA 7,733.

125. See David Rijser, *Raphael's Poetics: Art and Poetry in High Renaissance Rome* (Amsterdam: Amsterdam University Press, 2012), ch. 3.

126. Vossberg, *Im Heiligen Rom*, 14.

127. WAT 6,349–50,#7035.

128. WA 47,817. For Luther's reference to a depiction in Rome of Peter as a fisherman, see WA 1,617.

129. The original was supposed to have been in Constantinople, brought there by the fifth-century empress Eudocia. Perhaps the most famous of the Hodogetria icons was in Smolensk, where it is believed to have perished during World War II.

130. See Kristen Noreen, "The Icon of Santa Maria Maggiore, Rome: An Image and Its Afterlife," *Renaissance Studies* 19 (2005): 660–72.

131. There were many other famous icons associated with Luke in Luther's Rome, including one in S. Agostino (supposedly brought to Rome from Hagia Sophia after Constantinople fell), S. Maria in Ara Coeli (the Madonna Avvocata), and the church formerly known as S. Maria Nuova, now S. Francesca Romana (the Glycophilousa). The Madonna di San Sisto was moved to S. Maria del Rosario (on Monte Mario) in the early 1930s. A Lukan icon supposedly brought to S. Matteo in Merulana from Crete in the late fifteenth century is now in S. Alphonsus Liguori.

132. Luther was aware of Venice and mentions it more than once (e.g., WAT 1,4,#5; WAT 3,372,#3517), but if he was making his way home via

the Brenner Pass, it would have taken him considerably out of his way to visit the city.

133. According to Böhmer (*Luthers Romfahrt*, 80–81), at the time of Luther's trip to Rome, there were over three hundred Augustinian conventual houses in Italy. The Lombard congregation had at least twenty-two cloisters in the Piedmont alone.

134. WAT 5,455,#6042. For the identification of this monastery as S. Benedetto Po and not the abbey of San Sisto in Piacenza, see Böhmer, *Luthers Romfahrt*, 82. S. Benedetto Po is much closer to Mantua than Padua, which is over one hundred kilometers away.

135. WAT 5,676,#6463.

136. WAT 5,638–39,#6392.

137. Böhmer, *Road to Reformation*, 72.

138. She did eat the Host every Sunday (Böhmer, *Road to Reformation*, 73).

139. WAT 4,583,#4925. In 1518, Luther stayed at the church of Saint Anne in Augsburg. The church became Lutheran in 1545.

140. The situation around Bologna was already dangerous in early 1511 (Böhmer, *Luthers Romfahrt*, 79).

141. For relevant arguments, see Schneider, "Luthers Romreise," in *MLiR*, 19–20; and Schneider, *Martin Luthers Reise nach Rom*, 124–26. There are persistent local traditions regarding Luther's sojourn in Augustinian monasteries in southern France (Nice, Aix-en-Provence, und Pernes-les-Fontaines). On the Via Francigena, see Reinhard Zweidler, *Der Frankenweg-Via Francigena: Der mittelalterliche Pilgerweg von Canterbury nach Rom* (Darmstadt, Germany: Wiss. Buchgesellschaft, 2003). Hilaire Belloc's *The Path to Rome* (New York: Longmans, Green, 1902) describes the westerly route the author took across the Alps on his way from France to Rome.

142. According to Besler, Staupitz sent Mechelen to Cologne at the end of February 1512 from Salzburg, after the latter's return from Rome (Schneider, *Martin Luthers Reise nach Rom*, 16).

143. Schneider, "Luthers Romreise," in *MLiR*, 19.

144. The title for this subchapter is a translation of the first line of Matthias Claudius's poem *Urians Reise um die Welt: Wenn jemand eine Reise tut, so kann er was erzählen*; see his *Werke* (Gotha, Germany: Perthes, 1871), 5,76.

145. See, for example, WA 47,394.

146. Schneider, *Martin Luthers Reise nach Rom*, 8.

147. See, for example, WAT 3,344,#3476.

148. Franz Posset, "Luther's Journey to Rome in 1511–1512: In Commemoration of its 500th Anniversary and in Search of the Historical Luther—a Sequel to the Real Luther," *Luther Digest* 20 (2012): 9–24, emphasizes the difficulties involved in using the *Tischreden* to document the trip to Rome. For more nuanced considerations of the *Tischreden*, see Helmar Junghans, "Die Tischreden Martin Luthers," in *Sonderedition der kritischen Weimarer Ausgabe; Begleitheft zu den Tischreden* (Weimar: Böhlau, 2000), 26–50, and the articles included in Katherina Bärenfänger, Volker Leppin, and Stefan Michel, eds., *Martin Luthers Tischreden: Neuansätze der Forschung* (Tübingen: Mohr Siebeck, 2013).

149. Melanchthon (CR 6,157) praises Luther's "faithful and reliable memory."

150. See Rita Voltmer, "Behind the 'Veil of Memory': About the Limitations of Narratives," *Magic, Ritual, and Witchcraft* 5 (2010): 96–102.

151. WAT 1,442,#884. See also Scott Hendrix, *Martin Luther: Visionary Reformer* (New Haven, CT: Yale University Press, 2015), 17.

152. WAT 5,75,#5344. The subordinate clause introduced by *ut* could be a purpose or a result clause. Luther went to Rome either "in order to see . . ." or "so that he saw. . . ." It seems more natural here to translate it as a purpose clause. See also WAT 5,76–77,#5347.

153. See Theodor Kolde, "Innere Bewegungen unter den Augustinern und Luthers Romreise," *Zeitschrift für Kirchengeschichte* 2 (1877): 460–80. The Augustinian order's records from the end of 1510 to 1512 are missing or exist only in fragmentary form (Schneider, *Martin Luthers Reise nach Rom*, 9–10).

154. Philipp Melanchthon, *Historia de vita et actis reverendiss. viri D. Mart. Lutheri* (Heidelberg, 1548).

155. Mathesius's biography, published in Nuremberg in 1566, consists of seventeen sermons on the life of Luther that he preached to his congregation in Joachimsthal in Bohemia. See Brown, *Sixteenth-Century Biographies*, 127–28.

156. Matthäus Dresser, *De vita et morte D. Pauli Lutheri Medici Oratio* (Leipzig: Lantzenberger, 1593).

157. Johannes Cochlaeus, *Commentaria Ioannis Cochlaei, de Actis et Scriptis Martini Lutheri Saxonis* (Mainz: F. Behem, 1549).

158. Karl Euling, ed., *Chronik des Johan Oldekop* (Stuttgart: Literarischer Verein, 1891).

159. Schneider (*Martin Luthers Reise nach Rom*, 4) reports that he saw a reference to Luther's visit to the Augustinian cloister of San Nicolò in Spoleto on a sign for tourists. There is no evidence that Luther stopped in Spoleto, nor is it likely that he did so; it would have been somewhat out of his way if he was passing through Siena on his way to Rome. For examples of other local legends in Parma, Arezzo, Todi, and Padua, equally difficult to substantiate, see Schneider, "Luthers Romreise," in *MLiR*, 17–18.

160. George Sullivan, *Not Built in a Day: Exploring the Architecture of Rome* (New York: Carroll & Graf, 2006), 51; Maier, "Aussagen Luthers," 281–82.

161. For a list of references to well over one hundred passages in the *Weimarer Ausgabe* in which Luther refers to the city of Rome in his time, see Maier, "Aussagen Luthers," 288–90.

162. A similar lack of external evidence for Ovid's exile other than his own poetry has led some Ovidian scholars (but by no means most of them) to suggest that the poet simply made up the story of his exile for his own literary purposes. See A. D. Fitton Brown, "The Unreality of Ovid's Tomitan Exile," *Liverpool Classical Monthly* 10 (1985): 18–22.

163. The trip to Rome was Luther's first extensive journey and, indeed, the longest he would ever take in his life. It certainly must have helped broaden the young monk's horizons considerably. See Gustav Türk, *Luthers Romfahrt in ihrer Bedeutung für seine innere Entwicklung* (Meissen, Germany: Klinkicht, 1897).

164. Böhmer, *Luthers Romfahrt*, 79, n. 2. The distances I have provided here are based on Google Maps. Schneider ("Luthers Romreise," in *MLiR*, 12) calculates that the distance between Wittenberg and Rome was approximately 1,600 kilometers based on the travel routes of the time. If Luther left Wittenberg at the beginning of October, Schneider estimates that he would have arrived in Rome before the end of November.

165. See, for example, one of the proverbs in Luther's collection (WA 51,659): "You write the way the road goes to Rome" (*Schreibst wie der Weg nach Rom gehet*). The point of the proverb is that someone's handwriting is as crooked and unpredictable as all the different roads that lead in various ways to Rome.

166. Böhmer, *Luthers Romfahrt*, 79–80.

167. On the many dangers facing medieval pilgrims on their way to Rome, see Birch, *Pilgrimage to Rome*, 68–71.

168. Böhmer, *Luthers Romfahrt*, 4.

169. Böhmer, 4.

170. WAT 4,136–37,#4104. For another version, see WAT 2,49,#1327.

171. François Retief and Louis Cilliers, "Diseases and Causes of Death among the Popes," *Acta Theologica* 26, *Supplementum* 7 (2006): 242–43.

172. WAT 4,285,#4385.

173. Brecht 1,100: "He noted the infertility of Switzerland, where there were only meadows and where the raising of crops was impossible."

174. Wilson, *Here I Walk*, 101. See Fergus Fleming, "The Alps and the Imagination," *Ambio* 13 (2004): 51–55. For a different perspective, see William Barton, *Mountain Aesthetics in Early Modern Latin Literature* (London: Routledge, 2016).

175. WA 47,392.

176. Oberman, 146.

177. Karl Simrock, *Deutsche Märchen* (Barsinghausen, Germany: Unikum-Verlag, 2012), 321.

178. There is possibly more complexity to Luther's sentence about onions and garlic than the translation "shit for shillings" would suggest. Luther did not return home entirely empty handed or with nothing but "shit." In Luther's time, garlic was less often used in German kitchens than onions, but in Mediterranean countries, it was highly prized. In the Virgilian poem *Moretum* (often translated as "salad" but more likely a kind of spreadable paste), the recipe includes four cloves of garlic. Might Luther be suggesting here that even though he was disappointed in Rome, at least he did return home with a bracing new perspective on the "holy" city that was more sharply defined and a tongue that was more "seasoned" (cf. Col 4:6) than the unsophisticated friar had possessed when he left Germany?

179. WA 54,179.

180. WAT 5,657,#6427.

181. WAT 5,657,#6427.

182. WA 54,179.

183. Reiterated by Leopold von Ranke, *Deutsche Geschichte im Zeitalter der Reformation* (Berlin: Duncker & Humblot, 1839), 1,300.

184. Leppin, "Salve, Sancta Roma," in *MLiR*, 33; Oberman, 150.

185. See Alister E. McGrath, *Luther's Theology of the Cross: Martin Luther's Theological Breakthrough*, 2nd ed. (Oxford: Wiley-Blackwell, 2011), especially ch. 4.

186. WA 54,185–86.

187. See Oberman, 150–74.

188. See Thomas Kaufmann, *Geschichte der Reformation* (Frankfurt: Insel Verlag, 2009), 138–39.

189. Oberman, 323.

190. For Bernard's expression, *Quae vidimus loquimur*, see *Epistula* 46 (PL 182,153).

191. WAT 3,345,#3478.

192. WAT 5,676,#6463.

193. WAT 5,181,#5484.

194. WA 10.2,125.

195. WA 43,421.

196. Ewald Plass, *What Luther Says* (St. Louis: Concordia, 1959), 1015, n. 20.

197. WA 6,431.

198. WA 6,426.

199. Schwiebert, *Luther and His Times*, 191.

200. WA 36,352.

201. WAT 3,432,#3582A.

202. WAT 5,227,#5543.

203. The Cancelleria is singled out for praise by the Italian humanist and historian Raffaele Maffei in his *Commentariorum urbanorum octo et triginta libri* (Rome, 1506). See Pier Nicola Pagliara, "Rom in den Jahren 1510/11," in *MLiR*, 479.

204. See Caroline Vincenti Montanaro and Andrea Fasolo, *Palazzi and Villas of Rome* (Venice: Arsenale Editrice, 1999), 46–49 and 176–77. On the annual incomes of various cardinals, see Böhmer, *Luthers Romfahrt*, 114–16.

205. WA 39.1,150. According to WAT 5,181#5484, Luther said that other priests in Rome were celebrating "six or seven Masses" before he could finish one.

206. Sheila Barker, "The Making of a Plague Saint," in *Piety and Plague: From Byzantium to the Baroque*, ed. Franco Mormando and Thomas Worcester (Kirksville, MO: Truman State University Press, 2007), 92.

207. WAT 5,451,#6036.

208. WAT 3,313,#3428.

209. WAT 3,313,#3428.

210. WA 38,211–12. For another reference to *Curtisanen* in Rome, see WA 26,198.

211. Böhmer, *Road to Reformation*, 67. One courtier is supposed to have said that the pope had more power "in his littlest finger" than all the rulers of all of Germany (WA 53,283).

212. Luther associated the Carthusians with the practice of homosexuality (WA 43,55).

213. WAT 3,313,#3428. Luther's *gauckel spiel* could also be translated as "magic show."

214. WAT 5,181,#5484.

215. WA 39.1,150.

216. Roland Bainton, *Here I Stand: A Life of Martin Luther* (New York: Abingdon-Cokesbury Press, 1950), 41.

217. WA 14,393–94.

218. WA 36,352.

219. WA 32,219.

220. WAT 4,405,#4619.

221. Oberman, 149.

222. Translation in LW 44,170, n. 140. There is a familiar tripartite German proverb about Rome that Luther adduces in WA 6,437 and 45,406. See Karl Friedrich Wilhelm Wander, *Deutsches Sprichwörter-Lexikon* (Darmstadt, Germany: Wissenschaftliche Buchgesellschaft, 1964), 72.

223. Oberman, 149.

224. Oberman, 149.

225. WAT 3,345,#3478.

226. I use the translation of Lee Piepho, "Mantuan's Eclogues in the English Reformation," *Sixteenth Century Journal* 25 (1994): 625. The Latin text can be found in WA 54,222–23.

227. Böhmer, *Luthers Romfahrt*, 173.

228. Böhmer, 103.

229. WAT 5,675,#6461.

230. Her house still stands on the Piazza Fiammetta, not far from S. Agostino. A Roman prostitute later associated with the basilica was supposed to have served as a model for Caravaggio's "Madonna of the Pilgrims" (1604–6), a painting still to be seen in the Cavalletti Chapel of the church.

231. Brecht 1,448. For Luther's observations on Savonarola's *Meditatio pia*, see WA 12,48.

232. WAT 3,219,#3201b.

233. WAB 1,45.

234. WA 43,57.

235. WAT 1,294,#624.

236. WA 1,625.

237. WAT 3,432,#3582A–B.

238. Brecht 1,117 and 1,179.

239. Stephen Greenblatt, *Hamlet in Purgatory*, exp. ed. (Princeton, NJ: Princeton University Press, 2013), 70.

240. For Luther's respect for the antiquity of "the holy Roman church," see WAB 12,17.

241. Bertrand Lançon, *Rome in Late Antiquity: Everyday Life and Urban Change, AD 312–609*, trans. Antonia Nevill (New York: Routledge, 2000), 161.

242. WAT 3,218–19,#3201b.

243. WA 1,655.

244. WAT 3,461–62,#3260. See also WA 54,256.

245. WA 54,254–55.

246. WADB 7,3.

247. WA 2,72.

248. WAT 4,290,#4391.

249. The adjectives are from Brecht 3,193. On the title of the work, see LW 41,8.

250. Euling, *Chronik des Johan Oldekop*, 31. In WAT 5,609,#6451, Luther entertains the idea that he might "have stayed in Rome" (*wer ich tzu Rom blieben*) but does not mention any request on his part to that effect.

251. WA 51,89.

252. Barbara Harrison, *Italian Days* (New York: Tichnor & Fields, 1989), 211.

253. Goethe's *Italienische Reise*, 1,3, as quoted in Arnold Nesselrath, "Mirabilia Urbis Romae 1511," in *MLiR*, 345. For a comparative analysis of Luther's and Goethe's experiences in and reactions to Italy, see Italo Michele Battafarano, *Mit Luther oder Goethe in Italien: Irritation und Sehnsucht der Deutschen* (Trento, Italy: Università degli Studi di Trento, 2007).

254. I use Haakon Chevalier's translation of Stendhal, *A Roman Journal* (New York: Collier, 1961), 24–25.

255. Stendhal, 27.

256. C. Innocenti, G. Fioravanti, R. Spiti, and C. Faravelli, "The Stendhal Syndrome between Psychoanalysis and Neuroscience," *Rivista di Psichiatria* 49 (2014): 61–66.

257. Stendhal, *Roman Journal*, 74.

258. Stendhal, 39.

259. Stendhal, 34.

260. Stendhal, 26.

261. Janice Hewlett Koelb, "Freud, Jung, and the Taboo of Rome," *Arethusa* 48 (2015): 391.

262. Henry Edelheit, "Jung's 'Memories, Dreams, Reflections,'" *Psychoanalytic Quarterly* 33 (1964): 561.

263. Charles Dickens, *American Notes and Pictures from Italy* (London: J. M. Dent, 1907), 400.

264. See William Vance, *America's Rome*, vol. 2, *Catholic and Contemporary Rome* (New Haven, CT: Yale University Press, 1989).

265. Mark Twain, *Innocents Abroad, or the New Pilgrim's Progress* (New York: Harper, 1911), 2,161.

266. Marius, *Martin Luther*, xiii.

267. Marius, 83.

268. WA 51,89.

269. The pronoun in Latin not only is generally demonstrative but can sometimes have a pejorative connotation.

270. Preserved Smith, "A Decade of Luther Study," *Harvard Theological Review* 14 (1921): 114, suggests that with these words Luther may have been questioning only the authenticity of the relic itself. Were these really the stairs that Jesus had climbed to get to Pilate's *praetorium*? The Latin adjective (*verum*) that Luther uses here could be translated as "genuine" instead of "true."

271. Oberman, 147.

272. Marius, *Martin Luther*, 498, n. 22.

273. WA 1,233.

274. As translated in Alvin Schmidt, *Hallmarks of Lutheran Identity* (St. Louis: Concordia, 2017), 148.

275. WA 35,463–67.

276. For Luther's recommendation that pilgrimages to Rome be discontinued altogether except in special instances, see WA 6,437.

277. WA 47,817.

278. WA 51,136–37.

279. Böhmer, *Luthers Romfahrt*, 9. In his *Alphabetum de monarchis & monasteriis Germaniae ac Sarmatiae citerioris ordinis eremitarum S. Augustini* (1613), Felix Milensius describes Luther as a "shameless and mouthy monk" (*monachus frontosus ac linguacissimus*); see Schneider, *Martin Luthers Reise nach Rom*, 28, n. 100.

280. Böhmer, *Luthers Romfahrt*, 140.

281. Schneider, *Martin Luthers Reise nach Rom*, 147. Luther addresses Staupitz as his "sweetest father in Christ" in a letter of 1518 (Oberman, 101).

282. WA 1,529.

283. *Peristephanon* 11.1–2. See Paula Hershkowitz, *Prudentius, Spain, and Late Antique Christianity: Poetry, Visual Culture and the Cult of Martyrs* (Cambridge: Cambridge University Press, 2017), 134. On Prudentius as a "poet-pilgrim," see Anne-Marie Palmer, *Prudentius on the Martyrs* (Oxford: Clarendon, 1989), 111.

284. *Par tibi, Roma, nihil, cum sis prope tota ruina. / Quam magni fueris integra, fracta doces* (PL 171,1409). See C. David Benson, *Imagined Romes: The Ancient City and Its Stories in Middle English Poetry* (University Park: Pennsylvania State University Press, 2019), 5.

285. *The Roman Breviary, Reformed by Order of the Holy Oecumenical*, vol. 2 (Edinburgh: Blackwood, 1879), 1148.

286. *Roman Breviary*, 2,1149.

287. Joyce Sugg, *John Henry Newman: Snapdragon in the Wall* (Leominster, UK: Gracewing, 2001), 46.

288. Jerome Bertram, "John Henry Newman and the English College," in *A Roman Miscellany: The English in Rome, 1550–2000*, ed. Nicholas Schofield (Leominster, UK: Gracewing, 2002), 123.

289. Brigitte Hoegemann, "Newman and Rome," in *John Henry Newman in His Time*, ed. Philippe Lefebvre and Colin Mason (Oxford: Family, 2007), 61.

290. Charles Stephen Dessain, ed., *The Letters and Diaries of John Henry Newman*, vol. 17, *Opposition in Dublin and London: October 1855 to March 1857* (London: Clarendon, 1967), 294.

291. Jeremiah Reedy, *O Roma Nobilis. . . . Memoirs of Studying Theology in Pre-Vatican II Rome* (Bloomington, IN: Xlibris, 2015), ch. 3.

292. Cheryl White, *Round Trip to Rome: The Travelogue of a Returning Catholic* (Bloomington, IN: WestBow, 2015), ch. 7.

293. Joshua Kinlaw, "Protestants in Rome," *First Things*, June 2020, https://tinyurl.com/protestantsinrome.

294. PL 25,375.

295. Fulton J. Sheen, *This Is Rome: A Pilgrimage in Words and Pictures* (New York: Hawthorn, 1960), 78.

296. Junno Arocho Esteves, "Almost Four Million Pilgrims Visited the Vatican in 2016," *Catholic Herald*, December 30, 2016, https://tinyurl.com/Catholic-Herald.

Chapter Two

1. Macaulay, *Pleasure of Ruins*, 166–67.

2. Carl Springer, *Cicero in Heaven: The Roman Rhetor and Luther's Reformation* (Leiden: Brill, 2017), 73.

3. *Merriam-Webster*, s.v. *Latinist*, accessed February 11, 2012, https://tinyurl.com/dictionarylatinist. In his "Virgil and Augustine in Luther's De servo arbitrio," *Ad Fontes Witebergenses: Select Proceedings of Lutheranism and the Classics: Reading the Church Fathers*, ed. James A. Kellerman and Carl P. E. Springer (Fort Wayne: Lutheran Legacy, 2014), Christian Kopff has gone

so far as to argue that Luther was a better classicist than Erasmus insofar as Luther takes into fuller account "the tragic vision of human nature found in important works of the humanist curriculum," such as Virgil's *Aeneid*, whose hero is driven by fate as he leaves Troy to found Rome (50).

4. On the various ways in which contemporary humanists regarded Luther, see Richard Rex, "Luther among the Humanists," in *Martin Luther: A Christian between Reforms and Modernity (1517–2017)*, ed. Alberto Melloni (Berlin: De Gruyter, 2017), 203–20.

5. For the term *biblical humanism*, see Schwiebert, *Luther and His Times*, 275–302. On Luther's knowledge of Greek and interest in ancient Greek authors, see my *Luther's Aesop* (Kirksville, MO: Truman State University Press, 2011), 22–28.

6. On the distinction between direct and indirect influence, see Springer, *Cicero in Heaven*, 145–46.

7. WAT 3,544,#3700.

8. Carole Richardson, *Reclaiming Rome: Cardinals in the Fifteenth Century* (Leiden: Brill, 2009), 176.

9. John Pemble, *The Rome We Have Lost* (Oxford: Oxford University Press, 2017), 80.

10. WA 41,222.

11. WA 41,150.

12. WAT 3,544–45,#3700.

13. The bridge is described in Dante's *Inferno* 18.28–33.

14. WAT 3,544–45,#3700.

15. WAT 3,372,#3517.

16. Böhmer, *Luthers Romfahrt*, 88, n. 7.

17. Macaulay, *Pleasure of Ruins*, 168–69.

18. WAT 3,349,#3479a.

19. Birch, *Pilgrimage to Rome*, 143.

20. WAT 3,347,#3478.

21. WAT 3,349,#3479a.

22. For an overview, see Keith Hopkins and Mary Beard, *The Colosseum* (Cambridge, MA: Harvard University Press, 2011).

23. Richard Deakin, *Flora of the Colosseum* (London: Groombridge and Sons, 1873).

24. Sullivan, *Not Built in a Day*, 244.

25. WAT 2,609,#2709b.

26. WAT 2,609,#2709b. See also WA 36,126.

27. See Pier Luigi Tucci, "A New Look at the Tabularium and the Capitoline Hill," *Atti della Pontifica Accademia Romana di Archeologia* 86 (2014): 43–123.

28. See the discussion in Gregorovius, *History of the City of Rome*, 1,476.

29. WAT 3,349,#3479a.

30. Piranesi's fascination with Roman ruins is central to Susan Stewart's recent consideration of the importance of ruins in the history of Western culture, *The Ruins Lessons: Meaning and Material in Western Culture* (Chicago: University of Chicago Press, 2019).

31. WAT 5,467,#6058.

32. On the Aqua Marcia, see Peter Aicher, *Guide to the Aqueducts of Ancient Rome* (Wauconda: Bolchazy-Carducci, 1995), 36–37.

33. See, for example, WA 1,415; 7,677; 51,156; and 51,496.

34. WAT 1,231,#507.

35. WA 50,271.

36. WAT 5,209,#5515.

37. See Edmund Thomas, "The Cult Statues of the Pantheon," *Journal of Roman Studies* 107 (2017): 146–212.

38. WAB 5,560; 11,261.

39. Of course, some of the remains of the ancient city visible today, such as Augustus's *Ara pacis* (buried for centuries near S. Lorenzo in Lucina and only rediscovered in 1568), could not possibly have been seen by Luther.

40. For the essential continuity of Latin prose over time, see the essays collected in Tobias Reinhardt, Michael Lapidge, and J. N. Adams, eds., *Aspects of the Language of Latin Prose* (Oxford: Oxford University Press, 2005).

41. See Pliny, *Natural History*, 3,39, on the importance of Latin for the development of the Roman Empire. On Luther's views on the Pax Romana as a necessary preparation for the gospel, see WA 31.2,149 and 31.2,201.

42. See my *Cicero in Heaven*, 55–56.

43. Erikson, *Young Man Luther*, 233.

44. See Friedrich Grundt, "Hat Luther der Reise nach Rom eine Förderung seiner hebräischen Kenntnisse zu verdanken?," *Zeitschrift für kirchliche Wissenschaft und kirchliches Leben* 9 (1888): 312–16; and Hartmann Grisar, *Luther*, trans. E. M. Lamond, vol. 1 (London: Kegan Paul, Trench, Trübner, 1913), 35. Giles of Viterbo learned Hebrew from Elias Levita, but the learned Jewish grammarian and poet only arrived in Rome some years after Luther's visit there.

45. See Helmar Junghans, *Der junge Luther und die Humanisten* (Göttingen: Vandenhoeck & Ruprecht, 1985).

46. WAB 8,177.

47. WAT 1,44,#116.

48. WAT 5,413,#5972. See the discussion in my *Cicero in Heaven*, x–xi.

49. The quote comes from Michael Praetorius's *Syntagmatis Musici Tomus Primus* (WA 19,50).

50. WAT 3,380,#3530a.

51. WAT 5,317–18,#5677.

52. WAT 3,472,#3637.

53. Brecht 1,12–21.

54. Oberman, 136: "The task Luther was then set was to memorize the Scriptures by heart, page by page."

55. Cameron MacKenzie, "Luther and the Latin Language," in *Ad Fontes Witebergenses: Select Proceedings of Lutheranism and the Classics: Reading the Church Fathers*, ed. James Kellerman and Carl Springer (Fort Wayne: Lutheran Legacy, 2014), 154.

56. Brecht 3,326.

57. Brecht points out that Luther declined "to write a new preface to a Latin edition of his postils in Strasbourg in 1539 because he was no longer accustomed to writing in Latin." Brecht observes, "This was not entirely true, but in fact the old Luther now did write his works intended for publication predominately in German" (3,251). Ironically enough, the letter in which Luther claims that his Latin is rusty (WAB 8,569) is written in Latin.

58. LW 4,262; 4,357; 33,205.

59. LW 10,44.

60. LW 22,x.

61. WAB 1,563.

62. WA 18,614.

63. Figures such as alloeosis and synecdoche play important roles in Luther's *Confession concerning Christ's Supper* of 1528 (e.g., LW 37,211 and 37,214).

64. WA 20,13.

65. WAT 2,41,#1319.

66. WAT 6,261,#6904.

67. WAT 1,204,#467.

68. WAT 1,119,#285.

69. WAT 1,430–31,#867.

70. WAB 1,361–62. See my *Cicero in Heaven*, 68–69.

71. CR 6,157.

72. See my "Martin's Martial: Reconsidering Luther's Relationship with the Classics," *International Journal of the Classical Tradition* 14 (2007): 23–50.

73. For the text of these two poems, see Udo Frings, *Martinus Lutherus—Poeta Latinus* (Aachen, Germany: Hauptabteilung Erziehung und Schule im Bischöflichen Generalvikariat, 1983), 9 and 11.

74. I use the Latin text as found in WA 35,605, with minor changes in capitalization and punctuation.

75. For a fuller discussion, see my "Martin Luther, the Oreads of Wittenberg, and *Sola Gratia*," in *Acta Conventus Neo-Latini Abulensis: Proceedings of the Tenth International Congress of Neo-Latin Studies Avila 4–9 August 1997*, ed. Rhoda Schnur et al. (Tempe: University of Arizona Press, 2000), 611–18.

76. See the title of Lothar Mundt's "Die sizilischen Musen in Wittenberg. Zur religiösen Funktionalisierung der neulateinischen Bukolik im deutschen Protestantismus des 16. Jahrhunderts," in *Die Musen im Reformationszeitalter*, ed. Walther Ludwig (Leipzig: Evangelische Verlagsanstalt, 2001), 265–88.

77. Brecht 2,242.

78. WAB 3,50.

79. WAT 3,312,#3425.

80. WA 30.2,61–62.

81. WA 15,52.

82. WA 6,458.

83. WA 15,46.

84. WAB 10,134.

85. WA 15,36.

86. WA 11,455.

87. WA 42,374.

88. WA 40.3,607. See also WA 53,490–91.

89. WA 51,242–43.

90. See Lewis Spitz, "Luther and Humanism," in *Luther and Learning: The Wittenberg University Luther Symposium*, ed. Marilyn J. Harran (Selinsgrove, PA: Susquehanna University Press, 1985), 69–94.

91. See Russell Kleckley, *The Supputatio Annorum Mundi and Luther's View of History: A Case Study in Historiography and Exegesis* (Philadelphia: Lutheran Theological Seminary, 1985); and James Barr, "Luther and Biblical Chronology," *Bulletin of the John Rylands Library* 72 (1990): 51–68.

92. When, for instance, Luther comments on the parable of the king who forgave a considerable debt owed to him by one of his servants who then refused to forgive a much smaller debt himself (Matt 18:21–35), he devotes several sentences to explaining what the *denarius*, the Roman coin mentioned in Matthew 18:28, was worth (WA 52,525).

93. LW 1,x: "We are in no position to determine with any degree of finality which of the classical quotations originated with Luther and which did not."

94. See LW 51,xiv, for Luther's insistence that his printers only print his sermons "if they have been prepared by my hand or previously printed here in Wittenberg at my behest."

95. Pettegree, *Brand Luther*, xiii.

96. Of his lectures on Galatians as prepared for publication by Georg Rörer (with the help of Veit Dietrich and Caspar Cruciger), Luther observes, "I recognize that all the thoughts set down by the brethren with such care in this book are my own" (LW 26,x).

97. Reinhard Schwarz, "Beobachtungen zu Luthers Bekanntschaft mit antiken Dichtern und Geschichtsschreibern," *Lutherjahrbuch* 54 (1987): 22.

98. Hardie, *Classicism and Christianity*, 60.

99. WA 11,295.

100. See my "Arms and the Theologian: Martin Luther's *Adversus Armatum Virum Cochlaeum*," *International Journal of the Classical Tradition* 10 (2003): 38–53.

101. More than once Luther refers to Rome simply as *Urbs* not only in his early correspondence but also as late as 1545 (e.g., WAB 1,155; 1,270; and 2,118; and WA 54,181).

102. WAT 4,631,#5042. A book earlier, Virgil uses the same line to describe the death of another one of Aeneas's opponents, Camilla (*Aeneid* 11.831). For the Latin text of the *Aeneid* here and elsewhere, I rely on R. A. B. Mynors, ed., *P. Vergili Maronis* (Oxford: Clarendon, 1972).

103. WAB 9,366.

104. WAB 2,137. Luther may have borrowed the expression not directly from Caesar (Suetonius, *Divus Iulius* 32) but from Ulrich von Hutten, who used it as a slogan (WAB 2,138, n. 7).

105. Schwarz, "Beobachtungen," 22.

106. Calvin Pater, *Karlstadt as the Father of the Baptist Movements: The Emergence of Lay Protestantism* (Toronto: University of Toronto Press, 1984), 65.

107. Peter Matheson, *The Rhetoric of the Reformation* (Edinburgh: T&T Clark, 1998), 102.

108. WA 50,578.

109. WA 53,95.

110. WA 14,688.

111. WA 54,143.

112. WA 43,633; 43,638; and 44,368.

113. WA 50,148. On doubts as to Luther's authorship of *Aliquot nomina propria Germanorum ad priscam etymologiam restituta*, see Lewis Spitz, "Headwaters of the Reformation: *Studia Humanitatis, Luther Senior, et Initia Reformationis*," in *Luther and the Dawn of the Modern Era: Papers for the Fourth International Conference for Luther Research*, ed. Heiko Oberman (Leiden: Brill, 1974), 106.

114. WA 54,143.

115. WA 25,265 and 23,10.

116. WA 25,204; 20,170; and 31.2,188.

117. WA 43,574. Luther refers to the wealth of Crassus in the Ninety-Five Theses (LW 31,33).

118. WAT 3,449,#3607. In WA 19,404, Luther evidently confuses Pompey's *praenomen* with that of Caesar's. Luther has it as C.—that is to say, Gaius—but Pompey's first name was actually Gnaeus, which is usually abbreviated as Cn.

119. WA 31.2,190.

120. WA 40.3,242.

121. WA 40.3,251.

122. WA 51,215. Since Brutus is included in the company of Cicero and Demosthenes in this context, Luther probably has in mind the first-century orator and politician Marcus Junius Brutus and not the earlier Lucius Junius Brutus, who helped establish the Roman Republic after the overthrow of the last of the Roman kings, Tarquin the Proud.

123. WA 51,215.

124. WAT 5,468,#6061.

125. WA 51,207.

126. WA 31.2,131. See the sixth book of Josephus's *Bellum Judaicum*.

127. WA 5,62. On the question of whether Domitian actually was a great persecutor of Christians, see Brian Jones, *The Emperor Domitian* (New York: Routledge, 1992), 115–17.

128. WA 10.1,2,425.

129. Gregorovius, *History of the City of Rome*, 2,81–83.

130. WA 20,84.

131. WA 1,511. See the life of Alexander Severus in *Historia Augusta* 4.1.

132. WA 53,132.

133. WA 50,550.

134. WA 50,548.

135. WA 14,655.

136. WA 16,636; 16,538; and 14,666.

137. WA 31.1,118.

138. See WA 23,10.

139. See, for example, WA 40.3,252; 42,185; 47,511; 51,244; and 51,496; as well as LW 13,119 and 36,199.

140. See, for example, WA 16,575; 28,609; 28,611; 30.1,3; and 41,392.

141. WAB 8,99.

142. WA 37,214–15.

143. WA 40.3,93.

144. See his poem against Erasmus (WAT 1,399,#823): "He who does not hate Satan should love your poems, Erasmus. And the same man should yoke the Furies and milk the gods of death" (*Qui Satanam non odit, amet tua carmina, Erasme, / Atque idem iungat Furias atque mulgeat Orcos*).

145. WA 44,65.

146. WA 25,414–15. See Kim Beerden, "Roman *dolia* and the Fattening of Dormice," *Classical World* 105 (2012): 227–35.

147. WA 34.1,159.

148. WA 44,221.

149. WA 43,647.

150. WA 31.2,619. See the discussion in Plutarch's *Moralia* (*Roman Questions* 14).

151. WA 23,510. The crowns regularly used in Roman triumphs were made of laurel or gold, while myrtle was reserved for the *ovatio*, a less celebratory version of a full-blown triumph.

152. WAT 3,545,#3700. On Leo X's grand papal procession in 1513, see Gregorovius, *History of the City of Rome*, 8.1,180–88.

153. WA 9,425.

154. WA 50,383.

155. WA 50,383–84.

156. WA 42,224.

157. WA 3,420. Ennius's *Annales* does not itself survive intact but only as quoted by others. Luther probably took this line from Augustine (*De civitate Dei* 2.21), who, in turn, took it from Cicero, *De Republica* 5.1.

158. WA 40.1,543.

159. WA 40.1,219.

160. WA 40.1,219.

161. WA 31.2,190.

162. WAT 5,567,#6271.

163. WA 51,244.

164. WA 42,274.

165. WA 18,651.

166. See my discussion in *Cicero in Heaven*, 88–89.

167. WAT 4,14,#3925.

168. WAT 1,73,#155.

169. WA 20,167.

170. WA 51,210. See Suetonius, *Vita divi Augusti* 28.

171. WA 31.1,440.

172. WA 31.1,440. Luther is quoting here (in translation) lines 65–67 of Terence's play *Adelphoe*: *et errat longe mea equidem sententia, / qui imperium credat gravius esse aut stabilius / vi quod fit quam illud quod amicitia adiungitur.* For the Latin text, see Sidney Ashmore, ed., *P. Terenti Afri Comoediae* (New York: Oxford University Press, 1910), 247.

173. WA 14,692.

174. See Suetonius, *Divus Augustus* 25.

175. WA 38,541–42.

176. See Peter Stein, *Roman Law in European History* (Cambridge: Cambridge University Press, 1999).

177. WA 28,331–32. See also WA 33,481 and 37,340.

178. WA 51,242–43.

179. WAT 2,456,#2412b.

180. WA 39.1,101.

181. WA 51,207.

182. WA 51,243.

183. WA 51,243.

184. WA 1,603. See Suetonius, *Tiberius* 32.

185. WA 14,702.

186. WA 14,655.

187. See my *Luther's Aesop*, especially chs. 3 and 4.

188. WA 51,215.

189. WA 31.2,618.

190. WA 51,252; see Suetonius, *Gaius Caligula* 30.1.

191. WA 42,193; see Suetonius, *Gaius Caligula* 30.2.

192. WA 45,259.

193. WA 34.2,430–31.

194. WA 20,51.

195. WA 20,84.

196. WA 40.2,325.

197. WA 20,12.

198. WA 15,622. See Suetonius, *Divus Iulius* 7.

199. WA 46,572–73.

200. WA 42,514.

201. LW 48,25. See the descriptions in Virgil, *Aeneid* 6.843–44; and Dante, *Purgatorio* 20.25–27.

202. WA 39.1,101.

203. WA 20,51.

204. WA 19,589.

205. WA 49,248.

206. WA 20,54.

207. WA 20,104–5. See Suetonius, *Divus Iulius* 26–30, on Caesar's extravagance.

208. WA 31.2,509–10.

209. WA 42,415.

210. WA 20,54. The scatological reference to Nero is found in the lecture notes of 1526 but not in the 1532 edition.

211. WA 3,420.

212. There are many variations of this expression in Latin. See, for example, Aurelius Victor, *De viris illustribus urbis Romae* 47.8. Scipio Nasica is not to be confused with his cousin, Scipio Africanus, who defeated Hannibal at Zama (WAT 3,449,#3607).

213. WA 1,624–25.

214. WA 31.1,214.

215. WAT 2,608,#2709a.

216. For Luther's own historical overview, see WA 54,296.

217. WA 41,141.

218. See Lucy Grig, "Deconstructing the Symbolic City: Jerome as Guide to Late Antique Rome," *Papers of the British School at Rome* 80 (2012): 125–43.

219. For Luther's youthful annotations on *De civitate Dei*, see WA 9,24–27.

220. WA 33,630–31.

221. WA 23,527.

222. While in Rome, Luther would not have seen Raphael's famous fresco depicting Leo's meeting with Attila in the Vatican's Stanze di Raffaello, as it was not completed until 1514.

223. WA 54,296.

224. On the identification of the third of Luther's "sackings" with Ricimer's siege, see the note in LW 13,282.

225. WA 53,141.

226. WA 40.2,232.

227. WA 31.1,127.

228. For the heading of this subchapter, see Shayari De Silva, "Beyond Ruin Porn: What's behind Our Obsession with Decay?," *ArchDaily* (blog), August 15, 2014, https://tinyurl.com/whatswithourobsession.

229. See, for example, the account in Appian, *Punica* 19.132. My translation of the lines from the *Iliad* is based on the Greek text of David B. Munro and Thomas W. Allen, *Homeri Opera*, vol. 3, 3rd ed. (Oxford: Clarendon, 1920).

230. WAT 1,452,#904.

231. My translation is based on the Latin text in Roberto Palla, trans., *San Gerolamo, Lettere: Introduzione e note die Claudio Moreschini*, 3rd ed. (Milan: RCS Rizzoli Libri, 2009), 436.

232. See Robert Martyn, trans., *The Letters of Gregory the Great*, books 1–4 (Toronto: Pontifical Institute of Medieval Studies, 2004), 3, n. 12.

233. WAB 10,525.

234. *Carm.* 9.37–38 (MGH, *Poetae Latini Aevi Carolini* 1,230).

235. As quoted in Macaulay, *Pleasure of Ruins*, 174.

236. Macaulay, 174–75.

237. Macaulay, 175–76.

238. As quoted by Victor Plahte Tschudi, "Two Sixteenth-Century Guidebooks and the Bibliotopography of Rome," in *Rome and the Guidebook Tradition: From the Middle Ages to the 20th Century*, ed. Anna Blennow and Stefano Fogelberg Rota (Berlin: De Gruyter, 2019), 89.

239. For background, see Ronald Musto, *Apocalypse in Rome: Cola di Rienzo and the Politics of the New Age* (Berkeley: University of California Press, 2003).

240. Macaulay, *Pleasure of Ruins*, 178.

241. Macaulay, 188.

242. Macaulay, 189.

243. Ravaglioli, *Heart of Rome*, 59.

244. As quoted in Christopher Kelly, *The Roman Empire: A Very Short Introduction* (Oxford: Oxford University Press, 2006), 117.

245. Macaulay, *Pleasure of Ruins*, 189–90.

246. See John Pinto, *City of the Soul: Rome and the Romantics* (New York: Morgan Library & Museum, 2016).

247. George Gordon Byron, *The Poetical Works of Lord Byron* (London: Oxford University Press, 1928), 230.

248. Thomas Hutchinson, ed., *The Complete Poetical Works of Percy Bysshe Shelley* (London: Oxford University Press, 1923), 437.

249. Macaulay, *Pleasure of Ruins*, 201.

250. Dickens, *American Notes*, 363.

251. Henry James, *Portrait of a Lady* (Boston: Houghton Mifflin, 1882), 2,454.

252. Vance, *America's Rome*, xvi.

253. See Richard Gummere, "Walt Whitman and His Reaction to the Classics," *Harvard Studies in Classical Philology* 60 (1951): 263–89.

254. As quoted in Susan Hanssen, "'Shall We Go to Rome?'—The Last Days of Henry Adams," *New England Quarterly* 86 (2013): 9.

255. Macaulay, *Pleasure of Ruins*, 203.

256. Carl Jung, *Memories, Dreams, Reflections*, trans. Richard and Clara Winston, ed. Aniela Jaffé (New York: Knopf Doubleday, 1989), 288.

257. Richard Thomas, *Why Bob Dylan Matters* (New York: HarperCollins, 2017), 73. The first stanza of "When I Paint My Masterpiece" is "Oh, the streets of Rome are filled with rubble / Ancient footprints are everywhere / You can almost think that you're seeing double / On a cold, dark night on the Spanish Stairs."

Chapter Three

1. Orrin Robinson, "Luther's Bible and the Emergence of Standard German," in *A New History of German Literature*, ed. David Wellbery (Cambridge, MA: Harvard University Press, 2004), 234.

2. Heinrich Heine, *Zur Geschichte der Religion und Philosophie in Deutschland,* vol. 5, *Gesammelte Werke* (Berlin: Grotesche Verlagsbuchhandlung, 1887), 40.

3. WAT 5,468,#6062.

4. Geoffrey Parker, *Emperor: A New Life of Charles V* (New Haven, CT: Yale University Press, 2019), 8.

5. For a discussion of Luther's harangue "Against Hans Wurst," see Harry Loewen, *Ink against the Devil: Luther and His Opponents* (Waterloo, ON: Wilfrid Laurier University Press, 2015), ch. 15.

6. WA 54,206.

7. WA 7,89.

8. "The sober, secular, practical, temporal, and above all relative term *betterment*" is preferable to such grandiose designations as "the glorious *Reformation*" (Oberman, 74).

9. Brecht 2,251.

10. WA 7,838.

11. Scott Dixon, *Protestants: A History from Wittenberg to Pennsylvania, 1517–1740* (Chichester: Wiley-Blackwell, 2010), 6–7.

12. For the German text, see WA 35,457. The translation is from *The Lutheran Hymnal* (St. Louis: Concordia, 1941), #262.

13. For the French original, see Malachi Haim Hacohen, *Jacob and Esau: Jewish European History between Nation and Empire* (Cambridge: Cambridge University Press, 2019), 138, n. 4. For a compelling counterargument, see Thomas Renna, "The Holy Roman Empire Is Neither Holy, nor Roman, nor an Empire," *Michigan Academician* 42 (2015): 60–75. Joachim Whaley, *Germany and the Holy Roman Empire*, vol. 1, *Maximilian I to the Peace of Westphalia, 1493–1648* (Oxford: Oxford University Press, 2012), chs. 2–4, offers a helpful historical overview.

14. For Belisarius's victory over the Vandals, see John Barker, *Justinian and the Later Roman Empire* (Madison: University of Wisconsin Press, 1966), 141–43.

15. Einhard, *Vita Karoli Magni* 28 (PL 97,51–52).

16. MGH, *Diplomata Karolinorum* 1,284.

17. Einhard, *Vita Karoli Magni* 31 (PL 97,55). On Charlemagne's titles, see Janet Nelson, *King and Emperor: A New Life of Charlemagne* (Berkeley: University of California Press, 2019), 2.

18. For a recent biography, see John Freed, *Frederick Barbarossa: The Prince and the Myth* (New Haven, CT: Yale University Press, 2016). Luther gives Barbarossa's reign as thirty-seven years in his *Supputatio annorum* (WA 53,157); it was actually thirty-five years long.

19. Benjamin Curtis, *The Habsburgs: The History of a Dynasty* (London: Bloomsbury Academic, 2013), 36.

20. WADB 7,415.

21. WA 51,242.

22. Einhard, *Vita Karoli Magni* 23 (PL 97,48). Luther refers to the event in WA 50,104 and 54,296. Like Einhard, Luther believed that Charlemagne did not really want to be crowned emperor by the pope.

23. WA 54,297.

24. Joan Barclay Lloyd, "Medieval Dominican Architecture at Santa Sabina in Rome, c. 1219–1320," *Papers of the British School at Rome* 72 (2004): 246.

25. See David Abulafia, *Frederick II: A Medieval Emperor* (New York: Oxford University Press, 1992), ch. 8.

26. See, for example, WA 7,89.

27. For an overview of Diocletian's and Constantine's political innovations, see Timothy Barnes, *The New Empire of Diocletian and Constantine* (Cambridge, MA: Harvard University Press, 1982).

28. WA 5,429.

29. WADB 7,415.

30. WA 41,227.

31. See Uta-Renate Blumenthal, *The Investiture Controversy: Church and Monarchy from the Ninth to the Twelfth Century* (Philadelphia: University of Pennsylvania Press, 1988), ch. 4.

32. Geoffrey Bullough, *Narrative and Dramatic Sources of Shakespeare*, vol. 5, *The Roman Plays* (New York: Columbia University Press, 1964), 19.

33. See, for example, WA 2,31.

34. WA 50,70. See David Whitford, "The Papal Antichrist: Martin Luther and the Underappreciated Influence of Lorenzo Valla," *Renaissance Quarterly* 61 (2008): 26–52.

35. WAT 5,181,#5484.

36. WAT 2,48,#1327.

37. WA 6,417–18.

38. WA 50,78.

39. WA 6,289.

40. WA 47,434.

41. WAT 2,48,#1327 (1532). See also WA 47,492–93.

42. For the expression "German beast" (*Todescola bestia*), see WA 5,436.

43. WA 54,212.

44. WA 54,351.

45. WAB 2,138.

46. Julius Köstlin, *Life of Luther* (London: Longmans, 1883), 15. Brecht (1,19) suggests that the "Cotta couple lived in the same house as the Schalbes," where Luther was lodging.

47. WAT 4,17–18,#3930.

48. There is now a garden square in Florence that was dedicated in April 2017 to Martin Luther on the Lungarno Torrigiani southeast of the Ponte Vecchio.

49. Böhmer, *Luthers Romfahrt*, 84. On the heavy reliance on the mule in Italian agriculture at the time, see the bracketed parenthetical observation in a sermon of 1519 (WA 9,426).

50. WA 31.2,582.

51. Böhmer, *Luthers Romfahrt*, 84; Brecht 2,202.

52. WA 43,330.

53. WAT 3,345,#3477.

54. Böhmer, *Luthers Romfahrt*, 85.

55. WA 42,414.

56. WAB 2,307.

57. WAB 2,175–76.

58. WAB 2,177. Bainton's rather free translation (*Here I Stand*, 151) evokes Acts 25:11: "For three years I have sought peace in vain. I have now but one recourse. I appeal to Caesar."

59. WAB 2,300.

60. Oberman, 29.

61. WAT 5,466–67,#6058.

62. *MLiR*, xvii.

63. Gregorovius, *History of the City of Rome*, 8.2,523; Richard Viladesau, *The Triumph of the Cross: The Passion of Christ in Theology and the Arts from the*

Renaissance to the Counter-Reformation (Oxford: Oxford University Press, 2008), 184.

64. WAB 4,222.

65. WAB 4,280.

66. On the regular flooding of the Tiber and the flood of 1530, see Peter Partner, *Renaissance Rome 1500–1559: A Portrait of a Society* (Berkeley: University of California Press, 1976), 81–82.

67. I use the text of the poem as it is found in WA 35,599. Rörer's copy of the poem has *Quam* instead of *Quum* in the first line and *deas* instead of *deos* in the fourth line (WADB 4,417).

68. WAT 5,466,#6058.

69. For general background, see E. R. Chamberlin, *The Sack of Rome* (New York: Dorset, 1979).

70. For more on Clement VII, see Kenneth Gouwens and Sheryl Reiss, eds., *The Pontificate of Clement VII: History, Politics, Culture* (Aldershot, UK: Ashgate, 2005).

71. "How blind all you people of Rome were, and how little you understood God! Every hour you met in the streets men who had already turned their souls into stables for vices, and yet you thought nothing of it. But when a stable was needed for horses and they were sheltered in the church of St. Peter, you tell me that it was a great evil, and that it breaks your heart to think about it." As quoted in Russel Lemmons, "'If There Is a Hell, Then Rome Stands upon It': Martin Luther as Traveler and Translator," in *Travel and Translation in the Early Modern Period*, ed. Carmine G. Di Biase (Amsterdam: Rodopi, 2006), 36.

72. Adolf Häckermann, "Mohnike, Gottlieb Christian Friedrich," *Allgemeine Deutsche Biographie, Historische Kommission bei der Bayerischen Akademie der Wissenschaften* 22 (1885): 62–64.

73. It is hard to imagine what sort of motive Mohnike could possibly have had for such deception. There has never been that much interest in Luther's Latin poetry, especially when compared to the research that has been devoted over the years to his German hymns. Even if discovering a hitherto unknown work of Luther's might be regarded as a scholarly coup of some sort that could advance one's academic career, such a dubious strategy for self-aggrandizement could also easily backfire, effectively

wrecking one's chances for ever achieving legitimate success in the field. By 1832, when Mohnike first published his findings, he was already a well-established and even renowned scholar.

74. WAB 5,176–77.

75. WAT 3,390,#3543A.

76. For this line and other variations, see WA 35,597–98.

77. Oberman, 329.

78. WA 35,599.

79. See WAT 1,442,#884.

80. WA 50,660. See my "The Uses of *Tentatio*: Satan, Luther, and Theological Maturation," in *The Hermeneutics of Hell: Visions and Representations of the Devil in World Literature*, ed. Gregor Thuswaldner and Daniel Russ (Cham, Switzerland: Palgrave Macmillan, 2017), 39.

81. Oberman, 203.

82. WA 32,182.

83. WA 30.3,291.

84. WA 54,206.

85. See, for example, WAB 2,242.

86. For examples of Luther's prayers on behalf of the emperor in later letters, see WAB 10,525; 10,554; and 11,85.

87. WAB 6,37.

88. See Mark Edwards, *Luther's Last Battles: Politics and Polemics, 1531–46* (Ithaca: Cornell University Press, 1983), ch. 2, "The Question of Resistance."

89. WAB 8,367.

90. WAB 9,77.

91. WAB 11,201.

92. WAT 5,317,#5676. The first four lines follow: "When Caesar engages in battle with unsubdued foes, he is accustomed always to return with his Mars unconquered. But whenever he tries to scatter the assemblies of the saints, he will fall vanquished like one who has taken up arms against heaven" (*Caesar in indomitos ubi proelia suscipit hostes, / Invicto semper Marte redire solet. / Ast ubi sanctorum coetus disperdere tentet, / Victus, ut in coelum qui tulit arma, ruet*).

93. Brecht 2,424.

94. WAT 4,631,#5042.

95. WAB 5,373.

96. Clement was laid to rest in S. Maria sopra Minerva across the apse from the tomb of his cousin, Leo X.

97. WA 54,207.

98. Eric Metaxas, *Martin Luther: The Man Who Rediscovered the Gospel and Changed the World* (New York: Viking, 2017), 433. See also Hendrix, *Martin Luther: Visionary Reformer*, 287; and Brecht 3,380.

99. See Brent Sockness, "Luther's Two Kingdoms Revisited: A Response to Reinhold Niebuhr's Criticism of Luther," *Journal of Religious Ethics* 20 (1992): 93–110; and William Wright, *Martin Luther's Understanding of God's Two Kingdoms: A Response to the Challenge of Skepticism* (Grand Rapids: Baker, 2010).

100. WAT 4,388,#4582.

101. On Luther's deeply rooted Augustinianism, see Eric Saak, *Luther and the Reformation of the Later Middle Ages* (Cambridge: Cambridge University Press, 2017).

102. *De civitate Dei* 15.1 (PL 41,437–38). Luther's political thought developed far beyond its Augustinian foundations; see W. D. J. Cargill Thompson, *The Political Thought of Martin Luther* (Sussex: Harvester, 1983), 3. See also Robert Kolb, *Martin Luther: Confessor of the Faith* (Oxford: Oxford University Press, 2009), 176–78.

103. WA 36,385.

104. WA 51,238–39.

105. WAT 2,308,#2062.

106. WA 51,207. It is not clear which of the Holy Roman emperors who were named Frederick is meant here.

107. See Michael Gaddis, *There Is No Crime for Those Who Have Christ: Religious Violence in the Christian Roman Empire* (Berkeley: University of California Press, 2005), chs. 3–4.

108. The gospel will prevail "not by force but by the word" (*non vi, sed verbo*); see Oberman, 45.

109. WA 51,258.

110. WA 30.3,278–79.

111. WA 51,209.

112. On Duke George's determined opposition to Luther, see Edwards, *Luther's Last Battles*, ch. 3.

113. WAB 11,56.

114. WA 18,361. See Oberman, 289.

115. On Flacius's radical theology and its political implications, see Luka Ilić, *Theologian of Sin and Grace: The Process of Radicalization in the Theology of Matthias Flacius Illyricus* (Göttingen: Vandenhoeck & Ruprecht, 2014).

116. Leonard Trinterud, *Elizabethan Puritanism* (Oxford: Oxford University Press, 1971), 101–6.

117. For a diachronic overview, see George Mosse, *The Crisis of German Ideology: Intellectual Origins of the Third Reich* (New York: Grosset & Dunlap, 1964). But see also Uwe Siemon-Netto, *The Fabricated Luther: Refuting Nazi Connections and Other Modern Myths*, 2nd ed. (St. Louis: Concordia, 2007).

118. See my "Luther's Latin Poetry and Scatology," *Lutheran Quarterly* 23 (2009): 373–87.

119. Brecht 2,444.

120. WA 47,669.

121. Brecht 3,280.

122. From his preface to Justus Menius, *Defense and Thorough Exploration* (1526), as quoted in Pettegree, *Brand Luther*, 275–76.

123. Benjamin Mayes, *Counsel and Conscience: Lutheran Casuistry and Moral Reasoning after the Reform* (Göttingen: Vandenhoeck & Ruprecht, 2011), 33.

124. Brecht 3,381.

125. LW 50,277; 50,286; 50,300; and 50,305. See also Brecht 3,241.

126. WAT 1,554,#1110.

127. Oberman, 289.

128. WAT 3,370–71,#3514; Brecht 3,1–4 and 221.

129. See Luther's preface to his never-completed edition of Aesop's fables (translation in my *Luther's Aesop*, 82–87).

130. WA 5,450.

131. WA 6,292–93.

132. WA 45,83.

133. WA 5,57.

134. Already in 1519 in preparation for the Leipzig Debate, Luther had read Rufinus's translation of Eusebius's history of the early church (Oberman, 262).

135. Oswald Bayer, *Martin Luther's Theology: A Contemporary Interpretation*, trans. Thomas H. Trapp (Grand Rapids: Eerdmans, 2008), 278.

136. WA 50,250. See Sam Chan, *Preaching as the Word of God: Answering an Old Question with Speech-Act Theory* (Eugene: Pickwick, 2016), 59–60.

137. WA 2,448.

138. WA 47,425.

139. See Daniel Rodgers, *As a City on a Hill: The Story of America's Most Famous Lay Sermon* (Princeton, NJ: Princeton University Press, 2018); and Richard Gamble, *In Search of the City on a Hill: The Making and Unmaking of an American Myth* (London: Continuum, 2012).

140. See, for example, Cullen Murphy, *Are We Rome? The Fall of an Empire and the Fate of America* (New York: Houghton Mifflin, 2007).

141. Oberman, 46.

142. Brecht 3,262–65.

143. LW 50,278.

144. The adjective is James Nestingen's; see his *Martin Luther: A Life* (Minneapolis: Fortress, 2003), 17.

145. Brecht 3,265.

146. See Hartmut Lehmann, "Nineteenth-Century American Tourists in Wittenberg, the 'Protestant Mecca,'" *Lutheran Quarterly* 29 (2015): 420–38.

147. Gregorovius, *History of the City of Rome*, 1,9, n. 2.

148. *Enchiridion*, 513.

149. WA 22,371–72.

150. Luther mentions Ronciglione, a town located approximately halfway between Orvieto and Rome, in WA 54,219.

151. WA 14,72.

152. WAB 5,377–78.

153. *Enchiridion*, 514.

Chapter Four

1. Marina Münkler, "Luthers Rom: Augenzeugenschaft, Invektivität und Konversion," in *Transformationen Roms in der Vormoderne*, ed. Volker Leppin and Christoph Mauntel (Basel, Switzerland: Schwabe/Kohlhammer, 2019), 227.

2. Luther was quite familiar with the history of the papacy and the popes. The popes who reigned during Luther's lifetime were the following: Sixtus IV (della Rovere), Innocent VIII (Cibo), Alessandro VI (Borgia), Pius III (Piccolomini), Julius II (della Rovere), Leo X (Medici), Adrian (or Hadrian) VI, Clement VII (Medici), and Paul III (Farnese).

3. See Edwards, *Luther's Last Battles*, 6–19.

4. Oberman, 327–28, mentions a number of these. See also Edwards, *Luther's Last Battles*, 9–10.

5. Edwards, *Luther's Last Battles*, 10. A substantial body of research has been devoted to the question of Luther's health; see Edwards, 214, n. 10.

6. Edwards, 19.

7. See Heiko Oberman, "*Teufelsdreck*: Eschatology and Scatology in the Old Luther," *Sixteenth Century Journal* 19 (1988): 435–50.

8. Herman Selderhuis, *John Calvin: A Pilgrim's Life*, trans. Albert Gootjes (Downers Grove, IL: InterVarsity, 2009), 15.

9. WAT 1,294,#623. See also Erikson, *Young Man Luther*, 144–45.

10. Brecht 1,7–9.

11. See Marlene Winell, "Religious Trauma Syndrome," *Journey Free*, accessed February 12, 2021, https://tinyurl.com/17wlwrej.

12. WAT 2,132,#1557.

13. WA 54,207.

14. For recent scholarly perspectives, see P. David Marshall, Christopher Moore, and Kim Barbour, eds., *Persona Studies: An Introduction* (Hoboken, NJ: Wiley-Blackwell, 2020).

15. Pettegree, *Brand Luther*, especially chs. 4–6.

16. See WAT 2,132–33,#1557.

17. Brecht 3,186.

18. WAT 5,700,#6503.

19. WA 54,207.

20. WA 6,347.

21. WA 2,195 and 2,643.

22. WA 10.2,134; 49,683; 47,692; 51,193; 49,802; 54,298; 22,192; 8,214; 8,185; 21,302; 7,717; 50,103; 38,118; 7,403; 7,395; 2,195; and 54,228.

23. WAB 2,305.

24. WAB 3,229.

25. Brecht 3,359.

26. WAB 1,270.

27. WAB 2,214; 2,164.

28. WAB 11,142; 11,144.

29. For historical overviews, see Hans Preuss, *Die Vorstellungen vom Antichrist im späteren Mittelalter, bei Luther und in der Konfessionellen Polemik* (Leipzig: J. C. Hinrichs, 1906); and Bernard McGinn, *Antichrist: Two Thousand Years of the Human Fascination with Evil* (New York: HarperSanFrancisco, 1994).

30. Stefan Zweig, *Triumph und Tragik des Erasmus von Rotterdam* (Berlin: Karl-Maria Guth, 2015), 71.

31. See John Duerk, "Elijah P. Lovejoy: Anti-Catholic Abolitionist," *Journal of the Illinois Historical Society* 108 (2015): 103–21.

32. As quoted in Daniel Harmelink, "C.F.W. Walther Publishes an Impassioned Plea: 'Compare the Word of Christ with the Decrees of the Pope!' Missouri Synod's 1878 Saint Louis Edition of Martin Luther's *Passional Christi und Antichristi*," *Concordia Historical Institute Quarterly* 93 (2020): 27.

33. Karen DeYoung, "European Parliament Ejects Paisley after He Denounces Pope," *Washington Post*, October 12, 1988, https://tinyurl.com/ulsterantichrist.

34. See Susan Wood and Timothy Wengert, *A Shared Spiritual Journey: Lutherans and Catholics Traveling toward Unity* (New York: Paulist, 2016). On changing conceptions of Luther by Catholic theologians in more recent years, see David Steinmetz, "The Catholic Luther: A Critical Appraisal," *Theology Today* 61 (2004): 187–201.

35. "1999 Official Common Statement by the Lutheran World Federation and the Catholic Church," Pontifical Council for Promoting Christian Unity, accessed February 22, 2021, https://tinyurl.com/JDDJ-1999.

36. See the first chapter of John McHugo, *A Concise History of Sunnis and Shi'is* (Washington, DC: Georgetown University Press, 2017).

37. For the Latin original, see John Headley, ed., *The Complete Works of St. Thomas More*, vol. 5, pt. 1 (New Haven, CT: Yale University Press, 1969), 682.

38. *Sanctus Grobianus*, a fictional creation of Sebastian Brant, was the supposed saint of vulgarians. A humorous manual on manners entitled *Grobianus et Grobiana: De morum simplicitate libri tres*, published in 1558 by Friedrich Dedekind, a student of Melanchthon at Wittenberg, was translated into English as *The Schoole of Slovenrie: Or, Cato turnd wrong side outward* (1605).

39. For the Italian text, see Geoffrey Bickersteth, trans., *The Divine Comedy of Dante Alighieri* (Oxford: Blackwell, 1981), 716.

40. As quoted in Izora Scott, *Controversies over the Imitation of Cicero* (Davis, CA: Hermagoras, 1991), 11.

41. As quoted in James Atkinson, *Martin Luther: Prophet to the Church Catholic* (Grand Rapids: Eerdmans, 1983), 9.

42. I use the Latin epithets (with some emendations) as they are found in James Townley, *Illustrations of Biblical Literature Exhibiting the History and Fate of the Sacred Writings from the Earliest Period to the Present Century*, vol. 3 (London: Longmans, 1821), 214. The translations of the epithets are my own.

43. Luther's literary model in this regard might well be the Latin church father with whom he was otherwise relatively unimpressed, Jerome. See David Wiesen, *St. Jerome as a Satirist: A Study in Christian Latin Thought and Letters* (Ithaca: Cornell University Press, 1964), especially ch. 3, "The Church and the Clergy."

44. WA 50,128–30. The letter is not included in early editions of Luther's works, but the WA editors argue for its authenticity.

45. WAT 2,60,#1346. For some of the characteristics of Juvenal's satire, see S. C. Fredericks, "Irony of Overstatement in the Satires of Juvenal," *Illinois Classical Studies* 4 (1979): 178–91.

46. See Brean Hammond, "The City in Eighteenth-Century Poetry," in *The Cambridge Companion to Eighteenth-Century Poetry*, ed. John Sitter (Cambridge: Cambridge University Press, 2001), 83–108.

47. See, in general, Eric Gritsch, *The Wit of Martin Luther* (Minneapolis: Augsburg Fortress, 2006).

48. WA 7,666.

49. WA 54,207; and 5,441.

50. See my "Luther's Latin Poetry and Scatology," 373–87. Here, as elsewhere, Luther's vulgar invective tends to be scatologically rather than sexually oriented.

51. I use the Latin text as found in WAT 4,89–90,#4032.

52. In one of the *Tischreden* of 1532 (WAT 3,228,#3232b), Luther may be understood as assigning his momentous *Durchbruch* to an insight he had while relieving himself in the *cloaca*. See Erikson, *Young Man Luther*, 204. Oberman (155) observes, "The cloaca is not just a privy, it is the most degrading place for man and the Devil's favorite habitat." On the other hand, he continues, "no spot is unholy for the Holy Ghost; this is the very place to express contempt for the adversary through trust in Christ crucified."

53. John Pollack, *The Pun Also Rises: How the Humble Pun Revolutionized Language, Changed History, and Made Wordplay More Than Some Antics* (New York: Gotham, 2012), 88.

54. See John Morreall, "Enjoying Incongruity," *Humor: International Journal of Humor Research* 2 (1989): 1–18; and Tomas Kulka, "The Incongruity of Incongruity Theories," *Estetika* 30 (1993): 1–10.

55. On the popularity of the *Passional Christi und Antichristi*, with its twenty-six woodcuts vividly illustrating the differences between the conduct of Christ and that of the pope, see R. W. Scribner, *For the Sake of Simple Folk: Popular Propaganda for the German Reformation* (Cambridge: Cambridge University Press, 1981), 156–57.

56. WAT 2,152,#1612; and WA 54,220. Luther says that he himself heard the saying when he was in Rome (WA 26,198).

57. WAT 5,468,#6060.

58. WA 7,45.

59. There are variations of this expression in WA 6,437; WA 34.1,109; WA 47,410; WAB 6,274; and WAB 10,306.

60. José Antonio Rios González, *Roma, andar y ver* (Madrid: Vision Libros, 2009), 109.

61. On irony and its relationship to satire and humor, see Howard Hong, "The Comic, Satire, Irony, and Humor: Kierkegaardian Reflections," *Midwest Studies in Philosophy* 1 (1976): 98–105.

62. On the difficulties involved in determining whether emotions expressed in words can be accurately understood, see Eliot Wirshbo, "Can Emotions Be Determined from Words? A Reconsideration of Recent Military Usage," *American Behavioral Scientist* 33 (1990): 287–95.

63. WA 10.2,140.

64. WA 6,347.

65. WAB 2,249. See Brecht 2,337: "In 1525, and later as well, Luther himself maintained that compulsion should not be employed in matters of faith and conscience."

66. WA 6,468–69.

67. WAB 9,366. For a discussion of *Against Hanswurst* and its reception, see Brecht 3,219–22.

68. WAT 2,455–56,#2410b. On this topic, see Brecht, "Der Schimpfer Luther," *Luther. Zeitschrift der Luthergesellschaft* 52 (1981): 97–113.

69. WAB 6,73–74. See Edwards, *Luther's Last Battles*, 45.

70. WA 30.2,68–69.

71. On the issue of authorial intent in general, see John Farrell, *Varieties of Authorial Intention: Literary Theory beyond the Intentional Fallacy* (Cham, Switzerland: Palgrave Macmillan, 2017). In his "The Death of the Author," in *Image, Music, Text*, trans. Stephen Heath (New York: Hill & Wang, 1977), Roland Barthes acknowledges the difficulty of determining authorial intentions and suggests that a literary work's "origins" matter far less than its readerly "destination" (148).

72. Thomas, *Why Bob Dylan Matters*, 152.

73. WA 32,390.

74. Henri Bergson, *Laughter: An Essay on the Meaning of the Comic*, trans. Fred Rothwell and Cloudesley Brereton (New York: Macmillan, 1911), 5. See also Dwight Van de Vate, "Laughter and Detachment," *Southern Journal of Philosophy* 3 (1965): 163–71.

75. WAB 1,344.

76. Maria Plaza, *The Function of Humour in Roman Verse Satire: Laughter and Lying* (Oxford: Oxford University Press, 2006), 24–25.

77. William Anderson, *Essays on Roman Satire* (Princeton, NJ: Princeton University Press, 1982), 293.

78. See Birgit Stolt, *Martin Luthers Rhetorik des Herzens* (Tübingen: Mohr Siebeck, 2000).

79. WA 35,465.

80. See Olaf Kramer, *Goethe und die Rhetorik* (Berlin: De Gruyter, 2010), 55.

81. WA 1,529.

82. WAT 3,460,#3619.

83. Erikson, *Young Man Luther*, 237.

84. Robert Christman, Review of Andrew Pettegree's *Brand Luther*, *Faith-Life* 90 (2017): 52.

85. Erikson, *Young Man Luther*, 51. Hans Luther was much more than a simple miner. On his relatively high economic and social status as a successful "businessman" in the smelting industry in Mansfeld, see Brecht 1,3–6.

86. On the divisive relationship between Erasmus and Luther and its long-term consequences, see Michael Massing, *Fatal Discord: Erasmus, Luther, and the Fight for the Western Mind* (New York: HarperCollins, 2018). Luther, of course, was not always assertive or monologic, and he was perfectly capable of expressing skepticism and self-doubt. The question he asked himself at the top of the Scala sancta—"Who knows whether it's true?"—is hardly typical of someone who has the answer to everything.

87. Oberman, 326.

88. See Matheson, *Rhetoric of the Reformation*, chs. 5–7.

89. Constance Furey, "Invective and Discernment in Martin Luther, D. Erasmus, and Thomas More," *Harvard Theological Review* 98 (2005): 469–88.

90. Erikson, *Young Man Luther*, 241.

91. As quoted in Edwards, *Luther's Last Battles*, 27.

92. WAB 1,313.

93. WAB 1,408.

94. WAB 1,409–10, n. 6.

95. Bruno was born two years after Luther died, but he had a connection with Lutheranism, if not with Luther himself. He lectured on Aristotle at the university in Wittenberg for two years (1586–88), although he was excommunicated a year later by the Lutherans when he was teaching at Helmstedt. See Thomas Leinkauf, ed., *Giordano Bruno in Wittenberg,*

1586–1588: *Aristoteles, Raimundus Lullus, Astronomie* (Pisa: Istituti editoriali e poligrafici internazionali, 2004).

96. Oberman, 55.

97. For the effect of the executions on Luther, see Robert Christman, *The Dynamics of the Early Reformation in Their Reformed Augustinian Context* (Amsterdam: Amsterdam University Press, 2020), ch. 7. For Luther's views on contemporary martyrdoms, including that of Robert Barnes, see Oberman, 264–71. See Robert Kolb, *For All the Saints: Changing Perceptions of Martyrdom and Sainthood in the Lutheran Reformation* (Macon, GA: Mercer University Press, 1987), on the evolution of Lutheran views of saints and martyrs in the sixteenth century.

98. G. K. Chesterton, *Orthodoxy* (New York: John Lane, 1908), 75.

99. WAT 3,391#3543A.

100. See Piotr Wilczek, "Hate Speech or Brotherly Admonitions? Discourse between Jesuits and 'Heretics' in Early Modern Polish Literature," in *(Mis)translation and (Mis)interpretation: Polish Literature in the Context of Cross-cultural Communication* (Frankfurt: Peter Lang, 2005), 79–101.

101. WAB 1,294.

102. WAB 1,293.

103. WA 8,47.

104. CR 11,729–30.

105. WA 54,199.

106. Mikhail Bakhtin, *Rabelais and His World*, trans. Helene Iswolsky (Bloomington: Indiana University Press, 1984), 12.

107. WA 45,312.

108. Luther is drawing on the familiar analogy between the physical body and collective bodies such as the church and the state used not only by the apostle Paul (1 Cor 12:12–27) but also by Livy (*Ab urbe condita* 2.32) and other classical authors.

109. WA 6,469.

110. WA 35,462–63.

111. WAB 1,293. Augustine personifies the church as *mater ecclesia* in his *Psalmus contra partem Donati*.

112. WA 47,670.

113. WAT 5,181,#5484.

114. WA 8,575–76.

115. Franz Posset, *The Real Luther: A Friar at Erfurt and Wittenberg* (St. Louis: Concordia, 2011), 57.

116. WA 54,179.

117. WAB 1,110–12.

118. WAB 1,292.

119. WA 1,529.

120. WAB 1,306.

121. On the "balanced" character of this treatise, see Neil Leroux, "Luther's Middle Course: Balancing Freedom and Service in *De Libertate Christiana* (1520)," *Studia Historiae Ecclesiasticae* 36 (2010): 1–6.

122. As quoted in Chamberlin, *Bad Popes*, 118.

123. As quoted in Brecht 3,208.

124. Brecht 3,180.

125. As quoted in Brecht 2,351.

126. WA 40.1,357.

127. Brecht 3,223.

128. For recent psychological studies on the importance of place in religion, see Victor Counted and Fraser Watts, eds., *The Psychology of Religion and Place: Emerging Perspectives* (Cham, Switzerland: Palgrave Macmillan, 2019).

129. WA 1,625.

130. Lyndal Roper, *Martin Luther: Renegade and Prophet* (New York: Penguin Random House, 2016).

131. WAB 1,356.

132. WAT 1,96,#225.

133. WAT 1,177,#409.

134. For this designation, see Eric Hoffer, *The True Believer: Thoughts on the Nature of Mass Movements* (New York: Harper & Row, 1951).

135. Hausrath, *Martin Luthers Romfahrt*, 78.

136. WA 51,543.

137. WAT 5,201,#5506.

138. WA 32,328–29.

139. Paulson, *Luther's Outlaw God*, 2,345.

140. Graham Greene, *The Honorary Consul* (New York: Simon and Schuster, 1973), 261.

141. WA 4,147.

142. WA 49,180.

143. Roland Bainton, ed., *Martin Luther's Christmas Book* (Philadelphia: Westminster, 1948), 33.

144. *Enchiridion*, 511.

145. Theodore Tappert, trans. and ed., *The Book of Concord: The Confessions of the Evangelical Lutheran Church* (Philadelphia: Fortress, 1959), 150.

146. Translation in *The Lutheran Hymnal*, #377.

147. WA 5,63–64.

148. WA 2,449.

149. Erasmus's brilliant satire *In Praise of Folly* was first published in 1511.

150. Melanchthon's response to the news of Luther's death was couched in the words of Elisha upon witnessing Elijah being transported to heaven (2 Kgs 2:12): "My father, my father, the chariot of Israel, and the horsemen thereof" (Oberman, 8).

151. See Robert Kolb's useful analysis of perspectives on Luther as "the German prophet" in *Martin Luther as Prophet, Teacher, and Hero: Images of the Reformer, 1520–1620* (Grand Rapids: Baker, 1999), 75–101.

152. WA 30.3,290.

153. WA 6,468.

154. WAT 4,290,#4391.

155. See WA 56,488–89. Luther connects the two cities in WA 1,573; 4,24–26; 7,441; 13,281; 13,452; 31.1,508; 31.2,97; 31.2,375; 31.2,379; 44,787; 47,531; 51,356; and elsewhere.

156. WA 12,398.

157. WAB 2,163–64.

158. WA 40.2,270.

159. Scott Hendrix, in *Luther and the Papacy: Stages in a Reformation Conflict* (Philadelphia: Fortress, 1981), traces the steady deterioration of the relationship.

160. Gregorovius, *History of the City of Rome*, 8.1,186.

161. WA 54,180.

162. WA 30.3,470. See Edwards, *Luther's Last Battles*, 50–51.

163. Cultural prejudice and national pride, no doubt, were factors as well, but not the overriding ones. The threat that the Turks posed to Europe was

seen by Luther not as a political problem primarily but as a danger to true religion. For more on his nuanced perspective in this regard, see his 1529 treatise *On War against the Turk.*

164. LW 41,260.

165. WA 19,239.

166. WA 30.3,421.

167. Erikson, *Young Man Luther,* 65.

168. *Enchiridion,* 511.

169. James Martel, *Love Is a Sweet Chain: Desire, Autonomy, and Friendship in Liberal Political Theory* (New York: Routledge, 2001), 8.

170. WAT 3,348,#3479.

171. WAT 5,317–18,#5677. The entry concludes, "These were the last thoughts of Doctor Martin Luther the day before he died." For Aurifaber's slightly different version of Luther's final note, see WAT 5,168,#5468. According to Aurifaber, the words were written "two days" before Luther's death (February 16, 1546) on a scrap of paper and left lying on a table. Aurifaber made a copy, and the original was entrusted to Justus Jonas.

172. Oberman, 3.

173. WA 31.1,230.

174. Luther is apparently quoting from memory; his version departs somewhat from the standard text: *nec tu diuinam Aeneida tempta, / sed longe sequere et uestigia semper adora.* See Ruth Parkes, "Reading Statius through a Biographical Lens," in *Brill's Companion to Statius*, ed. William J. Dominik, Carole E. Newlands, and Kyle Gervais (Leiden: Brill, 2015), 476.

175. What makes the ministry of John the Baptist and Christ and the apostles such a "great miracle" for Luther is that they were able to proclaim the word of God with such insight and to such effect without much apparent preparation or formal education. As Luther puts it in WAT 5,168,#5468, it is not the "know-it-alls" (*scioli*) and the "big shots" but "the lowly and the simple" who really understand the Holy Scriptures.

176. Actually, only the second clause is to be found in Augustine's *Serm.* 131.10: *causa finita est.* See William Harmless, ed., *Augustine in His Own Words* (Washington, DC: Catholic University Press, 2010), 413.

177. LW 26,ix.

178. WAT 1,320,#674.

179. WA 10.1,1,593.

180. WA 38,105. See Erikson, *Young Man Luther*, 81.

181. WA 8,685. For this and other similar expressions of Luther's regarding the body, see Charles Cortright, "Poor Maggot-Sack That I Am: The Human Body in the Theology of Martin Luther" (PhD diss.; Marquette University, 2011). For the same thought (and an elaborate pun on the Diet of Worms), see Shakespeare's *Hamlet*, act 4, scene 3: "Not where he eats, but where he is eaten: a certain convocation of politic worms are e'en at him. Your worm is your only emperor for diet: we fat all creatures else to fat us, and we fat ourselves for maggots: your fat king and your lean beggar is but variable service, two dishes, but to one table: that's the end" (M. R. Ridley, ed., *Hamlet by William Shakespeare* [London: J. M. Dent & Sons, 1935], 118).

182. In his exposition of Luke 1:52 ("He hath put down the mighty from their seats"), Luther includes Rome among the successful kingdoms that rise only to fall (WA 7,590).

183. WA 56,272.

184. WA 42,254.

Bibliography

Abulafia, David. *Frederick II: A Medieval Emperor.* New York: Oxford University Press, 1992.

Aicher, Peter J. *Guide to the Aqueducts of Ancient Rome.* Wauconda, IL: Bolchazy-Carducci, 1995.

Allen, Bruce Ware. *Tiber: Eternal River of Rome.* Lebanon, NH: University Press of New England, 2018.

Anderson, Darran. *Imaginary Cities: A Tour of Dream Cities, Nightmare Cities, and Everywhere in Between.* Chicago: University of Chicago Press, 2017.

Anderson, William. *Essays on Roman Satire.* Princeton, NJ: Princeton University Press, 1982.

Atkinson, James. *Martin Luther: Prophet to the Church Catholic.* Grand Rapids: Eerdmans, 1983.

Bagchi, David. "The German Rabelais? Foul Words and the Word in Luther." *Reformation and Renaissance Review* 7 (2005): 143–162.

Bainton, Roland H. *Here I Stand: A Life of Martin Luther.* New York: Abingdon-Cokesbury Press, 1950.

———. *Martin Luther's Christmas Book.* Philadelphia: Westminster, 1948.

Baker, Patrick, Johannes Helmrath, and Craig Kallendorf, eds. *Beyond Reception: Renaissance Humanism and the Transformation of Classical Antiquity.* Berlin: De Gruyter, 2019.

Bakhtin, Mikhail. *Rabelais and His World.* Translated by Helene Iswolsky. Bloomington: Indiana University Press, 1984.

Bärenfänger, Katherina, Volker Leppin, and Stefan Michel, eds. *Martin Luthers Tischreden: Neuansätze der Forschung.* Tübingen: Mohr Siebeck, 2013.

Barker, John W. *Justinian and the Later Roman Empire.* Madison: University of Wisconsin Press, 1966.

Barker, Sheila. "The Making of a Plague Saint." In *Piety and Plague: From Byzantium to the Baroque*, edited by Franco Mormando and Thomas Worcester, 90–131. Kirksville, MO: Truman State University Press, 2007.

Barnes, Timothy D. *The New Empire of Diocletian and Constantine*. Cambridge, MA: Harvard University Press, 1982.

Barr, James. "Luther and Biblical Chronology." *Bulletin of the John Rylands Library* 72 (1990): 51–68.

Barthes, Roland. "The Death of the Author." In *Image, Music, Text*. Translated by Stephen Heath, 142–148. New York: Hill & Wang, 1977.

Barton, William M. *Mountain Aesthetics in Early Modern Latin Literature*. London: Routledge, 2016.

Battafarano, Italo Michele. "Luthers Romreise in den erinnernden 'Tischreden.'" In *Deutsche Handwerker, Künstler und Gelehrte im Rom der Renaissance*, edited by Stephan Füssel and Klaus Vogel, 214–237. Wiesbaden: Harrassowitz, 2001.

———. *Mit Luther oder Goethe in Italien: Irritation und Sehnsucht der Deutschen*. Trento, Italy: Università degli Studi di Trento, 2007.

Bayer, Oswald. *Martin Luther's Theology: A Contemporary Interpretation*. Translated by Thomas H. Trapp. Grand Rapids, MI: Eerdmans, 2008.

Beerden, Kim. "Roman *dolia* and the Fattening of Dormice." *Classical World* 105 (2012): 227–235.

Belloc, Hilaire. *The Path to Rome*. New York: Longmans, Green, 1902.

Benson, C. David. *Imagined Romes: The Ancient City and Its Stories in Middle English Poetry*. University Park: Pennsylvania State University Press, 2019.

Bergson, Henri. *Laughter: An Essay on the Meaning of the Comic*. Translated by Fred Rothwell and Cloudesley Brereton. New York: Macmillan, 1911.

Bertram, Jerome. "John Henry Newman and the English College." In *A Roman Miscellany: The English in Rome, 1550–2000*, edited by Nicholas Schofield, 123–132. Leominster, UK: Gracewing, 2002.

Birch, Debra J. *Pilgrimage to Rome in the Middle Ages: Continuity and Change*. Woodbridge, UK: Boydell & Brewer, 1998.

Blumenthal, Uta-Renate. *The Investiture Controversy: Church and Monarchy from the Ninth to the Twelfth Century*. Philadelphia: University of Pennsylvania Press, 1988.

Boas, Adrian J. *Jerusalem in the Time of the Crusades: Society, Landscape and Art in the Holy City under Frankish Rule*. London: Routledge, 2001.

Böhmer, Heinrich. *Luthers Romfahrt*. Leipzig: Deichert, 1914.

———. *Road to Reformation: Martin Luther to the Year 1521*. Translated by John W. Doberstein and Theodore G. Tappert. Philadelphia: Muhlenberg Press, 1946.

Bolgia, Claudia. *Reclaiming the Roman Capitol: Santa Maria in Aracoeli from the Altar of Augustus to the Franciscans, c. 500–1450*. New York: Routledge, 2017.

Brecht, Martin. "Der Schimpfer Luther." *Luther. Zeitschrift der Luthergesellschaft* 52 (1981): 97–113.

Brown, Christopher Boyd, ed. *Luther's Works Companion Volume: Sixteenth-Century Biographies of Martin Luther*. Translated by Matthew Carver and Kevin Walker. St. Louis: Concordia, 2018.

Bullough, Geoffrey. *Narrative and Dramatic Sources of Shakespeare*. Vol. 5, *The Roman Plays*. New York: Columbia University Press, 1964.

Burgess, Anthony. *Anthony Burgess's Rome*. New York: Learning Corp. of America, 1978. https://tinyurl.com/anthonyburgessrome.

Butler, Shane, ed. *Deep Classics: Rethinking Classical Reception*. London: Bloomsbury Academic, 2016.

Byron, George Gordon. *The Poetical Works of Lord Byron*. London: Oxford University Press, 1928.

Cahill, Susan. *The Smiles of Rome: A Literary Companion for Readers and Travelers*. New York: Ballantine, 2005.

Camille, Michael. "Dr Witkowski's Anus: French Doctors, German Homosexuals and the Obscene in Medieval Church Art." In *Medieval Obscenities*, edited by Nicola McDonald, 17–38. York, UK: York Medieval Press, 2006.

Cattani, Riccardo. *St John Lateran*. Rome: Macart, n.d.

Chamberlin, E. R. *The Bad Popes*. New York: Barnes & Noble, 1969.

———. *The Sack of Rome*. New York: Dorset, 1979.

Chan, Sam. *Preaching as the Word of God: Answering an Old Question with Speech-Act Theory*. Eugene: Pickwick, 2016.

Chesterton, G. K. *Orthodoxy*. New York: John Lane, 1908.

Christman, Robert J. *The Dynamics of the Early Reformation in Their Reformed Augustinian Context*. Amsterdam: Amsterdam University Press, 2020.

———. Review of Andrew Pettegree's *Brand Luther*. *Faith-Life* 90 (2017): 46–56.

Claudius, Matthias. *Werke*. Gotha, Germany: Perthes, 1871.

Cochlaeus, Johannes. *Commentaria Ioannis Cochlaei, de Actis et Scriptis Martini Lutheri Saxonis*. Mainz: F. Behem, 1549.

Corrigan, John, ed. *Religion, Space, and the Atlantic World*. Columbia: University of South Carolina Press, 2017.

Cortright, Charles Lloyd. "Poor Maggot-Sack That I Am: The Human Body in the Theology of Martin Luther." PhD diss.; Marquette University, 2011.

Counted, Victor, and Fraser Watts, eds. *The Psychology of Religion and Place: Emerging Perspectives*. Cham, Switzerland: Palgrave Macmillan, 2019.

Cruickshank, J. W., and A. M. *Christian Rome*. 2nd ed. London: Grant Richards, 1911.

Curtis, Benjamin. *The Habsburgs: The History of a Dynasty*. London: Bloomsbury Academic, 2013.

Curtius, Ernst Robert. *European Literature and the Latin Middle Ages*. Translated by Willard R. Trask. Princeton, NJ: Princeton University Press, 1953.

Dante. *The Divine Comedy of Dante Alighieri*. Translated by Geoffrey L. Bickersteth. Oxford: Blackwell, 1981.

Deakin, Richard. *Flora of the Colosseum*. London: Groombridge and Sons, 1873.

Della Portella, Ivana, Giuseppina Pisani Sartorio, and Francesca Ventre. *The Appian Way: From Its Foundation to the Middle Ages*. Los Angeles: J. Paul Getty Museum, 2004.

Demacopoulos, George E. *The Invention of Peter: Apostolic Discourse and Papal Authority in Late Antiquity*. Philadelphia: University of Pennsylvania Press, 2013.

Denecke, Dietrich. "Wege und Städte zwischen Wittenberg und Rom um 1510: Eine historisch-geographische Studie zur Romreise Martin Luthers." In *Genetische Ansätze in der Kulturlandschaftsforschung: Festschrift für Helmut Jäger*, edited by Wolfgang Pinkwart, 77–106. Würzburg, Germany: Steiner, 1983.

De Silva, Shayari. "Beyond Ruin Porn: What's behind Our Obsession with Decay?" *ArchDaily* (blog), August 15, 2014. https://tinyurl.com/whatswithourobsession.

Dessain, Charles Stephen, ed. *The Letters and Diaries of John Henry Newman*. 32 vols. London: Clarendon, 1961–2007.

DeYoung, Karen. "European Parliament Ejects Paisley after He Denounces Pope." *Washington Post*, October 12, 1988. https://tinyurl.com/ulsterantichrist.

Dickens, Charles. *American Notes and Pictures from Italy*. London: J. M. Dent, 1907.

Dixon, C. Scott. *Protestants: A History from Wittenberg to Pennsylvania, 1517–1740*. Chichester: Wiley-Blackwell, 2010.

Doyle, Arthur Conan. *The Complete Sherlock Holmes*. New York: Barnes & Noble, 1992.

Dresser, Matthaeus. *De vita et morte D. Pauli Lutheri Medici Oratio*. Leipzig: Lantzenberger, 1593.

Duerk, John A. "Elijah P. Lovejoy: Anti-Catholic Abolitionist." *Journal of the Illinois Historical Society* 108 (2015): 103–121.

Eastman, David L. *Paul the Martyr: The Cult of the Apostle in the Latin West*. Atlanta: Society of Biblical Literature, 2011.

Edelheit, Henry. "Jung's 'Memories, Dreams, Reflections.'" *Psychoanalytic Quarterly* 33 (1964): 561–566.

Edwards, Mark U., Jr. *Luther's Last Battles: Politics and Polemics, 1531–46*. Ithaca: Cornell University Press, 1983.

Eirich, Stefan-Bernhard. "'Ich wolt nich gros geldt nemen, das ich zu Roma nicht gewesen war.' Martin Luther und seine römischen Erinnerungen." *Korrespondenzblatt: Collegium Germanicum et Hungaricum* 101 (1992): 77–97.

Erikson, Erik H. *Young Man Luther: A Study in Psychoanalysis and History*. New York: Norton, 1962.

Esteves, Junno Arocho. "Almost Four Million Pilgrims Visited the Vatican in 2016." *Catholic Herald*, December 30, 2016. https://tinyurl.com/Catholic-Herald.

Euling, Karl, ed. *Chronik des Johan Oldekop*. Stuttgart: Literarischer Verein, 1891.

Farrell, John. *Varieties of Authorial Intention: Literary Theory beyond the Intentional Fallacy*. Cham, Switzerland: Palgrave Macmillan, 2017.

Fasola Umberto. "La 'regio IV' del cimitero di S. Agnese sotto l'atrio della basilica costantiniana." *Rivista di Archeologia Cristiana* 50 (1974): 175–205.

Febvre, Lucien. *Martin Luther: Un Destin*. Paris: Presses Universitaires de France, 1928.

Fitton Brown, A. D. "The Unreality of Ovid's Tomitan Exile." *Liverpool Classical Monthly* 10 (1985): 18–22.

Fleming, Fergus. "The Alps and the Imagination." *Ambio* 13 (2004): 51–55.

Fredericks, S. C. "Irony of Overstatement in the Satires of Juvenal." *Illinois Classical Studies* 4 (1979): 178–191.

Freed, John B. *Frederick Barbarossa: The Prince and the Myth.* New Haven, CT: Yale University Press, 2016.

Frings, Udo. *Martin Lutherus—Poeta Latinus.* Aachen, Germany: Hauptabteilung Erziehung und Schule im Bischöflichen Generalvikariat, 1983.

Furey, Constance. "Invective and Discernment in Martin Luther, D. Erasmus, and Thomas More." *Harvard Theological Review* 98 (2005): 469–488.

Gaddis, Michael. *There Is No Crime for Those Who Have Christ: Religious Violence in the Christian Roman Empire.* Berkeley: University of California Press, 2005.

Gallia, Andrew. "'Some of My Best Friends . . .': Reading Prejudice in Juvenal's Third Satire." *Classical Journal* 111 (2015/2016): 319–346.

Gamble, Richard M. *In Search of the City on a Hill: The Making and Unmaking of an American Myth.* London: Continuum, 2012.

Genthe, Hans-Albert, ed. *Auf Luthers Spuren unterwegs: Eine Reise durch Deutschland, die Schweiz und Italien.* Göttingen: Vandenhoeck & Ruprecht, 2010.

Gouwens, Kenneth, and Sheryl Reiss, eds. *The Pontificate of Clement VII: History, Politics, Culture.* Aldershot, UK: Ashgate, 2005.

Greenblatt, Stephen. *Hamlet in Purgatory.* Expanded ed. Princeton, NJ: Princeton University Press, 2013.

Greene, Graham. *The Honorary Consul.* New York: Simon and Schuster, 1973.

Gregorovius, Ferdinand. *The History of the City of Rome in the Middle Ages.* Translated by Annie Hamilton. 2nd ed. London: G. Bell & Sons, 1900.

Gregory. *The Letters of Gregory the Great.* Books 1–4. Translated by Robert Martyn. Toronto: Pontifical Institute of Medieval Studies, 2004.

Grig, Lucy. "Deconstructing the Symbolic City: Jerome as Guide to Late Antique Rome." *Papers of the British School at Rome* 80 (2012): 125–143.

Grisar, Hartmann. *Luther.* Translated by E. M. Lamond. Vol. 1. London: Kegan Paul, Trench, Trübner, 1913.

Gritsch, Eric W. *The Wit of Martin Luther.* Minneapolis: Augsburg Fortress, 2006.

Grundt, Friedrich. "Hat Luther der Reise nach Rom eine Förderung seiner hebräischen Kenntnisse zu verdanken?" *Zeitschrift für kirchliche Wissenschaft und kirchliches Leben* 9 (1888): 312–316.

Gummere, Richard Mott. "Walt Whitman and His Reaction to the Classics." *Harvard Studies in Classical Philology* 60 (1951): 263–289.

Häckermann, Adolf. "Mohnike, Gottlieb Christian Friedrich." *Allgemeine Deutsche Biographie, Historische Kommission bei der Bayerischen Akademie der Wissenschaften* 22 (1885): 62–64.

Hacohen, Malachi Haim. *Jacob and Esau: Jewish European History between Nation and Empire.* Cambridge: Cambridge University Press, 2019.

Haile, Harry Gerald. *Luther: An Experiment in Biography.* New York: Doubleday, 1980.

Hammond, Brean. "The City in Eighteenth-Century Poetry." In *The Cambridge Companion to Eighteenth-Century Poetry*, edited by John Sitter, 83–108. Cambridge: Cambridge University Press, 2001.

Hanssen, Susan. "'Shall We Go to Rome?'—The Last Days of Henry Adams." *New England Quarterly* 86 (2013): 5–28.

Hardie, Philip. *Classicism and Christianity in Late Antique Latin Poetry.* Oakland: University of California Press, 2019.

Harmelink, Daniel N. "C.F.W. Walther Publishes an Impassioned Plea: 'Compare the Word of Christ with the Decrees of the Pope!' Missouri Synod's 1878 Saint Louis Edition of Martin Luther's *Passional Christi und Antichristi.*" *Concordia Historical Institute Quarterly* 93 (2020): 9–39.

Harmless, William, ed. *Augustine in His Own Words.* Washington, DC: Catholic University Press, 2010.

Harrison, Barbara Grizzuti. *Italian Days.* New York: Tichnor & Fields, 1989.

Hausrath, Adolf. *Martin Luthers Romfahrt nach einem gleichzeitigen Pilgerbuche erläutert.* Berlin: Grotesche Verlagsbuchhandlung, 1894.

Hawthorne, Nathaniel. *The Marble Faun: or, the Romance of Monte Beni.* Boston: Houghton Mifflin, 1891.

———. *The Scarlet Letter: A Romance.* Boston: James R. Osgood, 1871.

Headley, John M., ed. *The Complete Works of St. Thomas More.* Vol. 5, part 1. New Haven, CT: Yale University Press, 1969.

Heine, Heinrich. *Gesammelte Werke.* Vol. 5, edited by Gustav Karpeles. Berlin: Grotesche Verlagsbuchhandlung, 1887.

Hendrix, Scott H. *Luther and the Papacy: Stages in a Reformation Conflict.* Philadelphia: Fortress, 1981.

———. *Martin Luther: Visionary Reformer.* New Haven, CT: Yale University Press, 2015.

Hershkowitz, Paula. *Prudentius, Spain, and Late Antique Christianity: Poetry, Visual Culture and the Cult of Martyrs.* Cambridge: Cambridge University Press, 2017.

Herwaarden, Jan van. *Between Saint James and Erasmus: Studies in Late-Medieval Religious Life: Devotion and Pilgrimage in the Netherlands.* Leiden: Brill, 2003.

Hillerbrand, Hans J. "Martin Luther and the Bull *Exsurge Domine*." *Theological Studies* 30 (1969): 108–112.

Hoegemann, Brigitte Maria. "Newman and Rome." In *John Henry Newman in His Time*, edited by Philippe Lefebvre and Colin Mason, 61–81. Oxford: Family, 2007.

Hoffer, Eric. *The True Believer: Thoughts on the Nature of Mass Movements.* New York: Harper & Row, 1951.

Holt, Jim. *Why Does the World Exist? An Existential Detective Story.* New York: Liveright, 2012.

Homer. *Homeri Opera.* Edited by David B. Munro and Thomas W. Allen. Vol. 1, 3rd ed. Oxford: Clarendon, 1920.

Hong, Howard V. "The Comic, Satire, Irony, and Humor: Kierkegaardian Reflections." *Midwest Studies in Philosophy* 1 (1976): 98–105.

Hopkins, Keith, and Mary Beard. *The Colosseum.* Cambridge, MA: Harvard University Press, 2011.

Hubert, Hans W. "Luther und die Peterskirche." In *MLiR*, 435–470.

Ilić, Luka. *Theologian of Sin and Grace: The Process of Radicalization in the Theology of Matthias Flacius Illyricus.* Göttingen: Vandenhoeck & Ruprecht, 2014.

Innocenti, C., G. Fioravanti, R. Spiti, and C. Faravelli. "The Stendhal Syndrome between Psychoanalysis and Neuroscience." *Rivista di Psichiatria* 49 (2014): 61–66.

James, Henry. *Portrait of a Lady.* Boston: Houghton Mifflin, 1882.

Jedin, Hubert. "Die römischen Augustinerquellen zu Luthers Frühzeit." *Archiv für Reformationsgeschichte* 25 (1928): 256–270.

Jerome. *San Gerolamo, Lettere: Introduzione e note die Claudio Moreschini.* Translated by Roberto Palla. 3rd ed. Milan: RCS Rizzoli Libri, 2009.

Jones, Brian W. *The Emperor Domitian.* New York: Routledge, 1992.

Jung, Carl G. *Memories, Dreams, Reflections.* Translated by Richard and Clara Winston, edited by Aniela Jaffé. New York: Knopf Doubleday, 1989.

Junghans, Helmar. *Der junge Luther und die Humanisten.* Göttingen: Vandenhoeck & Ruprecht, 1985.

———. "Die Tischreden Martin Luthers." In *Sonderedition der kritischen Weimarer Ausgabe; Begleitheft zu den Tischreden*, 25–50. Weimar: Böhlau, 2000.

Jung-Inglessis, Eva-Maria. *Auf den Spuren Luthers in Rom*. St. Ottilien: EOS Verlag, 2006.

Kaufmann, Thomas. *Geschichte der Reformation*. Frankfurt: Insel Verlag, 2009.

Kawerau, Gustav. "Aus den Actis generalatus Aegidii Viterbiensis." *Zeitschrift für Kirchengeschichte* 32 (1911): 603–606.

Kelly, Christopher. *The Roman Empire: A Very Short Introduction*. Oxford: Oxford University Press, 2006.

Kessler, Herbert L., and Johanna Zacharias. *Rome 1300: On the Path of the Pilgrim*. New Haven, CT: Yale University Press, 2000.

Kinlaw, Joshua. "Protestants in Rome." *First Things*, June 2020. https://tinyurl .com/protestantsinrome.

Kinney, Dale. "Fact and Fiction in the Mirabilia Urbis Romae." In *Roma Felix*, edited by Éamonn Ó Carragáin and Carol Neuman De Vegvar, 235–252. Aldershot, UK: Ashgate, 2007.

Kirsch, Adam. "The Empire Strikes Back: Rome and Us." *New Yorker*, January 9, 2012, 66–74.

Kleckley, Russell C. *The Supputatio Annorum Mundi and Luther's View of History: A Case Study in Historiography and Exegesis*. Philadelphia: Lutheran Theological Seminary, 1985.

Koelb, Janice Hewlett. "Freud, Jung, and the Taboo of Rome." *Arethusa* 48 (2015): 391–430.

Kolb, Robert. *For All the Saints: Changing Perceptions of Martyrdom and Sainthood in the Lutheran Reformation*. Macon, GA: Mercer University Press, 1987.

———. *Martin Luther as Prophet, Teacher, and Hero: Images of the Reformer, 1520–1620*. Grand Rapids: Baker, 1999.

———. *Martin Luther: Confessor of the Faith*. Oxford: Oxford University Press, 2009.

Kolde, Theodor. "Innere Bewegungen unter den Augustinern und Luthers Romreise." *Zeitschrift für Kirchengeschichte* 2 (1877): 460–480.

Kopff, E. Christian. "Virgil and Augustine in Luther's De servo arbitrio." In *Ad Fontes Witebergenses: Select Proceedings of Lutheranism and the Classics: Reading the Church Fathers*, edited by James Kellerman and Carl Springer, 39–52. Fort Wayne: Lutheran Legacy, 2014.

Köstlin, Julius. *Life of Luther*. London: Longmans, 1883.

———. *The Theology of Luther in Its Historical Development and Inner Harmony*. Translated by Charles E. Hay. Philadelphia: Lutheran Publication Society, 1897.

Kramer, Olaf. *Goethe und die Rhetorik*. Berlin: De Gruyter, 2010.

Krebs, Christopher B. *A Most Dangerous Book: Tacitus's* Germania *from the Roman Empire to the Third Reich*. New York: Norton, 2011.

Krüger, Jürgen, and Martin Wallraff. *Luthers Rom: Die ewige Stadt in der Renaissance*. 2nd ed. Darmstadt, Germany: Philipp von Zabern, 2015.

Kulka, Tomas. "The Incongruity of Incongruity Theories." *Estetika* 30 (1993): 1–10.

Lançon, Bertrand. *Rome in Late Antiquity: Everyday Life and Urban Change, AD 312–609*. Translated by Antonia Nevill. New York: Routledge, 2000.

Landi, Corinna. *Con Luthero nella Roma del 1510*. Rome: Com Nuovi Tempi, 2013.

Laurence, Ray, and David J. Newsome, eds. *Rome, Ostia, Pompeii: Movement and Space*. Oxford: Oxford University Press, 2011.

Lehmann, Hartmut. "Nineteenth-Century American Tourists in Wittenberg, the 'Protestant Mecca.'" *Lutheran Quarterly* 29 (2015): 420–438.

Leinkauf, Thomas, ed. *Giordano Bruno in Wittenberg, 1586–1588: Aristoteles, Raimundus Lullus, Astronomie*. Pisa: Istituti editoriali e poligrafici internazionali, 2004.

Lemmons, Russel. "'If There Is a Hell, Then Rome Stands upon It': Martin Luther as Traveler and Translator." In *Travel and Translation in the Early Modern Period*, edited by Carmine G. Di Biase, 33–44. Amsterdam: Rodopi, 2006.

Leppin, Volker. "'Salve, Sancta Roma': Luthers Erinnerungen an seine Romreise." In *MLiR*, 33–54.

Leroux, Neil R. "Luther's Middle Course: Balancing Freedom and Service in *De Libertate Christiana* (1520)." *Studia Historiae Ecclesiasticae* 36 (2010): 1–6.

Lloyd, Joan Barclay. "Medieval Dominican Architecture at Santa Sabina in Rome, c. 1219–1320." *Papers of the British School at Rome* 72 (2004): 231–292.

Loewen, Harry. *Ink against the Devil: Luther and His Opponents*. Waterloo, ON: Wilfrid Laurier University Press, 2015.

Macaulay, Rose. *Pleasure of Ruins*. London: Thames & Hudson, 1953.

MacKenzie, Cameron. "Luther and the Latin Language." In *Ad Fontes Witebergenses: Select Proceedings of Lutheranism and the Classics: Reading the Church*

Fathers, edited by James A. Kellerman and Carl P. E. Springer, 151–161. Fort Wayne: Lutheran Legacy, 2014.

Maier, Peter. "Aussagen Luthers über die Stadt Rom seiner Zeit." In *Lutheriana: Zum 5. Geburtstag Martin Luthers von den Mitarbeitern der Weimarer Ausgabe*, edited by Gerhard Hammer and Karl-Heinz zur Mühlen, 281–290. Cologne: Böhlau Verlag, 1984.

Marius, Richard. *Martin Luther: The Christian between God and Death*. Cambridge, MA: Harvard University Press, 1999.

Marshall, P. David, Christopher Moore, and Kim Barbour, eds. *Persona Studies: An Introduction*. Hoboken, NJ: Wiley-Blackwell, 2020.

Martel, James R. *Love Is a Sweet Chain: Desire, Autonomy, and Friendship in Liberal Political Theory*. New York: Routledge, 2001.

Massing, Michael. *Fatal Discord: Erasmus, Luther, and the Fight for the Western Mind*. New York: HarperCollins, 2018.

Matheson, Peter. *The Rhetoric of the Reformation*. Edinburgh: T&T Clark, 1998.

Matheus, Michael, ed. *S. Maria dell'Anima. Zur Geschichte einer "deutschen" Stiftung in Rom*. Berlin: De Gruyter, 2010.

Mattes, Mark. *Martin Luther's Theology of Beauty: A Reappraisal*. Grand Rapids: Baker Academic, 2017.

Mayes, Benjamin T. G. *Counsel and Conscience: Lutheran Casuistry and Moral Reasoning after the Reform*. Göttingen: Vandenhoeck & Ruprecht, 2011.

McGinn, Bernard. *Antichrist: Two Thousand Years of the Human Fascination with Evil*. New York: HarperSanFrancisco, 1994.

McGrath, Alister E. *Luther's Theology of the Cross: Martin Luther's Theological Breakthrough*. 2nd ed. Oxford: Wiley-Blackwell, 2011.

McHugo, John. *A Concise History of Sunnis and Shi'is*. Washington, DC: Georgetown University Press, 2017.

Melanchthon, Philipp. *Historia de vita et actis reverendiss. viri D. Mart. Lutheri*. Heidelberg, 1548.

Metaxas, Eric. *Martin Luther: The Man Who Rediscovered the Gospel and Changed the World*. New York: Viking, 2017.

Montanaro, Caroline Vincenti, and Andrea Fasolo. *Palazzi and Villas of Rome*. Venice: Arsenale Editrice, 1999.

Morreall, John. "Enjoying Incongruity." *Humor: International Journal of Humor Research* 2 (1989): 1–18.

Morris, John G. *To Rome and Back Again, or The Two Proselytes*. English adaptation of a German novel by Karl Gottlieb Bretschneider. Baltimore: T. Newton Kurtz, 1856.

Mosse, George L. *The Crisis of German Ideology: Intellectual Origins of the Third Reich*. New York: Grosset & Dunlap, 1964.

Mundt, Lothar. "Die sizilischen Musen in Wittenberg. Zur religiösen Funktionalisierung der neulateinischen Bukolik im deutschen Protestantismus des 16. Jahrhunderts." In *Die Musen im Reformationszeitalter*, edited by Walther Ludwig, 265–288. Leipzig: Evangelische Verlagsanstalt, 2001.

Münkler, Marina. "Luthers Rom: Augenzeugenschaft, Invektivität und Konversion." In *Transformationen Roms in der Vormoderne*, edited by Volker Leppin and Christoph Mauntel, 213–242. Basel, Switzerland: Schwabe/Kohlhammer, 2019.

Murphy, Cullen. *Are We Rome? The Fall of an Empire and the Fate of America*. New York: Houghton Mifflin, 2007.

Musto, Ronald G. *Apocalypse in Rome: Cola di Rienzo and the Politics of the New Age*. Berkeley: University of California Press, 2003.

Nadeau, Barbie Latza. "Rome's Sad Decline Sums up Italy's Problems." CNN, March 4, 2018. https://tinyurl.com/romes-sad-decline.

Nelson, Janet. *King and Emperor: A New Life of Charlemagne*. Berkeley: University of California Press, 2019.

Nesselrath, Arnold. "Mirabilia Urbis Romae 1511." In *MLiR*, 345–377.

Nestingen, James Arne. *Martin Luther: A Life*. Minneapolis: Fortress, 2003.

Nestori, Aldo. "La basilica di S. Pancrazio in Roma." *Rivista di Archeologia Cristiana* 36 (1960): 213–248.

Noreen, Kristen. "The Icon of Santa Maria Maggiore, Rome: An Image and Its Afterlife." *Renaissance Studies* 19 (2005): 660–672.

Oberman, Heiko. "*Teufelsdreck*: Eschatology and Scatology in the Old Luther." *Sixteenth Century Journal* 19 (1988): 435–450.

O'Malley, John W. *Giles of Viterbo on Church and Reform: A Study in Renaissance Thought*. Leiden: Brill, 1968.

Pagliara, Pier Nicola. "Rom in den Jahren 1510/11." In *MLiR*, 471–496.

Palmer, Alan. *Fictional Minds*. Lincoln: University of Nebraska Press, 2004.

Palmer, Anne-Marie. *Prudentius on the Martyrs*. Oxford: Clarendon, 1989.

Pardoe, Elizabeth Lewis. "Confessional Spaces and Religious Places: Lutherans in America, 1698–1748." In *Religion, Space, and the Atlantic World*, edited by John Corrigan, 246–266. Columbia: University of South Carolina Press, 2017.

Parker, Geoffrey. *Emperor: A New Life of Charles V.* New Haven, CT: Yale University Press, 2019.

Parkes, Ruth. "Reading Statius through a Biographical Lens." In *Brill's Companion to Statius*, edited by William J. Dominik, Carole E. Newlands, and Kyle Gervais, 463–480. Leiden: Brill, 2015.

Partner, Peter. *Renaissance Rome 1500–1559: A Portrait of a Society*. Berkeley: University of California Press, 1976.

Pater, Calvin Augustine. *Karlstadt as the Father of the Baptist Movements: The Emergence of Lay Protestantism*. Toronto: University of Toronto Press, 1984.

Paulson, Stephen. *Luther's Outlaw God*. Vol. 2. Minneapolis: Fortress, 2019.

Pemble, John. *The Rome We Have Lost*. Oxford: Oxford University Press, 2017.

Pettegree, Andrew. *Brand Luther*. New York: Penguin, 2015.

Piepho, Lee. "Mantuan's Eclogues in the English Reformation." *Sixteenth Century Journal* 25 (1994): 623–632.

Pinto, John A. *City of the Soul: Rome and the Romantics*. New York: Morgan Library & Museum, 2016.

Plass, Ewald. *What Luther Says*. St. Louis: Concordia, 1959.

Plaza, Maria. *The Function of Humour in Roman Verse Satire: Laughter and Lying*. Oxford: Oxford University Press, 2006.

Poli, Marco, and Simona Costato. "Martin Lutero in un Affresco alla Misericordia? Ipotesi per una ricerca storico-artistica." *Strenna Storica Bolognese / Comitato per Bologna Storica e Artistica* 47 (1997): 425–438.

Pollack, John. *The Pun Also Rises: How the Humble Pun Revolutionized Language, Changed History, and Made Wordplay More Than Some Antics*. New York: Gotham, 2012.

Posset, Franz. *The Front-Runner of the Catholic Reformation: The Life and Works of Johann von Staupitz*. Aldershot, UK: Ashgate, 2003.

———. "Luther's Journey to Rome in 1511–1512: In Commemoration of its 500th Anniversary and in Search of the Historical Luther—a Sequel to the Real Luther." *Luther Digest* 20 (2012): 9–24.

———. *The Real Luther: A Friar at Erfurt and Wittenberg.* St. Louis: Concordia, 2011.

Preuss, Hans. *Die Vorstellungen vom Antichrist im späteren Mittelalter, bei Luther und in der Konfessionellen Polemik.* Leipzig: J. C. Hinrichs, 1906.

Ranke, Leopold von. *Deutsche Geschichte im Zeitalter der Reformation.* Berlin: Duncker & Humblot, 1839.

Ravaglioli, Armando. *The Heart of Rome.* Rome: Edizione di Roma Centro Storico, 1984.

Reedy, Jeremiah. *O Roma Nobilis. . . . Memoirs of Studying Theology in Pre-Vatican II Rome.* Bloomington, IN: Xlibris, 2015.

Reinhardt, Tobias, Michael Lapidge, and J. N. Adams, eds. *Aspects of the Language of Latin Prose.* Oxford: Oxford University Press, 2005.

Renna, Thomas. "The Holy Roman Empire Is Neither Holy, nor Roman, nor an Empire." *Michigan Academician* 42 (2015): 60–75.

Retief, François P., and Louis Cilliers. "Diseases and Causes of Death among the Popes." *Acta Theologica* 26, *Supplementum* 7 (2006): 233–246.

Rex, Richard. "Luther among the Humanists." In *Martin Luther: A Christian between Reforms and Modernity (1517–2017)*, edited by Alberto Melloni, 203–220. Berlin: De Gruyter, 2017.

Richardson, Carole Mary. *Reclaiming Rome: Cardinals in the Fifteenth Century.* Leiden: Brill, 2009.

Ridley, M. R., ed. *Hamlet by William Shakespeare.* London: J. M. Dent & Sons, 1935.

Rijser, David. *Raphael's Poetics: Art and Poetry in High Renaissance Rome.* Amsterdam: Amsterdam University Press, 2012.

Rios González, José Antonio. *Roma, andar y ver.* Madrid: Vision Libros, 2009.

Roberts, Michael. "Rome Personified, Rome Epitomized: Representations of Rome in the Poetry of the Early Fifth Century." *American Journal of Philology* 122 (2001): 533–565.

Robinson, Orrin W. "Luther's Bible and the Emergence of Standard German." In *A New History of German Literature*, edited by David E. Wellbery, 231–235. Cambridge, MA: Harvard University Press, 2004.

Rodgers, Daniel T. *As a City on a Hill: The Story of America's Most Famous Lay Sermon.* Princeton, NJ: Princeton University Press, 2018.

The Roman Breviary, Reformed by Order of the Holy Oecumenical. Vol. 2. Edinburgh: Blackwood, 1879.

Roper, Lyndal. *Martin Luther: Renegade and Prophet.* New York: Penguin Random House, 2016.

Saak, Eric L. *Luther and the Reformation of the Later Middle Ages.* Cambridge: Cambridge University Press, 2017.

Salvo, James M. *Reading Autoethnography: Reflections on Justice and Love.* New York: Routledge, 2020.

Sanoff, Alvin P. "One Must Not Forget." *US News and World Report,* October 27, 1986, 68.

Schilling, Heinz. *Martin Luther: Rebel in an Age of Upheaval.* Translated by Rona Johnston Gordon. Oxford: Oxford University Press, 2017.

Schmidt, Alvin J. *Hallmarks of Lutheran Identity.* St. Louis: Concordia, 2017.

Schneider, Hans. "Luthers Romreise." In *MLiR,* 3–31.

———. *Martin Luthers Reise nach Rom—neu datiert und neu gedeutet.* Berlin: De Gruyter, 2011.

Schücking, Levin. *Luther in Rome; or, Corradina, the Last of the Hohenstaufen: A Religio-historical Romance.* Translated by Eudora Lindsay South. Boston: Thayer, 1890.

Schwarz, Reinhard. "Beobachtungen zu Luthers Bekanntschaft mit antiken Dichtern und Geschichtsschreibern." *Lutherjahrbuch* 54 (1987): 7–22.

Schwiebert, Ernest George. *Luther and His Times: The Reformation from a New Perspective.* St. Louis: Concordia, 1950.

Scott, Izora. *Controversies over the Imitation of Cicero.* Davis, CA: Hermagoras, 1991.

Scribner, Robert W. *For the Sake of Simple Folk: Popular Propaganda for the German Reformation.* Cambridge: Cambridge University Press, 1981.

Selderhuis, Herman J. *John Calvin: A Pilgrim's Life.* Translated by Albert Gootjes. Downers Grove, IL: InterVarsity, 2009.

Shaw, Christine. *Julius II: The Warrior Pope.* Oxford: Blackwell, 1996.

Sheen, Fulton J. *This Is Rome: A Pilgrimage in Words and Pictures.* New York: Hawthorn, 1960.

Shelley, Mary. *Rambles in Germany and Italy in 1840, 1842, and 1843.* London: Edward Moxon, 1844.

Shelley, Percy Bysshe. *The Complete Poetical Works of Percy Bysshe Shelley*. Edited by Thomas Hutchinson. London: Oxford University Press, 1923.

Siemon-Netto, Uwe. *The Fabricated Luther: Refuting Nazi Connections and Other Modern Myths*. 2nd ed. St. Louis: Concordia, 2007.

Simrock, Karl. *Deutsche Märchen*. Barsinghausen, Germany: Unikum-Verlag, 2012.

Smith, Preserved. "A Decade of Luther Study." *Harvard Theological Review* 14 (1921): 107–135.

Sockness, Brent W. "Luther's Two Kingdoms Revisited: A Response to Reinhold Niebuhr's Criticism of Luther." *Journal of Religious Ethics* 20 (1992): 93–110.

Spitz, Lewis W. "Headwaters of the Reformation: *Studia Humanitatis, Luther Senior, et Initia Reformationis*." In *Luther and the Dawn of the Modern Era: Papers for the Fourth International Conference for Luther Research*, edited by Heiko Oberman, 89–116. Leiden: Brill, 1974.

———. "Luther and Humanism." In *Luther and Learning: The Wittenberg University Luther Symposium*, edited by Marilyn J. Harran, 69–94. Selinsgrove, PA: Susquehanna University Press, 1985.

Springer, Carl P. E. "Arms and the Theologian: Martin Luther's *Adversus Armatum Virum Cochlaeum*." *International Journal of the Classical Tradition* 10 (2003): 38–53.

———. *Cicero in Heaven: The Roman Rhetor and Luther's Reformation*. Leiden: Brill, 2017.

———. *Luther's Aesop*. Kirksville, MO: Truman State University Press, 2011.

———. "Luther's Latin Poetry and Scatology." *Lutheran Quarterly* 23 (2009): 373–387.

———. "Martin Luther, the Oreads of Wittenberg, and *Sola Gratia*." In *Acta Conventus Neo-Latini Abulensis: Proceedings of the Tenth International Congress of Neo-Latin Studies Avila 4–9 August 1997*, edited by Rhoda Schnur, J. Costas, R. Green, A. Iurilli, E. McCutcheon, A. Moreno, M. Mund-Dopchie, and H. Wiegand, 611–618. Tempe: University of Arizona Press, 2000.

———. "Martin's Martial: Reconsidering Luther's Relationship with the Classics." *International Journal of the Classical Tradition* 14 (2007): 23–50.

———. "The Uses of *Tentatio*: Satan, Luther, and Theological Maturation." In *The Hermeneutics of Hell: Visions and Representations of the Devil in World Literature,* edited by Gregor Thuswaldner and Daniel Russ, 27–46. Cham, Switzerland: Palgrave Macmillan, 2017.

Stein, Peter. *Roman Law in European History*. Cambridge: Cambridge University Press, 1999.

Steinmetz, David C. "The Catholic Luther: A Critical Appraisal." *Theology Today* 61 (2004): 187–201.

Stendhal. *A Roman Journal*. Translated by Haakon Chevalier. New York: Collier, 1961.

Stewart, Susan. *The Ruins Lessons: Meaning and Material in Western Culture*. Chicago: University of Chicago Press, 2019.

Stolt, Birgit. *Die Sprachmischung in Luthers Tischreden: Studien zum Problem der Zweisprachigkeit*. Uppsala: Almqvist & Wiksell, 1964.

———. *Martin Luthers Rhetorik des Herzens*. Tübingen: Mohr Siebeck, 2000.

Strittmatter, Eugene J. "Classical Elements in the Roman Liturgy." *Classical Journal* 18 (1923): 195–207.

Sugg, Joyce. *John Henry Newman: Snapdragon in the Wall*. Leominster, UK: Gracewing, 2001.

Sullivan, George H. *Not Built in a Day: Exploring the Architecture of Rome*. New York: Carroll & Graf, 2006.

Swann, Charles. *Nathaniel Hawthorne: Tradition and Revolution*. Cambridge: Cambridge University Press, 1991.

Tappert, Theodore G., trans. and ed. *The Book of Concord: The Confessions of the Evangelical Lutheran Church*. Philadelphia: Fortress, 1959.

Tela, Josephus, ed. *A Catalogue of the Most Eminently Venerable Relics of the Roman Catholic Church*. London: Souter, 1818.

Terence. *P. Terenti Afri Comoediae*. Edited by Sidney G. Ashmore. New York: Oxford University Press, 1910.

Thacker, Alan. "The Cult of Peter and the Development of Martyr Cult in Rome: The Origins of the Presentation of Peter and Paul as Martyrs." In *The Early Reception and Appropriation of the Apostle Peter (60–800 CE)*, edited by Roald Dijkstra, 250–276. Leiden: Brill, 2020.

Thomas, Edmund. "The Cult Statues of the Pantheon." *Journal of Roman Studies* 107 (2017): 146–212.

Thomas, Richard. *Why Bob Dylan Matters*. New York: HarperCollins, 2017.

Thompson, Michael A. *To Rome and Back with Martin Luther: The Pilgrimage That Would Ultimately Lead to the Protestant Reformation*. Kingwood, TX: Charis, 2010.

Thompson, W. D. J. Cargill. *The Political Thought of Martin Luther*. Sussex: Harvester, 1983.

Townley, James. *Illustrations of Biblical Literature Exhibiting the History and Fate of the Sacred Writings from the Earliest Period to the Present Century*. Vol. 3. London: Longmans, 1821.

Trinterud, Leonard J. *Elizabethan Puritanism*. Oxford: Oxford University Press, 1971.

Tschudi, Victor Plahte. "Two Sixteenth-Century Guidebooks and the Bibliotopography of Rome." In *Rome and the Guidebook Tradition: From the Middle Ages to the 20th Century*, edited by Anna Blennow and Stefano Fogelberg Rota, 89–114. Berlin: De Gruyter, 2019.

Tucci, Pier Luigi. "A New Look at the Tabularium and the Capitoline Hill." *Atti della Pontifica Accademia Romana di Archeologia* 86 (2014): 43–123.

Türk, Gustav. *Luthers Romfahrt in ihrer Bedeutung für seine innere Entwicklung*. Meissen, Germany: Klinkicht, 1897.

Twain, Mark. *Innocents Abroad, or the New Pilgrim's Progress*. New York: Harper, 1911.

Vance, William. *America's Rome*. Vol. 2, *Catholic and Contemporary Rome*. New Haven, CT: Yale University Press, 1989.

Van de Vate, Dwight. "Laughter and Detachment." *Southern Journal of Philosophy* 3 (1965): 163–171.

Viladesau, Richard. *The Triumph of the Cross: The Passion of Christ in Theology and the Arts from the Renaissance to the Counter-Reformation*. Oxford: Oxford University Press, 2008.

Virgil. *P. Vergili Maronis Opera*. Edited by R. A. B. Mynors. Oxford: Clarendon, 1972.

Voltmer, Rita. "Behind the 'Veil of Memory': About the Limitations of Narratives." *Magic, Ritual, and Witchcraft* 5 (2010): 96–102.

Vossberg, Herbert. *Im Heiligen Rom: Luthers Reiseeindrücke 1510–11*. Berlin: Evangelische Verlagsanstalt, 1966.

Walsh, Katherine. "The Observance: Sources for a History of the Observant Reform Movement in the Order of Augustinian Friars in the Fourteenth and Fifteenth Centuries." *Rivista di storia della chiesa in Italia* 31 (1977): 40–67.

Wander, Karl Friedrich Wilhelm. *Deutsches Sprichwörter-Lexikon*. Darmstadt, Germany: Wissenschaftliche Buchgesellschaft, 1964.

Whaley, Joachim. *Germany and the Holy Roman Empire*. Vol. 1, *Maximilian I to the Peace of Westphalia, 1493–1648*. Oxford: Oxford University Press, 2012.

White, Cheryl. *Round Trip to Rome: The Travelogue of a Returning Catholic*. Bloomington, IN: WestBow, 2015.

White, Hayden. *Metahistory: The Historical Imagination in Nineteenth-Century Europe*. Baltimore: Johns Hopkins University Press, 1973.

Whitford, David M. "The Papal Antichrist: Martin Luther and the Underappreciated Influence of Lorenzo Valla." *Renaissance Quarterly* 61 (2008): 26–52.

Wiesen, David S. *St. Jerome as a Satirist: A Study in Christian Latin Thought and Letters*. Ithaca: Cornell University Press, 1964.

Wilczek, Piotr. "Hate Speech or Brotherly Admonitions? Discourse between Jesuits and 'Heretics' in Early Modern Polish Literature." In *(Mis)translation and (Mis)interpretation: Polish Literature in the Context of Cross-cultural Communication*, 79–101. Frankfurt: Peter Lang, 2005.

Wilson, Andrew L. *Here I Walk: A Thousand Miles on Foot to Rome with Martin Luther*. Grand Rapids: Brazos, 2016.

Winell, Marlene. "Religious Trauma Syndrome." *Journey Free*. Accessed February 12, 2021. https://tinyurl.com/17wlwrej.

Wirshbo, Eliot. "Can Emotions Be Determined from Words? A Reconsideration of Recent Military Usage." *American Behavioral Scientist* 33 (1990): 287–295.

Wiśniewski, Robert. *The Beginnings of the Cult of Relics*. Oxford: Oxford University Press, 2019.

Wood, Susan K., and Timothy J. Wengert. *A Shared Spiritual Journey: Lutherans and Catholics Traveling toward Unity*. New York: Paulist, 2016.

Wright, William John. *Martin Luther's Understanding of God's Two Kingdoms: A Response to the Challenge of Skepticism*. Grand Rapids: Baker, 2010.

Zweidler, Reinhard. *Der Frankenweg-Via Francigena: Der mittelalterliche Pilgerweg von Canterbury nach Rom*. Darmstadt, Germany: Wissenschaftliche Buchgesellschaft, 2003.

Zweig, Stefan. *Triumph und Tragik des Erasmus von Rotterdam*. Berlin: Karl-Maria Guth, 2015. First published 1934 in Vienna by the Herbert Reichner Verlag.

Index of Authors and Subjects

Acts of Peter, 24
Adam of Usk, 22
Adams, Henry, 108
adiaphora, 141
Aesop, 96–97, 144, 245
Agricola, Rudolph, 42
Aland, Kurt, 74
alloeosis, 230
Ambrosian rite, 7
Anabaptists, 146, 198
Anderson, William, 172
animals: ape, 159, 164; bird, 198; boar, 163; cow, 68; dog, 96–97, 124, 163; donkey (ass), 95, 97, 159, 162, 164; dormouse, 91, 234; dragon, 157, 159; fox, 164, 198; frog, 123, 164; lamb, 146, 183; lion, 105, 144, 159; minotaur, 159; mule, 241; nightingale, 188; nightjar, 163; ostrich, 157; rat, 63, 159; screech owl, 159; sheep, 23, 95, 134, 183; turtle, 123; viper, 164; vulture, 163; werewolf, 159; wolf, 134, 144
antichrist, 60, 117, 119, 149–50, 157, 159–61, 167, 169, 248, 250
Appian, 237
Aqua Marcia (aqueduct), 69
Ara pacis, 228
arches: of Constantine, 70; of Titus, 10, 70
Aristotle, 62, 74, 93–95, 165, 252

Arius, 126
Arnold, Thomas, 106
artists and architects: Bernini, Gian Lorenzo, 23, 210; Bramante, 23–24, 40; Caravaggio, 223; Conte, Jacopo del, 32; Cranach, Lucas, 32, 146, 159, 214; della Robbia, Andrea, 123; Dürer, Albrecht, 25; Fontana, Domenico, 213; Lorrain, Claude, 68; Michelangelo, 22–23, 25, 32, 51, 68–69; Perugino, Pietro, 18; Piranesi, Giovanni Battista, 68, 228; Raphael, 25, 104, 127, 237; Signorelli, Luca, 150; Turner, J. M. W., 68
Athanasius, 126
Atticus, 92–93
Attila, 100, 237
Augustine, xxiii, 10–11, 45, 71, 73, 84, 92, 100, 135–36, 138, 181, 196, 210, 234, 253, 256
Augustinian(s), 3–7, 10–13, 16, 26, 33–34, 59, 135, 144, 149, 155, 177, 182, 197, 199, 208–9, 211, 217–19, 244
Aurelian Walls, xxiii, 10, 16, 20, 64, 103
Aurifaber, Joannes, xv, 8–9, 29, 256

Baedeker, 2
Bagot, Richard, xxiii